Realizing God

or

a form of godliness?

By Ray Smith

Realizing God
or a form of godliness?

Copyright © 2010 Ray Smith
All rights reserved.

ISBN: 1452814090
EAN-13: 9781452814094

Printed in the United States of America

Scripture quotations in this publication unless otherwise noted are taken from:
NIV—*Holy Bible: New International Version*, copyright 1973, 1978, 1984 by the International Bible Society. Used by permission of Zondervan Bible Publishers.
Other quotations are noted as:
KJV—*King James Version*, Authorized King James Version.
NASB—Scripture quotations taken from the New American Standard Bible, copyright 1960, 1962, 1963, 1968, 1971, 1973, 1975, 1977, 1995 by the Lockman Foundation. Used by permission (www.Lockman.org).

Table of Contents

Foreword v
1. Realizing God 1
2. An Old Lady's Story 43
3. God or Coincidence 47
4. Born Again 55
5. Trusting God to Keep His Word 69
6. You're in the Army Now 77
7. Holy Land Bound 115
8. Homecoming Day 145
9. My Greatest Mistake 157
10. God Honors His Word Again and Again 171
11. College 189
12. Amazing Trip 197
13. Christmas 1964 203
14. Strength in Weakness 213
15. The Desires of Your Heart 229
16. Becoming a Missionary 241
17. Clouds on the Horizon 251
18. Becoming a Pastor 255
19. Becoming Missionaries Again 265
20. Conclusion 283

Foreword

To our believer friends in Europe, the United States, and those scattered around the world, to those that have supported us diligently with your prayers, we dedicate this book. We stand in awe as we see God answering your prayers. Many have asked (or perhaps wondered) how an old retired customs inspector at age seventy-five could become pastor of the International Baptist Church Sofia. The answer reveals the Lord using His power to accomplish His will in our time.

Two perplexing verses have troubled me for many years. The first is in the Gospel of **Luke 18:8**, where Jesus teaches about prayer in the parable of the persistent widow. Her prayers are answered by persistence. Jesus closes this parable by saying **(verse 8)**: **"However, when the Son of Man comes, will He find faith on the earth?"** From the time I first read this as a child, I wondered: "How could faith in God possibly vanish from the earth? There are so many church-goers, so many churches, so many Christians."

The second troublesome verse is found in **2 Timothy 3:1–5**. Paul writes: **"There will be terrible times in the last days."** He describes the people in those days. It sounds as if he is speaking of the present time. I believe we are living **"in *the last days*."** In **verse 5** Paul describes these people as **"having a form of godliness but denying its power. Have nothing to do with them."**

The Apostle Paul tells of a great apostasy or falling away from the faith. He portrays the church as **"having a form of godliness, but denying its power. Have nothing to do with them."** Paul is speaking of churches that perform rituals of worship. They go through all of the motions of appearing to be godly people. They sing their praise hymns with vigor, they read from the Bible, they even say all of the proper religious things, but sadly, they lack God's promised power.

After seventy-seven years, God's Holy Spirit is stirring my soul. Does our church fit into this category? Do our churches have **"a form of godliness but deny its power"**? We have rebelled against scripturally based lyrics in our songs of praise. In many churches our hymns are 24/7. We sing the same seven words twenty-four times. In the Sermon on the Mount, Jesus warned against using vain repetitions. **"The Lord does not look at the things man looks at. Man looks at the outward appearance, but the Lord looks at the Heart" (1 Samuel 16:7).**

In our churches we rejoice in the power of the blood of The Lamb to cleanse us from all sin. This is the central thrust of the Bible. What about all of God's other promises—promises of healing, of rest, of help in the time of need, of food, of blessing, even a blessing so big that **"there shall not be room enough to receive it?"** Do we worship in such a way that we are actually denying God's power? Or does God not stand behind His word today? Isn't the Lord **"Jesus Christ the same yesterday and today and forever" (Hebrews 13:8)?** If Jesus is Lord, then where is His power in the lives of church members? Does God limit His power to the salvation experience? The Lord is **"not slow in keeping His promise" (2 Peter 3:9).**

— Foreword —

John 16:24, "Until now you have not asked for anything in My name. Ask and you will receive, and your joy will be complete." Do we as Christians trust God? Do we **"ask and you will receive, and your joy will be complete"**? Very simply, do we merely have a form of godliness? Or, are we living in the joy of God's power?

Paul's solution is the Bible. **Second Timothy 3:16, "All Scripture is God-breathed and is useful for teaching, rebuking, correcting, and training in righteousness, (17) so that the man of God may be thoroughly equipped for every good work."**

Jesus told a man He healed **(Luke 8:39), "Return home and tell how much God has done for you."** Please take a moment and **"tell how much God has done for you"** in your life and in your church. Do you see the power of God at work? Or, do we merely have a form of godliness while denying the power of God in our lives?

One of the most quoted verses in the Bible begins: **"For God so loved the world…" (John 3:16).** Believers have narrowed this verse down to strictly a salvation experience. Salvation should be our number one priority. However, God's love extends to every area of our lives. Through many practical experiences I have learned that the love of God reaches out in everything, from the fall of a hair from your head to **"so much blessing that you will not have room enough for it" (Malachi 3:10).**

Listen to the Lord's promise of **John 10:10: "The thief comes only to steal and kill and destroy. I have come that they may have life, and have it to the full."** Is your life bubbling over with an **"abundant life" (King James Version)**?

God promises you a life in fullest measure. Does this describe you? Are you living your life **"to the full"**?

Recently, I asked our congregation in Sofia: "If you have received a blessing from God that you did not have room enough for it, please raise your hand." Approximately half of our people raised their hands. While my wife and I were at home in the United States, I asked our congregation there the same question. Only one hand went up; the hand of my wife.

Please permit me to ask you the same question: "Have you received such a blessing from the Lord that you did not have room enough for it?" If not—why not? If you have received such a blessing, are you telling **"how much God has done for you"**? Actually, the salvation experience is such a blessing. When your sins are covered by the blood of Christ Jesus, God gives you eternal life. His Holy Spirit comes and lives within you. This is a blessing that is as tremendous as eternity. My prayer is that you have received God's greatest gift—His Only Begotten Son, Christ Jesus.

But I am not talking about "pie in the sky by and by." What about right now in this life? Has God poured out such a wonderful blessing that you did not have room enough for it? This is what God promises. This is the thrust of what I am trying to convey in this book. God wants to empower you. Would you like to experience a living God who still touches your life today? Jesus said: **"I am willing…" (Matthew 8:3)**.

The Apostle Paul talked about a thorn in the flesh. We do not know what his physical problem was. Many believe he had an eye disease. Listen to these words of Paul **(2 Corinthians 12:7–10): "To keep me from becoming** conceited because of these surpassingly great revelations, there was given me a thorn in my flesh, a messenger of Satan, to torment me. Three times I pleaded with the Lord to take it away from me. But He said to me: 'My grace is sufficient for you, for My power is made perfect in weakness.' Therefore I will boast all the more gladly about my weaknesses, so that Christ's power may rest on me. That is why, for Christ's sake, I delight in weaknesses, in insults, in hardships, in persecutions, in difficulties. For when I am weak, then I am strong."**

When we pray for healing or for God's power, we must trust in God's unfailing wisdom. Many years ago I heard of a child in the Holy Land. The child was afflicted with a debilitating illness. Christians united together in prayer for the child. During the days while they were praying, an epidemic of fever began raging in the land. The Christians prayed even more fervently that God would spare the child from this outbreak of fever.

Despite all of their prayers to the contrary, the child caught the fever. Body temperatures reached as high as 105 degrees. Finally, the crisis passed; the fever receded. Then, they realized that the fever had burned away the child's illness. We need to understand that God knows best. We must always pray as did the Lord **(Luke 22:42): "Father, if you are willing, take this cup from me; yet not my will but yours be done."**

As a child, I was thrilled by the story of Peter walking on water. Within myself I asked, "Why can't I have that kind of faith?" The only recorded ones who walked on water are the Lord and Peter. After feeding the five thousand men with five loaves of bread and two fish, Jesus sent the disciples on ahead in a boat while He stayed behind to pray. After the boat sailed a considerable distance from land, strong winds and waves buffeted the boat.

"During the fourth watch of the night," (between 3:00 a.m. and 6:00 a.m.) Jesus went out to them walking on the lake. When the disciples saw Jesus walking on the water, they were terrified. They thought He was a ghost. But Jesus said, **"Take courage! It is I. Don't be afraid" (Matthew 14:22–34).**

"Peter replied, 'Lord, if it's you, tell me to come to you on the water.'

" 'Come,' Jesus said.

"Then Peter got down out of the boat, walked on the water and came toward Jesus. (30) But when he saw the wind, he was afraid and, beginning to sink, cried out, 'Lord, save me!'

(31) "Immediately Jesus reached out His hand and caught him. 'You of little faith,' He said, 'why did you doubt?' "

It is easy to see why Peter began to sink. Any time we begin fearing the wind and the waves, when we turn our faith away from the Lord, we are bound to sink. Why could Peter walk on water? Why not you and I? Because, Peter said, **"Lord, tell me (command me) to come to you on the water,"** and Jesus said, **"Come!"**

If Jesus commands you or me to come to Him, walking on water, then we could obey; we could walk on water. When God commands His servants, He also empowers them. However, Jesus has not given us this command. Never mind walking on water. Please search the scriptures and see the countless places where God commands us. What does the

Lord command His children? And also empower them? We need to stop denying the power of God by our actions. We need to wake up and *realize* that God is alive and well. God is still in business today.

Listen to these commands of God: **"Whoever believes in Him shall not perish but have eternal life" (John 3:16);** **"Come to Me, all you who are weary and burdened and I will give you rest" (Matthew 11:28–30);** **"Call upon Me in the day of trouble; I will deliver you, and you will honor Me" (Psalm 50:15);** **"Have I not commanded you? Be strong and courageous. Do not be terrified; do not be discouraged; for the Lord your God will be with you wherever you go" (Joshua 1:9);** **"Test Me in this and see if I will not throw open the floodgates of heaven and pour out so much blessing that you will not have room enough for it" (Malachi 3:10);** **"…He will give you the desires of your heart" (Psalm 37:4).**

Can you **"tell how much God has done for you"**? Or do you merely have "a form of godliness but deny its power"? My friends, if we are living in the power of the Almighty God, then we need to **"return home and tell how much God has done for you."** A lost and dying world is crying out for the power of God to come and bless their lives and their land. But, the people are smothered in false religions. People are confused by powerless beliefs that have become so popular in these last days.

A serious disappointment that I experienced more than once happened while I was pastor of a church in the United States. I visited someone in the hospital with a fellow member of our church. We talked and laid our hands on the person. We prayed for God's healing mercies.

As my colleague and I were leaving the hospital, my friend would say something like: "Did you see how bad he (or she) looked? He (or she) won't be long for this world."

Do you understand the problem? We just asked God's blessings of healing upon this sick person. Now, before we can even get out of the hospital, my colleague is denying the power of God by not trusting Him to keep His Word. You might say, "Oh, but your friend was merely realizing the reality of the situation." This is precisely my point! The reality is: God is still alive and well. God is still concerned about every aspect of His children's lives. God will still perform miracles today—but only through your faith.

Look in your Bible and see how many times people's lives were changed and healed because of their faith in the Lord **(Matthew 9:29): "According to your faith, will it be done to you."** We need to realize God in our own lives. We need to understand how much God loves us. Listen to the words of Jesus in **Matthew 11:27: "All things have been committed to Me by My Father. No one knows the Son except the Father, and no one knows the Father except the Son and those to whom the Son chooses to reveal Him."** When we accept the Lord's invitation and ask the Lord Jesus to come into our life and be our Savior, the Holy Spirit of God not only comes into our life, but the Lord reveals Himself to us. God establishes a close, intimate, personal relationship with those who trust Him with all of their heart.

When I was traveling in the Holy Land at the age of twenty-two, I met Pastor Ayoub. He was a wonderful man of God. God used him to establish churches and lead hundreds of people to faith in Christ. Ayoub was led to Christ by

— Foreword —

an Assembly of God missionary. I asked him about his faith and how physical healing fit into his ministry. He replied, "Our most important goal is to win people to a saving knowledge of Christ." Then he explained, "God, not only promises salvation; He also promises healing, and many other very special blessings. We consider these blessings as 'cream on the cake.' "

In this book I tell how the Lord Jesus became my personal Savior and changed my life forever. I also tell of many other vital situations in which I specifically asked God and trusted Him to keep His Word. I now understand what I once heard a wise old preacher say. He said, "You can get anything God has through faith."

Perhaps our most wonderful experiences of serving as foreign missionaries is seeing how the Lord answers the prayers of His people. My prayer for you is that you will begin to realize God in all of His fullness. We simply need to return to square one and literally trust God to keep His promises. We also must anticipate a positive response through our faith. **"He rewards those who earnestly seek Him" (Hebrews 11:6). "Listen my dear brothers: Has not God chosen those who are poor in the eyes of the world to be rich in faith and to inherit the kingdom He promised those who love him?" (James 2:5).** In our church in Sofia during the past year, people from thirty-five countries came to worship with us. Our congregation ranges from street dwellers to ambassadors.

In our prayer meetings, I listen to the prayers of the most destitute of people. These folks do not merely utter eloquent words. They speak from personal experience with a heart whose only hope is in God. Many people rely upon jobs, income, doctors, retirement, medicines, etc. These poor people only have God. Therefore, when they pray, you can feel their total dependence upon the Lord.

When we pray, **"Give us this day our daily bread,"** we trust in our well-stocked pantry at home, our jobs and income, our money in the bank, etc. When these poor folks pray, all they have is God. It is easy to see why **"God has chosen those who are poor in the eyes of the world to be rich in faith and to inherit the kingdom He promised those who love Him."**

When we trust the Lord implicitly, we too can benefit by the Almighty God who tells His children **(Psalm 84:11), "No good thing does He withhold from those whose walk is blameless."**

When I was a young man, Dr. Timothy Walton Callaway, our old pastor and my mentor, was the wisest man I knew. Serving as a news reporter in the Scopes evolution trial, he was there when Clarence Darrow and William Jennings Bryan defended their viewpoints regarding evolution. During World War I, Dr. Callaway was a chaplain in the military. He, as well as more than forty others in his family dating back into the 1700s, served as ministers of the Gospel. His son Royal baptized Jimmy Carter in Plains, Georgia, when Jimmy was a teenager. His son Merrill served as a missionary to Jordan and Morocco.

Dr. Callaway was pastor of the First Baptist Church of St. Andrews Parish in Charleston, South Carolina. At age eighty-four, he performed our wedding ceremony. A year later he died while participating in a revival in Waycross, Georgia. He spent his life preaching and teaching. He

— Foreword —

acquired so much wisdom during his lifetime. I often thought of the futility of a person gaining great wisdom over a long life span. Then, suddenly, he and all of his understanding passed away. I thought of how great it would have been if he had recorded many of his experiences. But now he is gone. It is too late.

Although I am not nearly as wise as my mentor, Dr. Callaway, I have three quarters of a century of experience with invaluable exposure in life, as well as in the Scriptures. So much learned! So much forgotten! What is pertinent? One preeminent figure stands above all others—the Lord Jesus Christ. When you know Him, you understand His titles: **"King of Kings!" "Lord of Lords!" The Almighty God!" "Everlasting Father!" "Prince of Peace!" "Light of the World!" "Water of Life!"** Please notice that I said *"when you know Him,"* not "when you know *about Him*." Herein is the difference of realizing God and tapping into His strength for your life.

Special thanks to our lifelong friends Robert P. and Shirley Dukes, who are now retired. Bobby is a retired minister; Shirley was honored several times as School Teacher of the Year in South Carolina. Some time ago Shirley suggested that I write about these experiences with God. Also, I honor my little bride, Charlene, who for more than one half of a century has been my one true love in this world.

Chapter 1

Realizing God

The dictionary defines "realize" as: 1. To comprehend fully or correctly. 2. To bring about or make real: fulfill <*realize* one's potential>. 3. To make realistic. 4. To obtain or achieve <*realize* a profit>. 5. To bring in (a sum) as profit by sale. *vi. (verb intransitive)*: To exchange holdings or goods for money.

According to the above definition, have you *realized* God? (1). Have you comprehended God fully or correctly? (2) Have you brought about or made God real in your life? Have you found fulfillment? Have you realized your potential? (3) Is God realistic in your life? Or just some abstract notion or belief? (4) Have you obtained God in your life? Have you realized a profit in God? (5) When you take stock of yourself, do you bring in a profit? Have you exchanged anything to achieve a profit in God?

You might say: "Wait just a minute! What are you talking about? I go to church on Sunday! I try to treat everyone fairly with dignity and respect! I give an offering! I also give every now and then to help the poor! I might not be the best person in the world, but I'm just as good as the next person!"

Or you could say: "Who are you talking about? Are you talking about the Buddha god, the Hindu god, the Muslim god, or the Christian God? Aren't they all the same? Haven't you heard? It does not matter who or what you believe just as long as you are sincere in your beliefs. Exactly which God are you talking about? Who is God anyhow? How do you even know that there is a God?"

A man woke up in the night with a splitting headache. He did not want to disturb his wife. He went to the bathroom in the dark. Opening the medicine cabinet, he took out a small bottle of what he sincerely believed to be aspirin. Pouring two tablets into his hand, he washed them down with water from the faucet and went back to sleep. In the morning the man was dead.

With absolutely no doubt, he earnestly, genuinely, sincerely believed he had taken two aspirin tablets. He did not realize the bottle contained poison. His sincere, genuine faith did not protect him. He was "dead wrong."

Today, we face a world full of religions, cults, sects, and strange beliefs. Eternity awaits us. How can we be sure which belief is right? Jesus warned of false prophets. Jesus said **(Matthew 7:16): "You shall know them by their fruits"**(KJV). Which belief is the correct way? How can I make the right choice? Since human beings are **"created in the image of God,"** each one of us has the right to choose. We have the right to choose any god, or no god, or The God. The problem with choosing is that our choice will have everlasting consequences or rewards.

This great choice of mankind has existed throughout the ages. Listen to this challenge by Moses to the Children of Israel **(Deuteronomy 30:19–20): "This day I call heaven and earth as witnesses against you that I have set before you life** and death, blessings and curses. Now choose life, so that you and your children may live (20) and that you may love the Lord your God, listen to His voice, and hold fast to him. For the Lord is your life and He will give you many years in the land He swore to give to your fathers, Abraham, Isaac, and Jacob."

When Moses had completed his work, he appointed Joshua to lead the people into the Promised Land. Listen to these words of Joshua **(Joshua 24:15): "If serving the Lord seems undesirable to you, then choose for yourselves this day whom you will serve, whether the gods your forefathers served beyond the River, or the gods of the Amorites, in whose land you are living. But as for me and my household, we will serve the Lord."** Many today have a problem because they have not made any choice. Listen to what God says about those who try to straddle the fence **(Revelation 3:16): "So, because you are lukewarm—neither hot nor cold—I am about to spit you out of My mouth."**

Our question is: **"Why Choose Jesus?"** Why should we choose Jesus, the Christ, the Messiah, over all of the other available choices? What makes Jesus the very best choice that we can make? **"Why Choose Jesus?"**

Please consider the following:

1. **The first reason we should choose Jesus:** The Bible was written in sixty-six parts over a period of sixteen hundred years in three languages on three continents. It has more than forty authors from all walks of life. Old Testament prophets were held to a very supreme standard. **Deuteronomy 18:20: "But a prophet who presumes to speak in My name anything I have not commanded him to say, or a

prophet who speaks in the name of other gods, must be put to death."

Any prophet who prophesied a thing that did not happen was put to death. A prophet's accuracy determined whether he lived or died. One false statement could cause him to forfeit his life. These were the men who wrote the Old Testament Scriptures. The Apostle Paul wrote to young Timothy **(2 Timothy 3:16–17): "All Scripture is God-breathed and is useful for teaching, rebuking, correcting, and training in righteousness (17) so that the man of God may be thoroughly equipped for every good work."**

2. <u>The second reason we should choose Jesus</u>: These Old Testament prophets were inspired by the Almighty God to write the things that are in the Bible. God inspired each one of these men to write a fact or facts about One who was to come into the world. Each prophet or man of God wrote about this One who would come.

The first five books in the Bible are called the Pentateuch. They are traditionally attributed to Moses. Moses wrote about God creating all things. He wrote of the Garden of Eden and how God created a man named Adam. Then, using one of Adam's ribs, God created a woman. He told of how Satan tempted Eve and she disobeyed God's command to not eat of the forbidden fruit. Adam also ate of the fruit.

Then God spoke to Satan **(Genesis 3:15): "And I will put enmity between you and the woman, and between your offspring and hers; He will crush your head and you will strike His heel."** Theologians believe this is the first promise of the Christ who would come into the world. They explain:

Jesus was not the offspring of a man and a woman. He was born of the **"offspring of a woman,"** the Virgin Mary. The Scriptures tell how the Holy Spirit of God brought about this miraculous birth.

When Jesus died on the Cross of Calvary, it was a **"strike of His heel,"** not a final death blow. Although Jesus suffered and died, He arose from the dead and is alive today. In all of His perfection as God's only begotten Son, when He gave His life as a sacrifice for our sins, He ultimately defeated Satan. In the Book of Revelation, Satan and his angels are cast into a burning hell—an eternal death—a **"crush of your head."**

Moses gives a direct reference of the Christ to come in **Deuteronomy 18:17: "The Lord your God will raise up for you a prophet like me from among your own brothers."** The Children of Israel began looking forward to this Holy One who would be raised up.

Throughout the Old Testament, prophets and men of God wrote many predictions of this one who would come into the world. David said His body would not decay in the grave. Isaiah said He would be born of a virgin. The Psalmist said: **"They pierced My hands and My feet...They divide my garments among them and cast lots for my clothing."** (Psalm 22 contains a vivid account of the crucifixion of Jesus hundreds of years before it happened.) The coming Messiah would cause the blind to see and the lame to leap as a deer. He would be born in Bethlehem. Another said He would come riding into Jerusalem on the back of a donkey (as Jesus did in His triumphal entry). Another quoted God as saying: **"Out of Egypt have I called My Son."**

Another said, **"Not one of His bones would be broken."** John the Baptist cried: **"Look! The Lamb of God who takes away the sin of the world!" (John 1:29). "I have seen and I testify that this is the Son of God!" (John 1:34).**

More than three hundred of these prophecies were written by different holy men in different centuries concerning the coming Christ. When the Lord Jesus Christ came into the world, he fulfilled every one of these prophecies to the very letter. These Old Testament prophecies are like the pieces of a jigsaw puzzle. When you put them all together, they form a vivid picture of Christ Jesus. A rational person would conclude that only the Almighty God could predict all of these incidents by different authors over many centuries and then have them fulfilled exactly in a single person.

3. <u>The third reason we should choose Jesus</u>: Listen to the writer of **Hebrews 4:12-13: "For the word of God is living and active. Sharper than any double-edged sword; it penetrates even to dividing soul and spirit, joints and marrow; it judges the thoughts and attitudes of the heart. (13) Nothing in all creation is hidden from God's sight. Everything is uncovered and laid bare before the eyes of Him to whom we must give account."**

A great correlation is the symbolism used throughout the Old Testament. **Hebrews 10:1: "The law is only a shadow of the good things that are coming—not the realities themselves."** Those mysterious writings and events of the Old Testament are actually **"a shadow of the good things that are coming—not the realities themselves."** They are shadows of Jesus, the Christ.

Consider the first Passover when Moses was leading the Israelites out of Egypt. The Passover meal consisted of unleavened bread and the meat of a lamb or male goat without spot or blemish. The blood of the lamb was to be smeared on the side posts and over the frame of the door. These are actually **"a shadow"** of the body of Christ that was broken for our sins and His blood that would be shed for our sins.

Those in Egypt whose homes had the blood of a spotless lamb on their doorpost and lintel were protected from death. It did not matter if they were poor or rich. The only thing that saved them was their obedience in placing the blood of a spotless lamb or goat on the doorpost of their home. Perhaps many Egyptians saw the Israelites "ruining" their homes with the blood and possibly joked and made fun of them. However, as dawn came, a great cry of despair throughout the land of Egypt could not be silenced. From the mighty pharaoh to the lowest peasant, they faced the death of the firstborn in their home and among their cattle.

In the same way, the Scriptures teach us when the Almighty God makes His final judgment, only those who have invited the Lord Jesus to forgive and cover their sins with His blood shed on the Cross of Calvary will be spared. In the book of **Revelation 20:14–15, "The lake of fire is the second death. If anyone's name was not found written in the book of life, he was thrown into the lake of fire."**

In **Genesis 22** we read where God instructed Abraham to offer his only son, the child of his old age, as a sacrifice on an altar. (I have read and heard many sensational statements about this Scripture from people who do not have even a clue about God and His love and His Word.)

God gave Abraham a supreme test of his faith. As Abraham and his son, Isaac, traveled along the trail to Mount Moriah, Isaac asked, **"Father?"**

"Yes, my son?" Abraham replied.

"The fire and wood are here," Isaac said, "but where is the lamb for the burnt offering?"

Abraham answered, "God Himself will provide the lamb for the burnt offering, my son." And the two of them went on together.

When Abraham obeyed God and was prepared to offer his son Isaac as a sacrifice to God on Mount Moriah, the Angel of God cried out from heaven **(Genesis 22:11–12):** "Abraham! Abraham!"

"Here I am," he replied.

"Do not lay a hand on the boy," he said, "Do not do anything to him. Now I know that you fear God, because you have not withheld from Me your son, your only son."

(Verse 3) "Abraham looked up and there in a thicket he saw a ram caught by its horns. He went over and took the ram and sacrificed it as a burnt offering instead of his son."

As a young person, I said to myself: "Abraham promised that God would provide a lamb for the offering. However, Abraham offered a Ram in the place of his son. Where was the lamb?"

Don't you see? Don't you understand? Abraham was speaking prophetically. He was predicting that the **"Lamb of God"** would be sacrificed, not only for Isaac but for all of us. Do you see **"a shadow of the good things that are coming"**?

See how this Old Testament story portrays the coming Messiah, who would offer His life on the Cross to take upon Himself the punishment we deserve for our sins?

Throughout the Old Testament, such **"shadows"** of the coming Christ are evident in many different ways—for example, the blood that the great high priest placed on the mercy seat on the Ark of the Covenant each year, the scarlet (red as blood) cord that Rahab the harlot was ordered to tie over the window of her home as protection from death by the attacking troops. The Messiah is plainly evident in so many ways through these **"shadows"** from the Old Testament.

4. <u>The fourth reason we should choose Jesus</u>: Consider Christ Jesus Himself. Read through the Bible and see what eyewitnesses said about Him. Everyone from His worst enemies to His best friends all spoke well of Him. Even God in heaven on a couple of occasions spoke of **"the Son whom I love."** (Later I will list some of these eyewitness reports.)

5. <u>The fifth reason we should choose Jesus</u>: Consider the miracles, the miraculous signs, that Jesus performed. Even His enemies admitted that He did these miracles. He cleansed people from leprosy. He caused the blind to see. He restored crippled limbs. He enabled the mute to speak. He forgave sins. He cast out demons. He comforted the brokenhearted. He even raised some from the dead. These miraculous signs that Jesus performed authenticate he is indeed the promised Messiah, the Savior of the world, Immanuel, God with us.

6. <u>The sixth reason we should choose Jesus</u>: Miracle of all miracles—after He suffered the brutal flogging, fists, spitting, and the curse and agony of being nailed to a cross, three days and three nights later he arose from the dead. He showed Himself to more than five hundred people before he ascended up into heaven. An interesting prophecy is recorded at the time of His ascension. After Jesus told His followers that they would receive power from God's Holy Spirit to be His witnesses to the world, He began to rise into the air. **Acts 1:10–11: "They were looking intently up into the sky as He was going, when suddenly two men dressed in white stood beside them. (11) 'Men of Galilee,' they said, 'why do you stand here looking into the sky? This same Jesus, who has been taken from you into heaven, will come back in the same way you have seen Him go into heaven.' "**

Although Jesus fulfilled hundreds of prophecies from Old Testament Scriptures, this prophecy in the New Testament is yet to be fulfilled: **"This same Jesus, who has been taken from you into heaven, will come back in the same way you have seen Him go into heaven."** Two thousand years have passed, and God's Word remains true. The Lord Jesus Christ will return to this earth. You have God's Word on it. The question is: "Are you ready to meet the Lord when He returns? Have you received Him as your Lord and Savior? Are you living in His power?"

7. <u>The seventh reason we should choose Jesus</u>: If you are not convinced that Christ Jesus is the answer to your life, let me mention one final fact. Today, you will find people from around the world whose lives have been miraculously changed. I know of alcoholics and drug addicts who have been lifted out of the despair of addiction into an abundant life of love and service for God. I have seen broken homes that were restored by those who invited Jesus to come and be their Savior. I have seen people cured of leukemia and other serious diseases. These folks are not only being blessed by God, but they are a blessing to others because they invited the Lord Jesus to come into their lives and bless them.

Our question is: **"Why Choose Jesus?"** After you consider all of these facts about the Lord consider **John 14:14: "Jesus answered, 'I am the way and the truth and the life. No one comes to the Father except through Me. If you really knew Me, you would know My Father as well.' "** Understand that Jesus who fulfilled every Old Testament prophecy concerning the promised Messiah or Christ tells us very bluntly that He alone is **"the way and the truth and the life. No one comes to the Father except through Me."** The Lord Jesus debunks those who say that "all roads lead to God."

These are not the words of a biased sect or pseudoreligion. These are the words of the One who fulfilled every Old Testament prophecy concerning the coming Messiah. Then, He validated His claim by performing miracles that only God can do. He sealed this validation by rising from the dead.

Today, He still performs miracles in the lives of those who have faith in Him. The only miracle He promises to a lost and dying world is the **"sign of the prophet Jonah. For as Jonah was three days and three nights in the belly of a huge fish, so the Son of man will be three days and three nights in the heart of the earth" (Matthew 12:39–40).** When you receive Jesus and place your trust in Him, He comes into your life and reveals Himself to you in many different ways, including miracles.

Please examine any other religion or god and see how they compare with the Lord Jesus Christ. If you are convinced that you should choose Christ Jesus, the question is: "How can I become His follower, His child?"

The Apostle Paul writes **(Romans 10:9–10) "that if you confess with your mouth, 'Jesus is Lord,' and believe in your heart that God raised Him from the dead, you will be saved. (10) For it is with your heart that you believe and are justified, and it is with your mouth that you confess and are saved."**

The Scriptures tell us **(1 Samuel 16:7), "The Lord does not look at the things man looks at. Man looks at the outward appearance, but the Lord looks at the heart."** Do you understand? We try to impress each other by our outward appearance. God looks through our outward appearance. God looks to our heart. God knows if we are genuine or not. We cannot deceive God.

Jeremiah 29:13: "You will seek Me and find Me when you seek Me with all your heart." Success with God is only found when, without reservation, you seek and love God with all of your heart.

"Why Choose Jesus?" My prayer for you is that the Holy Spirit of God will open your eyes and your heart to these truths from God's Word and that you will do as Moses said: **"This day I call heaven and earth as witnesses against you that I have set before you life and death, blessings and curses. Now choose life, so that you and your children may live and that you may love the Lord your God, listen to His voice, and hold fast to him. For the Lord is your life, and He will give you many years."**

Why choose Jesus? I would also like to answer by recounting personal experiences throughout my life. I would like to mention scriptures that have been a blessing. These verses and experiences have molded and helped me to *realize* God in His fullness. I am not a holy guru or a religious professional. I am merely an average person with no special skills or talents. I was born June 10, 1932, during the throes of the Great Depression, the fifth and least of six children. (Actually, there were seven of us, but Charles died at birth, long before my time.)

The most impressive, dynamic, powerful force in my life occurred when I realized God in all of His fullness and glory. Which God am I talking about? The One and only Almighty, Omnipotent, Omnipresent God of Abraham, Isaac, and Jacob—Jehovah, the One who created the heavens and the earth, the One whom prophets have proclaimed down through the centuries of historic time in the Holy Scriptures.

Our minds are overwhelmed by the mention of an Almighty, Everlasting God who has no beginning or end. Let me ask you a simple question about physical things. If you could leave the earth and go straight up into the air, if you could rise beyond the stars, when and where would you come to the end? Suppose you could reach "the end." What would be beyond the end on the other side? In school we learned that light travels at the speed of 186,000 miles per second. We also learned many heavenly creations are so far away in space that their light has not reached earth. Do you understand? Our finite minds cannot comprehend some physical things, much less spiritual things.

When I was in college, I remember a professor talking about Dr. Albert Einstein and his theory. The professor quoted Einstein as saying that if you could go straight up into space on such a journey, you would arrive back at the place from which you departed. The problem I have with this explanation is that it sounds as if he is talking about a gigantic circle, not a 180-degree straight line. It reminds me of the childhood story of the king who had no clothes.

A great realization concerning God extends beyond our finite mind's understanding. Just as man will never reach the end of space, God is the **"Alpha and the Omega, the beginning and the end."** Nothing was before God and nothing is after God. He is indeed "The Great I Am." **"In the beginning God created the heaven and the earth" Genesis 1:1** (KJV). **"In the beginning was the Word, and the Word was with God, and the Word was God" John 1:1** (KJV). We just read that God is "The Great I Am." Now, we read in the Gospel of John the past tense: **"In the beginning <u>was</u> The Word, and The Word <u>was</u> with God, and The Word <u>was</u> God"** (KJV).

Do you understand? "In the beginning," before the heavens and the earth were created, "The Word" <u>was</u> already in place. "The Word" extends back beyond our capacity to grasp the fact of God's ever-living omnipotence. Who is the Word? **"The Word was with God and The Word was God."** Verse 3: **"All things were made by Him; and without Him was not any thing made that was made."** Verse 14: **"And The Word was made flesh and dwelt among us."**

Who is The Word? **Verse 29: "The next day John saw Jesus coming toward him, and said, 'Look, the Lamb of God, who takes away the sin of the world.' "** The Word is Jesus! Jesus was in the beginning with God. Jesus was God. Jesus is God. Jesus made all things. Jesus (God) became flesh and dwelt among us. This is the meaning of the word **"Immanuel—which means: God with us" (Matthew 1:23).**

Why did God come to earth in the body of a man? **"No one has seen God at any time; the only begotten God who is in the bosom of the Father, He has explained Him" (John 1:18,** NASB). Another reason God came to earth: **"I lay down My life for the sheep" (John 10:15,** KJV).

Jesus, the Messiah, is proclaimed throughout both the Old and the New Testaments. Luke's Gospel Chapter 24 tells of Jesus walking along the road to Emmaus with two of his followers. Jesus had just risen from the dead and the two did not recognize Him. **"He said to them, 'How foolish you are, and how slow of heart to believe all that the prophets have spoken! (26) Did not the Christ have to suffer these things and then enter His glory?' (27) <u>And beginning with Moses and all the Prophets, He explained to them what was said in all the Scriptures concerning Himself</u>" (Luke 24:25–27).** (Emphasis added.)

Notice that Jesus did not show them the nail prints in His hands and His feet or the spear print in His side to prove who He is. Jesus used Old Testament Scriptures to **"explain to them what was said in all the Scriptures concerning Himself."** It is plainly evident that Jesus believed the Bible is the inspired, infallible, inerrant Word of God.

Jesus says: **"I tell you the truth, the man who does not enter the sheep pen by the gate, but climbs in by some other way, is a thief and a robber. (2) The man who enters by the gate is the shepherd of His sheep"** (John 10:1–2).

What is the gate by which **"the shepherd of His sheep"** (the Messiah, the Good Shepherd) must enter? Anyone who claims to be the promised Messiah, **"the anointed One,"** the one **"after the order of Moses," "the shepherd of His sheep,"** must enter through the front gate. If a person claims to be the Messiah, the Christ, the representative that God has been promising throughout recorded Biblical history, then that person must come through the front gate. I believe the front gate is the fulfillment of all of God's promises that God inspired His prophets to proclaim down through the centuries. Included in these prophecies is: **"But he was wounded for out transgressions, He was bruised for our iniquities; the chastisement of our peace was upon Him; and with His stripes we are healed,"** Isaiah 53:5 (KJV).

When Jesus came into the world, He fulfilled every Old Testament prophecy (more than three hundred) concerning the Messiah. Jesus also performed miraculous signs to prove conclusively His Divine claims. He walked on water; He calmed the raging seas with a word; He restored sight to the blind; He cleansed the rotting flesh of leprosy; He restored withered arms and legs so that the crippled could leap like a deer; by speaking to a fig tree, the tree withered and died; He fed five thousand men (not counting women and children) with a child's lunch and gathered twelve baskets of leftovers; He even raised some from the dead.

On at least a couple of occasions the crowd heard God speaking from the heavens of **"My beloved Son in whom I am well pleased."**

Exactly who is Jesus? Many today, some very highly educated, seem to speak with authority about Jesus of Nazareth. When I worked with the United States Customs Service, such testimony was considered as hearsay. The court system requires eyewitness accounts or substantial evidence in order to prove a case. Let us hold a hearing and recall some of those who knew the Lord Jesus. Let us ask these eyewitnesses one question: "What do you think of Jesus, the Christ?" We can look in the Scriptures for their answers: We shall discover that not only is God **"well pleased in His beloved Son**," but those who knew Jesus spoke well of Him—His friends, as well as His enemies.

As we call our hearing to order, listen to these witnesses from Bible times as they answer our question: "What do you think of Jesus, the Christ?" These are recorded, eyewitness accounts.

First, let us go back into Old Testament times and call some whose lives were changed by the Savior, even before He came into the world to live in a body of flesh. Consider Job. God allowed Satan to test Job's integrity and faith. Job lost everything he had—his wealth, his sons, his daughters, his health. Instead of being a respected, responsible person in the community, Job learned how what it is like to be rejected and despised by young and old alike.

"Job, after you experienced the severe testing that the Lord allowed Satan to bring into your life with such pain and sorrow: WHAT DO YOU THINK ABOUT THE CHRIST?"

"**Though He slay me, yet will I trust in Him!**" (**Job 13:15,** KJV) What an amazing testimony.

"Job, Is there anything else that you would like to add? Job, WHAT DO YOU THINK ABOUT THE CHRIST?"

"**I know that my redeemer lives, and that in the end He will stand upon the earth**" (**Job 19:25,** KJV).

The Bible says David was **"a man after God's own heart."** God elevated David from being a young shepherd boy to become the second king of Israel. God delivered the great giant, Goliath of the Philistines, into David's hand. David discovered what it is to sin and disobey God. He also learned how wonderful it is to be forgiven of sin by the Lord. God promised David that one would come from his family who would rule on his throne forever—the Messiah—the Christ!

"David, WHAT DO YOU THINK ABOUT THE CHRIST?"

"**The Lord is my shepherd, I shall not want**" (**Psalms 23:1,** KJV).

Isaiah was the son of Amos, a shepherd who became a prophet of Israel. In the year that King Uzziah died, Isaiah saw a vision of the Lord seated on a throne. He saw the six-winged seraphs flying and calling to one another, **"Holy, holy, holy is the Lord Almighty; the whole earth is full of his glory" (Isaiah 6:3).**

When Isaiah saw the vision, he cried out: **"Woe to me! I am ruined! For I am a man of unclean lips, and I live among a people of unclean lips, and my eyes have seen the King, the Lord Almighty" (Isaiah 6:5).** Then, Isaiah heard the voice of the Lord saying, **"Whom shall I send? And who will go for us?"** Isaiah said, **"Here am I. Send me" (Isaiah 6:8).**

"Isaiah, you were a major prophet in Old Testament times. The Holy Spirit revealed many things to you about the Savior—how He would be born of a virgin, how He would suffer and give His life for our sins!"

"Isaiah, WHAT DO YOU THINK ABOUT THE CHRIST?"

"His name shall be called Wonderful, Counselor, The Mighty God, The Everlasting Father, The Prince of Peace" (Isaiah 9:6).

Old Testament prophecy tells of one who would precede the coming of the Messiah, **"a voice of one calling: In the desert prepare the way for the Lord; make straight in the wilderness a highway for our God" (Isaiah 40:3)**. "John the Baptist, you baptized the Lord in the River Jordan. You proclaimed the message to small and great to repent for the kingdom of heaven is at hand. John the Baptist, WHAT DO YOU THINK ABOUT THE CHRIST?"

"Look! The Lamb of God who takes away the sin of the world!" (John 1:29) "I have seen and I testify that this is the Son of God!" (John 1:34)

On different occasions people heard a voice from heaven speak. When John the Baptist baptized the Lord Jesus in the River Jordan, a voice from heaven spoke out.

"Voice from Heaven, WHAT DO YOU THINK ABOUT THE CHRIST?"

"This is My beloved Son, in whom I am well pleased" (Matthew 3:17, KJV).

Jesus took Peter, James, and John up onto a high mountain. They saw Jesus transfigured before their very eyes. The face of Jesus shone like the sun. His clothing became as white as the light. They saw Moses and Elijah speaking with Jesus. Then the voice from heaven spoke again.

"Voice from Heaven: WHAT DO YOU THINK ABOUT THE CHRIST?"

"This is My Son, whom I love; with Him I am well pleased. Listen to Him" (Matthew 17:5).

Are you well pleased with the Son of God? Are you listening to Him?

Jesus said He had to go through Samaria. Since many Jews despised the Samaritans, Jews usually walked around Samaria, rather than through the country. Jesus sat at a well in the middle of the day to rest. He talked with a woman there. After asking the woman for a drink of water, Jesus offered her water she could drink and never thirst again.

"Woman at the Well, WHAT DO YOU THINK ABOUT THE CHRIST?"

"Could this be the Christ?" (John 4:29)

What do you think? **"Could this be the Christ?"**

After the woman at the well returned to her village, she spoke with the men. The men came out and also spoke with Jesus. These Samaritan men not only heard the testimony of the woman at the well, but they also saw and heard Jesus for themselves.

"Samaritan men: WHAT DO YOU THINK ABOUT THE CHRIST?"

"We have heard Him ourselves, and know that this is indeed the Christ, the Savior of the world" (John 4:42, KJV).

Do you know that Jesus really is the Christ, the Savior of the World?

Jesus spent many happy times visiting with Mary and Martha and their brother Lazarus. After Lazarus died and had been in the tomb for four days, Jesus raised him from the dead.

"Martha, WHAT DO YOU THINK ABOUT THE CHRIST?"

"I believe that He is the Christ, the Son of God who was to come into the world" (John 11:27).

Do you agree? Can you say: **"I believe that He is the Christ, the Son of God"**?

Judas was one of the twelve disciples. He walked and talked with Jesus. He saw the Lord perform miracles of healing and comfort. He was their treasurer. He carried the bag with their funds. Despite this, Judas betrayed Jesus with a kiss.

"Judas Iscariot, WHAT DO YOU THINK ABOUT THE CHRIST?"

"I have betrayed innocent blood!" (Matthew 27:4)

Even the one who betrayed Jesus testifies for Him: **"I have betrayed innocent blood!"**

Pilate was the Roman governor who tried Jesus. While he was involved in the proceedings of this trial, Pilate received a note from his wife.

"Wife of Pilate, WHAT DO YOU THINK ABOUT THE CHRIST?"

"Don't have anything to do with that innocent man!" (Matthew 27:19) Even the wife of the man who had Jesus crucified testifies of Christ's innocence.

Pilate, the Roman governor, was in charge of the trial of Jesus. He had the authority to listen to the facts and set Jesus free. In a Roman court one usually got justice. No mercy, but justice. However, in the trial of Jesus, Roman justice failed. Although Jesus was innocent and should have been set free, He was sentenced to be crucified.

"Pilate, as the Roman governor who condemned Jesus to death: WHAT DO YOU THINK ABOUT THE CHRIST?"

"I find in Him no fault at all" (John 18:38, KJV).

The temple guards were sent out by the Chief Priests to bring Jesus back. Yet, they returned empty handed without the Lord.

"Temple guards: WHAT DO YOU THINK ABOUT THE CHRIST?"

"No one ever spoke the way this man does" (John 7:46).

Peter was one of the twelve disciples. He was a fisherman. Peter's brother, Andrew, first brought him to Jesus. Peter was very impetuous. He was quick to speak. He was one of the special three disciples, along with James and John, who witnessed the Transfiguration.

"Peter: WHAT DO YOU THINK ABOUT THE CHRIST?"

"You are the Christ, the Son of the living God" (Matthew 16:16).

After Peter denied the Lord three times during His trial, and after the resurrection and ascension of the Lord, Peter became a true leader in the early church.

"Peter, once again: WHAT DO YOU THINK ABOUT THE CHRIST?"

"Salvation is found in no one else, for there is no other name under heaven given to men by which we must be saved" (Acts 4:12).

Two thieves were crucified along with Jesus. One of the criminals repented and turned to Jesus in his dying moments. He rebuked his companion and admitted that they both deserved to die.

"Criminal on the cross: WHAT DO YOU THINK ABOUT THE CHRIST?"

"This man has done nothing wrong!" (Luke 23:41)

The centurion was a leader of one hundred Roman soldiers. He was there on Calvary Hill. His men drove the nails through the hands and feet of Jesus. He heard the cries of the Lord from the cross. He watched as the sunlight turned to darkness.

"Centurion, you were an eyewitness to this great crucifixion. Centurion: WHAT DO YOU THINK ABOUT THE CHRIST?"

"Surely He was the Son of God!" (Matthew 27:54)

Do you understand? Do you believe?

Thomas became known as doubting Thomas. He was the kind of person who had to see for himself. Thomas said he would not believe that Jesus arose from the dead unless he could see the nail prints in His hands and put his hand in the wound in Jesus' side.

"Thomas, you saw Jesus for yourself: WHAT DO YOU THINK ABOUT THE CHRIST?"

"My Lord and my God!" (John 20:28, KJV)

Can you say with Thomas: **"My Lord and my God"**?

The Apostle Paul was an ardent Jew. As a young man he consented to the death of Stephen, the first deacon, and watched the coats of those who stoned Stephen to death. Paul was on the way to Damascus to capture Christians. He persecuted them. Paul saw a great light and heard the Lord calling to him from heaven. Paul became an outstanding Christian and wrote much of the New Testament.

"Paul: WHAT DO YOU THINK ABOUT THE CHRIST?"

"Therefore God exalted Him to the highest place and gave Him the name that is above every name, that at the name of Jesus every knee should bow...and every tongue confess that Jesus Christ is Lord to the glory of God the Father!" (Philippians 2:9–11)

After Jesus arose from the dead he was seen by more than five hundred people at once (1 Corinthians 15:6). As Jesus ate with His disciples, He told them: **"Do not leave Jerusalem, but wait for the gift My Father promised, which you have heard Me speak about. (5) For John baptized with water, but in a few days you will be baptized with the Holy Spirit" (Acts 1:4).**

In His final meeting with His disciples Jesus said: **"But you will receive power when the Holy Spirit comes on you; and you will be My witnesses in Jerusalem, and in all Judea and Samaria, and to the ends of the earth" (Acts 1:8).** After Jesus said this, he was taken up before their eyes, and a cloud hid Him from their sight.

As they were gazing up into the sky, suddenly, two men dressed in white stood beside them and spoke. Let us query these two men with our question: "You two men dressed in white: WHAT DO YOU THINK ABOUT THE CHRIST?"

"This same Jesus, who has been taken from you into heaven, will come back in the same way you have seen Him go into heaven" (Acts 1:11).

Two thousand years have passed since this promise was made. The promise from God's Word still stands. Jesus is coming to earth again. The Apostle Paul writes about Christ's return:

"Brothers, we do not want you to be ignorant about those who fall asleep, or to grieve like the rest of men, who have no hope. (14) We believe that Jesus died and rose again and so we believe that God will bring with Jesus those who have fallen asleep in Him. (15) According to the Lord's own word, we tell you that we who are still alive, who are left till the coming of the Lord, will certainly not precede those who have fallen asleep. (16) For the Lord Himself will come down from heaven, with a loud command, with the voice of the archangel and with the trumpet call of God, and the dead in Christ will rise first. (17) After that, we who are still alive and are left will be caught up together with them in the clouds to meet the Lord in the air. And so we will be with the Lord forever. (15) Therefore, encourage each other with these words" (1 Thessalonians 4:13–18).

Do not be disheartened because so much time has passed. Many centuries elapsed before God fulfilled the prophecies of His Old Testament prophets and sent the Messiah into the world. You have God's word. Christ will return. **"With the Lord a day is like a thousand years, and a thousand years are like a day. The Lord is not slow in keeping His promise as some understand slowness. He is patient with you, not wanting anyone to perish, but everyone to come to repentance" (2 Peter 3:8–9).**

Today, it matters little what these witnesses from olden days thought about Jesus. The thing that matters is what you think about the Lord Jesus! He promises everlasting life if you will trust Him! The question that you and I face is: "WHAT DO YOU THINK ABOUT THE CHRIST?" Your eternal destiny hinges upon your answer to this question. **"Whoever believes in the Son has eternal life, but whoever rejects the Son will not see life, for God's wrath remains on him" (John 3:36).**

A Pharisee and ruler of the Jews came to Jesus one night and said: **"Rabbi, we know that you are a teacher come from God: for no man can do these miracles that you do, except God be with Him" (John 3:2).** Although some envied Jesus even to the point of His execution, both His friends and His enemies testify of Christ's amazing power, wit, and compassion.

Many people talk about the scientific method. They rule out anything that they cannot see and fit into their test tube in the laboratory. If we were confining ourselves to physical science, their point might be valid. However, if these scientists open their eyes, they will see another branch of science that deals with human behavior. Social scientists know full well that human behavior does not fit into a test tube or laboratory. Yet learned scholars, utilizing the scientific method, have revolutionized medical science by delving into behavioral patterns. They have set many captives free from psychological and mental distresses.

When Jesus was with His disciples, He promised: **"I will ask the Father, and He will give you another Counselor to be with you forever—the Spirit of truth" (John 14:16).** Jesus said about the Spirit of truth: **"The world cannot accept Him, because it neither sees Him nor knows Him. But you know Him, for He lives with you and will be in you. I will not leave you as orphans; I will come to you" (John 14:17–18).**

Do you see the problem? The great Counselor—the Spirit of truth—that Jesus promised to send into the world is invisible. Because people cannot see Him, they can neither accept Him nor know Him. Even some who saw Jesus perform miracles and Godly signs would not believe in Him.

Listen to the words of the Apostle Paul: **"The man without the Spirit does not accept the things that come from the Spirit of God, for they are foolishness to him, and he cannot understand them, because they are spiritually discerned" (1 Corinthians 2:14).** Smug, know-it-all, learned people close their eyes and their understanding to these unseen truths. Yet, a tremendous spiritual dimension stretching throughout eternity is available to those with faith.

Does this seem too difficult to grasp? God is unlike anyone or anything you have ever experienced. God is the Master of paradoxes. Consider: **"He that is last shall be first and he that is first shall be last." "Anyone who would be great in the kingdom of God must be a servant." "Humble yourself and you will be exalted." "Exalt yourself and you will be humbled."** To the widow who put into the temple offering two small coins ("mites") worth less than a penny, Jesus said she had given more than all of the others who put in great riches.

A most amazing paradox is God's key to receiving. Listen to the Lord's instructions: **"Do not judge, and you will not be judged. Do not condemn, and you will not be condemned. Forgive, and you will be forgiven. (38) Give, and it will be given to you. A good measure, pressed down, shaken together and running over, will be poured into your lap. For with the measure you use, it will be measured to you" (Luke 6:37–38).**

When I was a child, my parents took me to the farmer's market in Charleston. Local farmers brought their harvests and sold them on Market Street. A quart of freshly shelled butter beans (the local people called them "sivvy" beans—similar to lima beans) sold in those days for twenty-five cents per quart. Using a quart-sized can as a measure, the farmer would scoop the can full of beans; then, he would shake the can to make the beans settled into the can; he pressed them down and then poured a handful on top to be sure the can was running over. When he poured the overflowing can of beans into a sack, he grabbed another handful and threw them into the sack to be sure the measure was more than adequate.

Jesus tells us that when we give, the Lord will give back to us: **"A good measure, pressed down, shaken together, and running over, will be poured into your lap."**

God's instructions for giving are found in **2 Corinthians 9:6–11. "Remember this: Whoever sows sparingly will also reap sparingly, and whoever sows generously will also reap generously. (7) Each man should give what he has decided in his heart to give, not reluctantly or under compulsion, for God loves a cheerful giver. (8) And God is able to make all grace abound to you, so that in all things at all times, having all that you need, you will abound in every good work. (9) As it is written: 'He has scattered abroad his gifts to the poor; his righteousness endures forever.' (10) Now he who supplies seed to the sower and bread for food will also supply and increase your store of seed and will enlarge the harvest of your righteousness. (11) You will be made rich in every way so that you can be generous on every occasion,** and through us your generosity will result in thanksgiving to God."

How does Jesus say we can receive? By giving! **"He who is kind to the poor lends to the Lord, and He will reward him for what he has done" (Proverbs 19:17).**

I am writing about Christians obeying God's commands and expecting God to keep His word. You have a choice of hoarding up for yourselves. You can be stingy with all that you have. When you do, you will also **"reap sparingly."** During the past year, we have given more of our pension back to God than ever before. Despite our giving (actually, because of our giving), God has blessed us in more ways than we can imagine, including available funds.

When we talk about realizing God, you do not need a PhD degree or some exceptional merit. Jesus says you **"must become as a little child in order to see the kingdom of God."**

How can we *realize* God? The first step is: **"And without faith it is impossible to please God, because anyone who comes to Him must believe that He exists and that He rewards those who earnestly seek Him" (Hebrews 11:6).** Without being able to see any proof, without any miraculous signs we must have faith in God. The only tangible sign that God promises is **"the sign of the prophet Jonah"**: **"as Jonah was three days and three nights in the belly of a huge fish, so the Son of Man will be three days and three nights in the heart of the earth" (Matthew 12:29–30).** The Crucifixion and Resurrection of Jesus are the only signs that God promises to a lost and dying world.

At the trial of Jesus when Pontius Pilate discovered that Jesus was a Galilean under the jurisdiction of Herod, Pilate sent Jesus to Herod. Herod was very pleased. For a long time he had heard about Jesus. Herod hoped to see Jesus perform a miracle. The chief priests and teachers of the law were vehemently accusing Jesus. Herod plied Him with many questions, **"but Jesus gave him no answer" (Luke 23:9).** The Lord does not do miracles to gain a believer.

Jesus fed five thousand men (not counting the women and children) with five small loaves of bread and two fish: **"After the people saw the miraculous sign that Jesus did, they began to say, 'Surely this is the Prophet who is to come into the world.' (17) Jesus, knowing that they intended to come and make Him king by force, withdrew again to a mountain by Himself" (John 6:14–15).**

Since Jesus came to earth to be King, why did He not take the easy way and let the people draft Him into being their king? Why not? For the same reason Jesus answered Satan's temptation: **"If you are the Son of God, tell these stones to become bread." (6) Jesus answered, 'It is written: 'Man does not live on bread alone, but on every word that comes from the mouth of God' " (Matthew 4:3–4; Revelation 13:8). "The Lamb that was slain from the creation of the world."** This is the central theme of both the Old and New Testaments. Jesus came to redeem us from our sins by shedding His blood in our place. He took upon Himself the punishment we deserve for our sins. He promises eternal life to **"whoever believes in Him."**

When we are willing to trust in God, to believe in Him, to come to Him in simple, childlike faith, believing that **"He exists and that He rewards those who earnestly seek Him," we are on the astounding way towards *realizing* God in all of His fullness. What is faith? **"Now faith is being sure of what we hope for and certain of what we do not see" (Hebrews 11:1).** Faith sees the invisible. Faith believes the incredible. Faith achieves the impossible. Does this describe your faith? Or is your faith merely an accumulation of facts? Do you merely have a form of godliness but deny God's power?

Realizing God does not come by simply believing facts. **"You believe that there is one God; you do well; the devils also believe, and tremble" (James 2:19,** KJV). If believing about God is not enough, what more do we need? We need to establish a close, intimate, personal relationship with God. James explains: **"Come near to God and He will come near to you.... (10) "Humble yourselves before the Lord, and He will lift you up" (James 4:8, 10).** Listen to the words of Jesus: **"I am the vine, you are the branches: He that abides in Me, and I in him, the same brings forth much fruit: for without Me you can do nothing" (John 15:5,** KJV). Jesus says we must "hang in there" with Him just as a branch is connected to the vine. Listen to Jesus: **"If you abide in Me, and My words abide in you, you shall ask what you will, and it shall be done unto you" (John 15:7,** KJV).

Faith is not merely positive thinking, as powerful as that may be. We are talking about believing that Jesus is the Messiah, the Christ, the Son of God, the Savior of the World, and trusting Him. Understand from the Scriptures: Jesus went to the Cross of Calvary. He shed His blood in our place. He died and rose again from the dead. Jesus took upon Himself the punishment we deserve for our sins. **"By His stripes we are**

healed." When we receive Jesus in faith, the Bible teaches that God's Holy Spirit comes and lives within us. The Holy Spirit teaches us all things. He reveals Christ Jesus to us. This is when we begin to *realize God*.

After Jesus arose from the dead, His disciples were locked in a room, fearing for their lives. Jesus came into the room and spoke with them. However, the disciple Thomas was not with them. When they told Thomas they had seen Jesus, Thomas said he would not believe unless he could see the nail prints in Christ's hands and thrust his hand into the wound in His side.

Later, the disciples gathered together in a room along with Thomas. The door was locked. Jesus appeared to them. Jesus said to Thomas: **"Put your finger here: see my hands. Reach out your hand and put it into My side. Stop doubting and believe."** Thomas cried out: **"My Lord, and my God!"** Jesus said to Thomas (as well as to you and me): **"Thomas, because you have seen me, you have believed; blessed are those who have not seen and yet have believed" (John 20:27–29).** When we believe without the benefit of physically seeing or touching, God blesses us.

"That which was from the beginning, which we have heard, which we have seen with our eyes, which we have looked upon, and our hands have handled, of the Word of life." (3–4) "That which we have seen and heard declare we unto you, that you also may have fellowship with the Father, and with His Son Jesus Christ. And these things write we unto you, that your joy may be full" 1 John 1:1, 3-4 (KJV).

John, the beloved disciple, says we have heard Him, we have looked upon Him, we have gazed in awe upon Him with our eyes; we have handled Him, the Word of Life. We are indeed eyewitnesses of what I am telling you. Now, we are declaring Him to you so that you too may have fellowship with the Father and with His Son, Jesus Christ. We are writing these things to you so that your joy may be full.

Is your joy full? Are you experiencing fellowship with God the Father and His Son Jesus Christ? John, the beloved disciple, says they are eyewitnesses of the fact that you can indeed have this special relationship with the Almighty God and His Son, Jesus Christ.

The Lord Jesus says **(John 6:37): "All that the Father gives Me will come to Me, and whoever comes to Me I will never drive away" (John 15:7).** What a promise from God! **"Whoever comes to Me I will never drive away."** If you would like to *realize* God in all of His fullness, you need to **"come to Jesus."** However, merely believing about God is not enough. **"You believe that there is one God. Good! Even the demons believe that—and shudder" (James 2:19).** What do we need besides simply believing? How can we actually *realize* God?

Over the years I have read of various poor people who barely made a living. They lived in poverty and lacked the basic essentials of life. Their clothes were ragged; they struggled with hunger; they usually walked wherever they went and would not waste money on a bus or taxi. They were malnourished and needed medical assistance. Finally, the person died. When the authorities came to close-out their humble dwelling place, a cache of hundreds of thousands of dollars was found stuffed into their mattress or some other hiding place.

These "poor" people scrimped and saved all of their lives. They could have used their money to live very comfortably or even in luxury. But they chose to disregard all of their readily available wealth that was at their fingertips. They clung to their lifestyle rather than enjoy the bountiful plenty easily within their grasp.

Could this be a picture of many Christians today? Do we plod our way through life? Do we refuse to avail ourselves of the bountiful plenty that God offers to us in the precious promises of His Word? Jesus promised us **"life to the full" (John 10:10).**

God's promises are like money in the bank. Our Heavenly Father owns **"the cattle on a thousand hills" (Psalm 50:10).** God's account is never out of funds. Throughout the Bible God offers special blessings to His children. Money in the bank does us no good unless we either write a check or make a withdrawal. In the same way the gifts that God offers to us must be claimed. If we desire God's gifts, we must make a withdrawal. How do we withdraw from God's great offers to us? Simply by faith.

My three children taught me this principle very well. Sometimes they would say, "But Daddy! You promised!" I only know one way to resolve such an issue. I must keep my word. Otherwise, I have not told the truth. The Almighty God makes precious, wonderful promises to His children. Any child of God can get on his or her knees and say, "Almighty Father, you promised. Now, I am asking you to keep Your Word."

With this close, personal, intimate, spiritual relationship with God, we pass **"from death unto life."** We begin a relationship that grows and empowers us. His Holy Spirit lives within us. We begin to experience God in every aspect of our lives. We have begun to *realize* God. **"Therefore, since we have a great high priest who has gone through the heavens, Jesus the Son of God, let us hold firmly to the faith we profess. For we do not have a high priest who is unable to sympathize with our weaknesses, but we have one who has been tempted in every way, just as we are—yet was without sin. Let us then approach the throne of grace with confidence, so that we may receive mercy and find grace to help us in our time of need" (Hebrews 4:14–16.**

For example: **"For it is by grace you have been saved, through faith—and this not from yourselves, it is the gift of God—not by works, so that no one can boast" (Ephesians 2:8–9).** Many can quote these verses and talk about how good God is and how He loves us. What a wonderful gift of God! How many of us take the time to accept God's free gift? How many take time to say, "Heavenly Father, You promised me this gift of your grace. Now, I am asking You and trusting You to keep Your promise of love to me, personally." This is the way we make withdrawals from our account with the Lord. When we establish such a close, personal relationship with the Lord, we see firsthand how God **"rewards those who earnestly seek Him" (Hebrews 11:6).**

The Scriptures give us reasons why God will not answer our request: **"You do not have, because you do not ask God" (James 4:2).** First, we must ask God to keep His promise. Then, another problem: **"When you ask, you do not receive, because you ask with wrong motives, that you may spend what you get on your pleasures" (James 4:3).**

We can easily deceive people by the way we act, dress, and speak. However, we cannot deceive God. **"The Lord does not look at the things man looks at. Man looks at the outward appearance, but the Lord looks at the heart" (1 Samuel 16:7).** God always sees our inner, real self. David writes: **"If I had cherished sin in my heart, the Lord would not have listened" (Psalm 66:18).** Jesus says: **"If you remain in Me and My words remain in you, ask whatever you wish, and it will be given you. (8) This is to My Father's glory, that you bear much fruit, showing yourselves to be My disciples" (John 15:7–8).** Jesus points out that we must stay as close to Him as a branch to a vine. Our prayers should always consider God's will and not our personal, selfish desires.

King David gives a splendid model for our prayers in **2 Samuel 12**: After David committed his great sins of coveting another man's wife, committing adultery with Bathsheba, and then having her husband, Uriah, murdered in combat, the prophet Nathan confronted King David. The child that Uriah's wife bore to David became very ill. David pleaded with the Lord for the child. He fasted and went into his house and spent the nights lying on the ground. The elders tried to get David up to eat, but he would not eat any food with them. On the seventh day the child died.

After the child died, David got up from the ground, washed, put on lotions, and changed his clothes. He went into the house of the Lord and worshiped. Then he requested food and ate.

His servants asked: **"Why are you acting this way? While the child was alive, you fasted and wept, but now that the child is dead, you get up and eat!"**

David's answer is a very good model for our prayers: "While the child was still alive, I fasted and wept. I thought, **'Who knows? The Lord may be gracious to me and let the child live. But now that he is dead, why should I fast? Can I bring him back again? I will go to him, but he will not return to me.' "**

When we present our prayers and requests to the Lord, we must trust God's perfect judgment and will, regardless of the answer that we receive from God. I remember a lady in a church we once attended. She had a son who was born with a serious heart problem. The child was truly beautiful and completely innocent. The mother loved her son dearly.

Everyone in the church prayed for the child and his mother. The doctors were unable to correct the problem. After several weeks, the child died. The entire church and community came to the funeral. Through her agonizing distress, the mother was closer to God than she had ever been. Although her heart was broken, she was able to rejoice in God's nurture and compassion for her in her deepest hour of need.

The second most important verse in the Bible to me—after **John 3:16**, where I found Christ—is **1 John 1:9: "If we confess our sins, He is faithful and just and will forgive us our sins and purify us from all unrighteousness."** After we have a saving relationship with the Lord, after we have our sins forgiven and are gloriously saved, what can we do if we miserably fail God and sin against Him? Do you see why this verse is my second most favorite verse? God promises forgiveness and cleansing when we stumble and fail. Never mind those self-righteous critics. Confess your sins to Jesus. We have His promise, not only of forgiveness, but also of purifying from all unrighteousness.

I have heard people say, "Oh, there he goes again! He keeps thinking that God will forgive him every time he sins!" This brings to mind some other favorite verses: **"Then came Peter to Him, and said, Lord, how often shall my brother sin against me, and I forgive him? Till seven times? Jesus said unto him, 'I say not unto you, until seven times: but, until seventy times seven" (Matthew 18:21–22**, KJV).

Do you know why I love that verse? If God expects me to forgive my brother **"seventy times seven,"** how many times do you think God is going to forgive me of my sins as long as I continue to love the Lord and forgive my brothers? One thing I have learned about tithing money to God: You cannot outgive God! The same can be said about forgiveness: You cannot outforgive God. **"As a father has compassion on his children, so the Lord has compassion on those who fear Him; for He knows how we are formed, He remembers that we are dust. As for man, his days are like grass, he flourishes like a flower of the field; the winds blows over it and it is gone, and its place remembers it no more. But from everlasting to everlasting the Lord's love is with those who fear Him, and His righteousness with their children's children— with those who keep His covenant and remember to obey His precepts" (Psalm 103:13–14).**

A few years ago I talked with a young lady in North Charleston, South Carolina. She grew up in California. Her mother was a practicing witch. As a teenager this young lady mocked Christians and ridiculed them. She had received no Biblical teaching, except for things she heard from her peers. In her late twenties, problems within her marriage became overwhelming. One dark night she walked out into the back yard of her home, looked up into the star-filled sky, and in desperation cried out: "God! If you are there, I need you!"

She said, "Immediately, I felt the Spirit of God come into my life." The next days she went to some Christian friends, learned about Jesus, and invited Christ to be her Savior. Today, this woman is actively serving the Lord Jesus and testifying of how God reached out to her when she called upon Him.

God gives us the simple solution to finding Him in all of His fullness: **"And you shall seek Me, and find Me, when you shall search for Me with all your heart"** (Jeremiah 29:13, KJV). An old preacher once said, "Marriage is not a fifty-fifty proposition." He explained, "Marriage is a 100-100 proposition." He said, "If you get married, you cannot merely go half way. Both of you must go all of the way." So it is with a relationship with God. God says you will find Him when **"you shall search for me with all your heart."**

Paul writes: **"Continue to work out your salvation with fear and trembling, for it is God who works in you to will and to act according to His good purpose" (Philippians 2:12).**

Some think when a person becomes a child of the Lord; he will no longer have problems and trials. Jesus said: **"He causes His sun to rise on the evil and the good, and sends rain on the righteous and the unrighteous" (Matthew 5:45).** Although trials come to everyone, a believer obtains strength and shelter from God. Many can quote Psalm 23 from memory. In verse 4 David says: **"Yea, though I walk**

through the valley of the shadow of death, I will fear no evil: for thou art with me; thy rod and thy staff they comfort me" (KJV).

Every time God allows one of His children to face the serious complications of life, including death, God empowers and lives within His child. As the believer relies upon and trusts the Lord for His guidance, strength, and mercy, God sustains. Even as the believer confronts **"the valley of the shadow of death,"** and faces his enemies, he can rejoice: **"My cup runs over!"** The believer has the confidence that God's **"goodness and mercy shall follow me all the days of my life; and I will dwell in the house of the Lord for ever."**

To many these words from the Twenty-third Psalm are merely beautiful poetry. To a believer who is *realizing* God, these words are God's steadfast guarantee of ultimate success, regardless of the trials and temptations we face in life.

Many pastors like to paint a harsh, tough struggle for being a Christian. Some even say: "Jesus never said it will be easy." However, Jesus says, **"My yoke is easy and My burden is light" (Matthew 11:30).** The difference is in whom you are trusting. If you are trusting in your strength, your commitment, your willpower, your abilities, and your determination—then you will indeed have a most difficult life. You will ultimately fail.

When you *realize* God, when God is real in your life; when you are wholly looking to Him for His strength and power and guidance, you find success. You can say with the Apostle Paul: **"I can do everything through Him who gives me strength" (Philippians 4:13).** The key is found in God's

Word: **"Not by might nor by power, but by My Spirit, says the Lord Almighty" (Zechariah 4:6).**

The most elementary fact of God's Word is **"Jesus Saves!"** You cannot save yourself. If Christ does not save you, then you are eternally lost, regardless of how much you struggle, fight, promise, and vow. As a youth, we sang a chorus:

Let go and let God have His wonderful way.
Let go and let God have His way.
Your burdens will vanish, your night turn to day;
Let go and let God have His way. (Harry D. Clarke)

Even in small struggles, we sometimes torture ourselves by looking to our strength and not God's. Christians need to begin living in God's power. We can do this by trusting all of God's Word as a little child, relying upon the Lord to keep each of His precious promises to us. Jesus quoted from Deuteronomy 8:3: **"Man does not live on bread alone, but on every word that comes from the mouth of God" (Matthew 4:4).**

The Lord sums up this teaching in the Gospel of John, Chapter 15. **Verse 5: "I am the vine; you are the branches. If a man remains in Me and I in him, he will bear much fruit; apart from Me you can do nothing."** What kind of fruit does a believer bear? **Galatians 5:22–23: "But the fruit of the Spirit is love, joy, peace, patience, kindness, goodness, faithfulness, gentleness, and self-control. Against such things there is no law."** Is this a reflection of your temperament and life?

Chapter 2

An Old Lady's Story

Several years ago I was speaking with an elderly lady. She told me of a Sunday evening, many years ago, when she was sitting in the swing on her mother's front porch in Brunswick, Georgia. It was twilight time. Her two small daughters and a son were playing on the steps and in the front yard. She said her husband had a good-paying job with the railroad. They did not lack for any necessary thing. Although she was blessed in practically every way, she said her life had lost its luster. She wondered what had gone wrong. An empty longing that would not be satisfied gnawed away inside of her.

As she sat there pondering these things, the folks in a little church down the street began to sing a hymn. She listened to the words of their song: **"What a friend we have in Jesus, all our sins and griefs to bear; what a privilege to carry everything to God in prayer. O what peace we often forfeit, O what needless pain we bear; all because we do not carry everything to God in prayer"** (Joseph Scriven, 1819–1886).

"Suddenly," she said, "I realized what had gone wrong in my life. My father died before I was born. I had two brothers and a sister. Mother worked from sun-up to sun-down for one dollar per day, six days each week. On Sunday mornings she scrubbed her children and took us to Sunday school and church. She honored God with all of her heart. She even gave a tithe of her income. After I married, had children, and became engrossed in many family problems, I began to leave God out of my life. Right then and there," she said, "I resolved within myself: from now on, every Sunday, I will scrub my children, dress them in their Sunday best, and take them to Sunday school and church. Fulfillment and joy immediately replaced my emptiness." This inner peace sustained her throughout her life—from the mid-1920s until 1994, when she passed away.

The elderly lady who was telling me this was my mother, "Momma Ruby." At that time Mom only had three children, Frances, Lavonia, and Pat. Eugene came next, then I was number five. When I was born, there was no question about Sunday. Every Sunday, Mom had us ready and in church without excuse. Finally, Luther (number six) was born. As long as we lived with our parents, we were faithfully in Sunday school and church each Sunday.

Why do I mention this part of our childhood? When my mother comprehended God fully and correctly, when she made God real in her life, she fulfilled her potential as a mother. When God became realistic in her life, she achieved or *realized* a profit, i.e., the empty longing within her gave way to a sense of accomplishment, fulfillment, and purpose. Mom exchanged her lonely emptiness for a profit that cannot be purchased with money. Mother had *realized* God. She discovered the dynamic difference of life with God.

By attending Sunday school and church virtually all of my life, I learned a great deal about the scriptures and how to apply them. My mother spoke of the difference that God made in her life. I have also seen many other people whose lives have been changed dramatically, when they *realized* God. Although my dad was never a deacon or Sunday school teacher, I never saw him stop to eat food (no matter how small an amount) without first pausing to thank God for his blessings.

I remember a young man (I'll call him Roger). We met in New York during the summer of 1970. I was teaching at the U.S. Customs Service National Training Center at Hofstra University. Roger said he began a drug habit by taking pills. He started with amphetamines and barbiturates. He advanced to marijuana and hallucinogens. Later, he stepped up to cocaine and finally heroin.

Roger said he felt a hollow emptiness inside, similar to what my mother had described. He said he enjoyed drugs because they dulled his senses. Drugs helped him cope with his feelings of emptiness. But he said when he was "high," even on heroin, the empty feelings were still there. Although drugs had dulled his senses, he knew drugs were not the answer to his problem.

One Saturday afternoon, Roger, the young drug addict, was in a mall on Long Island. A group of young people from church went to the mall. They sang hymns and passed out Gospel tracts. They told how Jesus had changed their lives. When Roger heard their testimonies, he decided to visit their church.

On Sunday Roger came to church. The pastor preached about God's love for every person. The pastor explained how God loves you so much He gave His only begotten Son, Jesus Christ, to die for our sins—to take upon himself the penalty that we deserve for our sins and failures. At the conclusion of the service, the pastor invited anyone to come down to the front and receive Jesus as his or her personal Savior.

Roger made his way down to the front of the church. He asked the pastor to pray for him. Roger said he wanted to receive Jesus Christ as his Savior. He wanted Jesus to come into his life. He wanted Jesus to help him with his serious drug problem. When we left New York at the end of that summer, Roger was an active, outstanding youth in church. He had completely quit using drugs. He even dedicated his life to become a minister so that he could help others who were struggling with drugs. Roger said, "When I invited the Lord Jesus to come into my life, at once my hollow emptiness was filled." Roger had *realized* God.

Chapter 3

God or Coincidence

One of my earliest recollections of what seemed to be an experience with God happened at age nine. I lived with my parents, three brothers, and two sisters in a two-bedroom home on the poor end of Grove Street in Charleston, South Carolina. In those days one end of Grove Street (the Ashley River end) was paved. On the end where we lived, the Seaboard Airline Railroad track ran down the middle of the unpaved, dirt street in front of our house. Dad worked for the railroad and liked to live close to his work. Consequently, our home fronted on the railroad tracks. It was neat to sit in the swing on the front porch and watch trains going by—almost in our front yard. Our rented house was behind a Sinclair service station on the corner of King and Grove streets.

A minor league baseball team, the Charleston Rebels, played at College Park two blocks from our home. Several of my friends and I were hired to sell soft drinks and peanuts at the ballpark. At the age of nine I received my Social Security card in order to get my first formal job.

I say "formal," because from about the age of seven I saw how my older brothers gathered and sold scrap metal. They took their junk two blocks away to Garfinkle's, the junk dealer. Copper, brass, and lead brought a much higher price than iron. I would take my little red wagon and search the neighborhood for scrap. At the railroad tower where my dad worked, electricians and railroad maintenance men would frequently have a great deal of copper wire scrap after working all day. Since I was just a little fellow, they brought all of their scrap and gave it to me. I could earn twenty-five to thirty-five cents per wagon load. In the late 1930s, those small coins had tremendous purchasing power. The railroad repair men gave me one of my first nicknames. They called me "Junk."

At the ballpark, a galvanized bucket with fifteen bottled soft drinks and ice was quite a load for a nine-year-old lad to carry through the stands. Coca-Colas were sold only in six-ounce bottles. Other bottled soft drinks contained twelve ounces. Despite its size, I sold more Coca-Colas than all of the other drinks. I can still sing the Pepsi-Cola jingle: *"Pepsi Cola hits the spot! Twelve full ounces that's a lot! Twice as much for a nickel, too! You know Pepsi is the drink for you! Nickel! Nickel! Nickel! Nickel! Nickel! Nickel! Nickel! Nickel."* As a child, I enjoyed "twice as much." Now I prefer Coke.

Soft drinks sold at the ballpark for ten cents each. I received a penny for each one I sold. During a game, I earned approximately $1.25 to $1.75. That was a small fortune for a nine-year-old in the early 1940s. I could attend the Palace Movie Theater for nine cents. For a nickel I could ride the streetcar to the other end of the city. A penny would buy a piece of candy, bubble gum, or a lollipop; a pack of chewing gum cost only five cents.

Sometimes, when we were playing at night, someone would shout: "Look at the shooting star!" They would talk about how bright and beautiful it was, but I could never look up fast enough to see what they had seen. Time and again this happened. All of my brothers, sisters, and friends had seen a falling star.

One night I was visiting with my best friend, Jimmy. Because his Dad was sick, Jimmy wanted to do something special to make him feel better. Jimmy had no job and no money. We went into a grocery store. We bought a can of chicken soup. Then we went into Jimmy's home. He opened the can, poured it into a pot, added a can of water, heated the soup, and served it in a bowl for his Dad. The fact that little Jimmy was able to do this was very special to his father. Jimmy was also pleased with himself. Although I was only a silent partner, I felt good because my small resources made such happiness possible.

When I left Jimmy's house that night, I walked along in the darkness towards home. I really felt good about what had happened. Suddenly, a bright light streaked across the sky, leaving huge sparks and a long trail of light. I had seen my first shooting star! What a spectacle it was! Although I did not hear an audible voice, in my heart I felt as if God were saying, "Well done, my son." From lessons in Sunday school I knew that God is pleased when we help someone in need. I discovered firsthand that it is more blessed to give than to receive.

Was this incident a small miracle or just a happy coincidence? During the years that have followed, my life has been a series of many such happy "coincidences." I am convinced the Bible is indeed the inspired Word of God. **"The Lord is not slack concerning his promise"** (**2 Peter 3:9**,

KJV). The Bible contains many amazing promises from God: promises of salvation, promises of forgiveness, promises of healing, promises of blessings, promises of joy, promises of "the desires of your heart." **"No good thing will he withhold from them that walk uprightly" (Psalms 84:11**, KJV).

Why do people not receive all of these wonderful blessings that God promises? Because they have not *realized* God. When anyone offers you a gift, you must receive the gift before it belongs to you. God tells us He loves us. God also promises many splendid things. However, we must claim each of the good things that God promises us. We must receive God's gifts. How do we receive God's gifts? We receive God's gifts through faith.

The basic rule for *realizing* God is: **"And without faith it is impossible to please God, because anyone who comes to Him must believe that He exists and that He rewards those who earnestly seek Him" (Hebrews 11:6).** James clearly gives us a vital key to receiving from God: **"But when he asks, he must believe and not doubt, because he who doubts is like a wave of the sea, blown and tossed by the wind. That man should not think he will receive anything from the Lord; he is a double-minded man, unstable in all he does" (James 1:6–8).**

Receiving from God involves unwavering faith. We are able to put up a front with our friends; we may even act deceitfully with each other. When we are seeking God, we must be completely honest and genuine. **"The Lord does not look at the things man looks at. Man looks at the outward appearance, but the Lord looks at the heart" (1 Samuel 16:7).** Does this seem to be an insurmountable problem?

Actually, it is very simple: **"You must become as a little child in order to see the kingdom of God."** I love a hymn in the hymnbook. It says: "Only trust Him" (John H. Stockton). It's just that simple. God wants us to simply trust Him implicitly with all of our heart. When you trust Him with **"all your heart**," God takes care of everything else.

His Eye Is on the Sparrow

My Dad was a telegraph operator for the Seaboard Airline Railroad. As long as I was his dependent, he could get a free pass on the train for me to anywhere in the United States. Actually, I had a pass in my wallet which was good on the Seaboard Railroad. The Seaboard ran from Miami to Mobile to Richmond.

I earned money during the school year delivering newspapers for the News and Courier (now called the Post and Courier). During the summer, I would get Dad to order a pass. I traveled by myself to see the USA. I visited Washington, D.C., Niagara Falls, New York City, Philadelphia, Tampa, and Miami. At the conclusion of my senior year in high school at age seventeen, I took the "granddaddy" trip of them all. I traveled to Los Angeles and San Francisco. It took five days of traveling by train to cross the wonderful United States of America!

During my early teens, I traveled one summer to the nation's capital, Washington, D. C. What an exciting time it was to visit the Capitol Building, the White House, the Smithsonian Institution, and the National Archives to see the actual Declaration of Independence. I marveled at the

Bureau of Printing and Engraving, where I saw American currency being printed. In the Smithsonian Institution, I saw the *Spirit of St. Louis,* the actual airplane that Charles Lindbergh flew solo across the Atlantic Ocean.

After seeing so many magnificent buildings and monuments, I decided to walk out to the Pentagon Building. I climbed the steps in the Washington Monument and walked along the mall around the reflecting pool to the Lincoln Memorial. Then, I walked across the bridge over the Potomac River that leads towards the Pentagon.

In those days the area was not developed as it is today. It was mostly wooded. Since I had limited funds, I tried to conserve as much as possible. I could not afford to ride in a taxi. The Pentagon is not a very long walk from the city.

After gazing at the Pentagon for quite a while, I began walking back to the city. Hunger gnawing away inside spoke loud and clear. I had not had lunch. There was no place along that road to buy food. The road seemed longer on the way back than it did on the trip out.

Walking along beside the road and feeling my hunger, I thought about what Jesus said in the Sermon on the Mount: **"Therefore I say unto you, Take no thought for your life, what you shall eat, or what you shall drink, nor yet for your body, what you shall put on. Is not the life more than meat, and the body than clothing? Behold the fowls of the air: for they sow not, neither do they reap, nor gather into barns; yet your heavenly Father feeds them. Are you not much better than they?" (Matthew 6:25–26**, KJV).

I thought of these words. I thought of how great it would be if the Lord were to give me something to eat. But there was no place to buy food. As I walked along thinking of these things, I saw a tree beside the road just to the left of the pathway. Within easy reach from the path were two shiny red, ripe apples, hanging from the tree. I walked around the tree and looked at all of the limbs. There were only two apples on the entire tree and they were within easy reach.

I picked both apples, rubbed them clean on my shirt, and said, "Thank you, Lord, for your love and mercy and kindness. Thank you, Lord, for keeping your promise and caring for a hungry little boy." As I continued to walk along eating the apples, I was sure that the Lord had kept His Word. I believe God saw the desire of my heart and answered. I did not realize at the time that early August is too soon to find ripe apples on a tree. Those two apples were not only ripe but delicious. The more I think of it, the more I realize how God's love extends to the very smallest and most insignificant of us.

Chapter 4

Born Again

I love the third chapter of the Gospel of John, perhaps more than any other scripture in the Bible. Why do I love this chapter so much? Because in this scripture I discovered Jesus! In this scripture I discovered a whole new life! Because of this scripture, Jesus became not just a Jew who walked the streets of Israel two thousand years ago. Jesus became not merely someone that you read about or hear about in church on Sundays. Jesus became not just an impersonal God.

Through this scripture Jesus became a close, intimate, personal friend who (as it says in **Proverbs 18:24**) **"is a friend who sticks closer than a brother"** (KJV). Through this scripture, Jesus became **"my hope!" "My Rock!" "My fortress!" "My deliverer!" "My Comforter!" "My Wonderful Counselor!" "My hiding place!" "My shelter in the time of storm!" "My eternal salvation!"** Jesus became my **"King of Kings and Lord of Lords!" "My Savior!" "My Master!" "My Redeemer!" "My Almighty God!" My Prince of Peace!" "My Friend!"**

Do you know the Lord Jesus today? Have you experienced the Love of God that you receive by inviting Jesus to come into your life, to forgive you of your sins—to give you a new beginning in life? Have you *realized* God?

Some time ago, I saw a short clip on television of Osama bin Laden, the terrorist. Bin Laden said he and his followers love death, but in the United States they love life. Jesus *is* life. Jesus says: **"The thief comes only to steal and kill and destroy; I am come that they may have life, and have it to the full" (John 10:10).**

What kind of life are you living today? Are you living your life **"to the full"?** Do you enjoy the **"abundant life"** (KJV) that Jesus offers to all who receive Him as Savior and Lord? Or is your life full of painstaking drudgery and anxiety? Full of death?

"Now there was a man of the Pharisees named Nicodemus, a member of the Jewish ruling council. (2) He came to Jesus at night and said, 'Rabbi, we know you are a teacher who has come from God. For no one could perform the miraculous signs you are doing if God were not with Him" (John 3:1).

Do you understand? A man named Nicodemus came to Jesus one night. This man was a Pharisee. The Pharisees considered themselves to be the best in Israel. They believed in the inspiration of the Old Testament; they believed in the coming of the Messiah, the Christ; they believed in miracles; they believed in the Resurrection. Although many of the Pharisees were against Jesus, Nicodemus was a sincere, genuine man of faith. In addition to being a Pharisee Nicodemus was also a member of the Jewish ruling council. Nicodemus was a teacher of the scriptures.

"Nicodemus came to Jesus at night." People like to imagine why Nicodemus came to Jesus at night. Was he afraid or ashamed to be seen by the other Pharisees coming to

Jesus? Was he trying to cover up his meeting with darkness? Or perhaps Nicodemus was a very busy man like so many today and only had the opportunity after working hours. It does not matter why Nicodemus came to Jesus at night. The important thing is that Nicodemus did indeed come to talk with Jesus.

Nicodemus begins the conversation by stating: **"Rabbi, we know you are a teacher who has come from God, because no one could perform the miraculous signs you are doing if God were not with him."** Today we find pseudoreligious people who are pompous. They think they know everything. They deny the virgin birth of Jesus. They deny His miracles. One thing that we learn from history and the Bible is that everyone recognized the miracles of Christ. Not just His friends, but His enemies also acknowledged the miracles that Jesus performed.

Among the things prophesied that the Messiah would do is restore sight to the blind. He would cause the deaf to hear again. The Messiah would enable the lame to leap into the air as a deer. Nicodemus was a teacher of the law. He knew all of these prophecies. Nicodemus also knew that Jesus had performed such miracles. Could Nicodemus have imagined that Jesus might possibly be the Messiah?

We have an expression: "beating around the bush." It means instead of directly coming to the point, people tend to talk about a subject without actually dealing with the matter at hand. Have you ever talked with someone, and after you finished, you still did not know what the person was talking about? This is one of the things that I love about the Lord Jesus. Jesus goes right to the point.

Listen to what Jesus says to Nicodemus: **"In reply Jesus declared, 'I tell you the truth, no one can see the kingdom of God unless he is born again' " (John 3:3).** Jesus says if you are born only once, you cannot see the kingdom of God. If you are born only once, you will never get to heaven. Unless you are born again, you will forever be separated from God and His kingdom.

Can you feel the impact of this statement? Nicodemus is a top leader and teacher in his synagogue and community. People respect him wherever he goes. Because of his honesty and sincerity, we would consider him to be a man of moral excellence. Jesus declares to Nicodemus: **"Unless you are born again, you will not even see the kingdom of God."**

What an earth-shaking revelation! Nicodemus probably thought because of his impeccable life style, his being a Pharisee, a teacher of the scriptures, a respected and all around splendid person in the community, he was closer to God and God's kingdom than anyone. If you look around today, you still find people who think their position, their lifestyle, their good name in the community, their willingness to teach and reach out to help the poor and others, - they think: certainly God would be glad to welcome me into heaven before almost anyone I know.

However, just as Jesus spoke to Nicodemus, Jesus speaks to you and me. Jesus says to every one of us: **"Unless you are born again, you will not even see the kingdom of God."**

Nicodemus replied: **"How can a man be born when he is old? Surely he cannot enter a second time into his mother's womb to be born!" (John 3:4)** Do you see Nicodemus' problem? We are all physical—flesh and blood. Our thinking is limited by our flesh-and-blood experiences. Jesus is talking about an entirely spiritual realm.

This is the reason why many people stumble at the doctrine of the "Trinity." The Bible teaches us of God the Father, God the Son, and God the Holy Spirit. Yet, the scriptures claim that God is One. Physical beings try to rationalize and understand this in physical terms. They say things like the Father, Son, and Holy Spirit are "One in purpose." They cannot grasp that God is **"One"** as the scriptures declare.

What is impossible for flesh and blood is possible for the Spirit. God, who created the heavens and the earth, can be anything He claims to be. One day when we take on a completely spiritual nature, we will understand how elementary this is. After Jesus arose from the dead, He entered a locked room where His disciples were. The Spirit does things the flesh cannot even understand.

Jesus answered Nicodemus by giving him a short discourse on the Spirit: **"Jesus answered: 'I tell you the truth, no one can enter the kingdom of God unless he is born of water and the Spirit. (4) Flesh gives birth to flesh, but the Spirit gives birth to spirit. (7) You should not be surprised at My saying, 'You must be born again." (8) The wind blows wherever it pleases. You hear its sound, but you cannot tell where it comes from or where it is going. So it is with everyone born of the Spirit"** (John 3:5).

Jesus said to Nicodemus: **"no one can enter the kingdom of God unless he is born of water and the Spirit."** Brilliant theologians talk about this verse. Some say *water* refers to "water baptism." Others say *water* refers to the Word of

God. Jesus keeps it very simple. He says,: **"Flesh gives birth to flesh, but the Spirit gives birth to spirit."** It sounds simple to me. Jesus says you are born once of flesh and blood. Now, you must be born of the Holy Spirit.

Jesus explains it is similar to the wind: **"The wind blows wherever it pleases; you hear its sound, but you cannot tell where it comes from or where it is going. So it is with everyone born of the Spirit."** You cannot see the Spirit, but you can look and see addicts freed from their horrible addiction. You can see drunks restored to sober health; you can see miracles caused in people's lives because of God's Spirit. You can see Momma Ruby's life transformed from doubt and uncertainty to a loving Grandmother full of peace and wisdom.

"How can this be?' Nicodemus asked" (9).

" 'You are Israel's teacher,' said Jesus, 'and do you not understand these things? I tell you the truth, we speak of what we know, and we testify to what we have seen, but still you people do not accept our testimony. I have spoken to you of earthly things and you do not believe; how then will you believe if I speak of heavenly things? No one has ever gone into heaven except the one who came from heaven— the Son of Man. Just as Moses lifted up the snake in the desert, so the Son of Man must be lifted up, that everyone who believes in Him may have eternal life" (John 3:10–15).

My dear mother took me to Sunday school and church every Sunday. Actually, I went to church nine months before I was born. Around the age of thirteen I began to understand some of the scriptures. I realized I was a sinner: **"For all have sinned and fall short of the glory of God"** (Romans

3:23, KJV). I also realized that because of my sin I was under God's death penalty: **"The soul who sins is the one who will die" (Ezekiel 18:4). "For the wages of sin is death" (Romans 6:23**, KJV). (I also knew the second part of this verse, **"but the gift of God is eternal life in Christ Jesus our Lord."**) I even knew the scripture where Jesus told Nicodemus: **"You must be born again."** My problem was: I did not know how to be born again.

I also knew **Luke 13:3 and verse 5**, where Jesus says: **"I tell you, no! But unless you repent, you too will all perish."** When the Lord repeats a message, it is extremely important. I had heard preachers talking about repentance. They explained that *repent* means turning away from sin and going in a different direction. At age thirteen I decided to stop sinning. I decided that I would only do and be what God wanted me to do and be. During the two years that followed my decision to be a Christian, I made an amazing discovery. I discovered I was a lost sinner and there was absolutely nothing I could do about it. I could not be the perfect person that God wants me to be.

New Year's Day came along. I made only one resolution: this year I would live for Christ and do no wrong. Before the sun set, I knew I was already in trouble. One thing I was saving for last: After getting my life in shape and living completely for God, then I would go down and tell the pastor: I believe in Jesus; I want to be baptized. Since I could not get my life completely holy for God, I decided that maybe if I were baptized this would help to make it happen.

On Sunday morning in church when they were singing the hymn of invitation, I went down and shook the pastor's hand. I told him: "I want to be baptized." The pastor asked me several questions about my faith in Jesus. I knew all of the right answers. I had learned them in Sunday school.

When I was being lifted out of the baptismal waters, in my heart I did something I had not done before. I said within myself: "Lord, I now directly promise you that I will never sin again." Do you know how sad this is? I lied to God. I was a miserable, lost sinner, and there was nothing I could do about it.

At age fifteen I was sitting on the side of my bed one night, reading the scripture from the Gospel of **John, chapter 3**. I knew I had to be born again, but how? In verse 14, Jesus explains to Nicodemus how to be born again. Jesus says: **"Just as Moses lifted up the snake in the desert, so the Son of Man must be lifted up."** I remembered having studied about Moses and the brass snake in the desert. I looked in my concordance and found the event recorded in Numbers 21 in the Old Testament.

"They traveled from Mount Hor along the route to the Red Sea, to go around Edom. But the people grew impatient on the way; they spoke against God and against Moses, and said, 'Why have you brought us up out of Egypt to die in the desert? There is no bread! There is no water! And we detest this miserable food!' Then the Lord sent venomous snakes among them; they bit the people and many Israelites died. The people came to Moses and said, 'We sinned when we spoke against the Lord and against you. Pray that the Lord will take the snakes away from us.' So Moses prayed for the people. The Lord said to Moses, 'Make a snake and put it up on a pole; anyone who is bitten can look at it and live.'

So Moses made a bronze snake and put it up on a pole. Then when anyone was bitten by a snake and looked at the bronze snake, he lived" (Numbers 21:4–9).

Do you understand this story? Moses was leading the Children of Israel out of slavery and bondage in Egypt to the land God had promised to give to them. When the people became very hungry, God began to rain down "manna" or bread from heaven to feed them. The Israelites could have gone directly into the Promised Land. Because of their lack of faith, they refused. Therefore, God caused them to wander for forty years in the desert. God would raise up a new generation to enter the Promised Land. The people continuously complained and fussed. They spoke against God and against God's man, Moses. God punished them by sending poisonous snakes into their camp. Everyone who was bitten by a snake died.

As people began to die, they realized they had sinned against God. They came and apologized to Moses. They asked him to pray to God to remove the snakes. God did not remove the snakes. Instead, God told Moses to make a bronze snake, place it on a pole in the camp, and tell everyone, "If you are bitten by a poisonous snake, just look to the bronze snake and you will live." From that day forward when a poisonous snake bit someone, if they looked to the bronze snake on the pole they lived. If they refused to look to the bronze snake, they died.

Jesus told Nicodemus: **"Just as Moses lifted up the bronze snake in the desert, in the same way I am going to be lifted up, that <u>everyone who believes in Me will have eternal life</u>."** Do you see how simple this is? Moses placed a bronze snake on a pole and told everyone: "If you are bitten by a snake, simply **look and live**." Now, Jesus says, I am going to be lifted up on a cross. You do not even need to roll your eyes up to see. All you need to do is believe in your heart—and you will live forever with Him in heaven.

Then, Jesus gives us perhaps the greatest verse in the Bible. This verse is a brief summary of the Gospel or Good News from God: **"For God so loved the world that He gave His only begotten Son that whosoever believes in Him should not perish but have everlasting life"** (John 3:16, KJV).

As a fifteen-year-old boy, when I read this verse, the Holy Spirit revealed something to me I had never understood. I realized God was making a direct promise to me. I did something that I had seen in Sunday school. The verse says: **"God so loved the <u>world</u>."** Who is the world? (Anyone!) The verse also says: **"that <u>whoever</u> believes in Him."** Who is whoever? (Anyone!) You can place your name in the parentheses to make it personal. I prayed the verse like this:

"For God so loved Ray (the world) that He gave His only begotten Son, that (if) Ray (whoever) believes in Him, he should not perish but have eternal life." You can also make this substitution in verse 17 as follows: **"For God did not send His Son into Ray (the world) to condemn Ray (the world), but to save Ray (the world) through Him."**

That night, as a fifteen-year-old boy, I got on my knees by my bed and prayed: "Lord, I see something here I never understood. You are promising me all I need to do to be saved, to be a Christian, is not to struggle, fight, quit anything, or do anything. You are telling me all I need to do to be saved is to believe in your Son, Jesus Christ."

I continued, "Lord, I believe Jesus is the Christ, the Messiah, the anointed One promised in the Old Testament; your only begotten Son. I believe He was perfect in every respect. I believe Jesus never committed a sin or did anything wrong. I believe He went to the Cross of Calvary and died in my place to pay the debt I owe for my sins. I believe Jesus shed His blood for me on that cross. I believe Jesus died, was buried in a tomb, and three days and three nights later, He arose from the dead. I believe He ascended up into heaven and is alive today at Your right hand.

"Lord, I believe with all of my heart. If I do not have the faith I need, I pray as did one of your followers: **'Lord, help my unbelief!'** Lord, you know how hard I have tried for the past two years to be a Christian. You know I cannot be a Christian in my own strength. Now, I see you are telling me all I need to do to be saved is to believe in Your Son. I believe in Jesus with all of my heart—to the best of my ability. Lord, You are my only hope."

Then, I prayed something I should not have prayed; I said: "Lord, If I am not saved now, then there is nothing I can do about it and you have lied to me, because Your Word says all I need to do to be saved is believe in Your Son, Christ Jesus, and I am doing this the best I know how!"

After that prayer, I fell asleep. When I woke up the next morning, something was different. I experienced inner strength, joy, and a love for others that I had never known. Jesus says when you receive Him, His Holy Spirit comes and lives within you. Today, more than sixty years later, I can tell you His promise still holds true. I take great confidence in

God's promise: **"I will never leave you; nor forsake you" (Hebrews 13:5**, KJV).

Today, God makes his offer of a new birth—of salvation—to you. If you would like to be saved, if you would like to be a Christian, if you would like to have everlasting life with God, then God invites you to receive His only begotten Son, the Lord Jesus Christ. You simply receive Him by faith, by trust. There is one key that can make your relationship with God successful. **"You will seek Me and find Me when you seek Me with all your heart" (Jeremiah 29:13**, KJV). If you desire a relationship with God, you must be willing to seek Him with all of your heart. God must be first above all else. Only then can you fully *realize* God.

Some folks believe they are so miserable and wicked God will not have anything to do with them. They do not understand how much God loves them. Jesus gives His personal promise: **"whoever comes to Me I will never drive away" (John 6:37)**. Some people claim God has already made up His mind about who will or will not be saved. **"God is patient with you, not wanting anyone to perish, but everyone to come to repentance" (2 Peter 3:9)**.

While Jesus was nailed on the Cross of Calvary, one of the two thieves being crucified with him looked to Him in faith and said: " **'Jesus, remember me when you come into your kingdom.' Jesus answered him, 'I tell you the truth, today you will be with Me in paradise' " (Luke 23:42–43)**.

It still works the same way today. If you will cry out to the Lord Jesus Christ In faith and say, "Master, remember me…" then God will hear your heart's cry. God will reach out to you. God will save you from your sins. God will receive you as His dear child. God will make a place for you in His kingdom. God offers you the free gift of His love. But, you must receive this free gift. You must invite the Lord to come into your life and be your Savior. You must do this **"with all your heart."** If you do, you will immediately begin to *realize God*.

Some people say, "I don't feel anything! I did what you said and I still feel the same." God is not offering you a feeling or an emotion. God is offering you His only begotten Son. God offers you eternal life with Him in heaven. God says you may have this free gift by believing in His Son. When you buy a home or a car, you go in and sign your name on a dotted line and the transaction is complete. You might not feel as if you own a new home or car, but the deal is settled when you sign your name.

In the same way, when you trust God and His Word and invite the Lord Jesus to come into your life to forgive your sins and cleanse you from all unrighteousness, your faith closes the deal. You do not need any special feelings. God honors His Word. This is simple faith in action. However, I fail to see how anyone cannot be moved by the gravity of *realizing* God.

Chapter 5

Trusting God to Keep His Word

In the summer of 1949 I graduated from the High School of Charleston and enrolled in the College of Charleston. Although tuition for the first semester was only $87, salaries were equally as low, especially for a part-time worker. As I remember, I earned seventy-five cents per hour in a department store. I struggled to make ends meet but finally managed to survive my first year.

When school was out, my aunt and uncle and cousins in Sycamore, South Carolina, invited me to live with them and get a job in Aiken County. My cousin Robert and I were both successful in getting jobs at the construction site known as *the Savannah River Project*. I was hired as a carpenter clerk.

From my very first check I gave 10 percent of the gross amount to the Lord in church as a tithe of my earnings. In addition I gave a small offering. I paid my necessary expenses, took a very small amount for a cheap weekend date, and banked the remainder to try to save enough to enter college in the fall.

One weekend at home in Charleston, summer was half gone. Looking at the amount I had saved for college, I knew I would not have enough money to enter school in the fall. I also knew I was saving virtually the maximum amount possible each week.

Late Sunday night, sitting on the side of my bed, I opened my Bible and read from **Malachi, chapter 3, verses 8 through 10:** *"Will a man rob God? Yet you have robbed me. But you say wherein have we robbed You? In tithes and offerings. Bring you all the tithes into the storehouse, that there may be meat in my house, and prove me now herewith, says the Lord of hosts, if I will not open the windows of heaven, and pour you out a blessing, that there shall not be room enough to receive it"* (KJV).

I fell to my knees beside my bed and prayed: "Lord, in these verses you promise me that if I give a tithe, you will pour out a blessing that is so big, I will not have room enough to receive it. Lord, I can't imagine such a blessing that I would not have room enough to receive it. I don't want such a tremendous blessing. However, I do need enough money to get back into school in the fall.

"Lord," I prayed, "You know I have given You a tithe of every cent I have earned from my first pay check until now. Also, I have given an offering in addition to my tithe. I have not given these tithes and offerings, expecting anything in return. I gave because I love You. If You don't help me, I shall continue to give You Your tithes and offerings. But, Lord, You promised. You tell me: **'prove Me, test Me.'** Now, I am asking You to keep Your Word and help me earn enough money to get back into college."

Monday morning at 5:00 a.m. I met my friend who had a car and also worked at the Savannah River Plant. A miraculous week was under way. When my friend dropped me off at my office in Aiken County, my boss, Mr. Miles, the superintendent of the area where I worked, did not even smile.

He was usually very friendly and outgoing. Today, however, he abruptly threw the keys of the company pickup truck on my desk and said, "Get the truck! We're going to Central Shops."

Central Shops was the head office for the entire plant. It was the place where they hired me when I began my job. Quickly, I drove the pickup truck to the front of the building and picked up my boss. As we drove along; he did not speak, smile, or offer a clue as to the reason for this strange assignment. He sat and shuffled through his papers.

Arriving at Central Shops, we entered the office of the big boss. He was sitting there at his desk reading some papers with his yellowed plastic framed spectacles drooped down on his nose. His half-bald head glistened in the light. In front of him superintendents and foremen were seated in chairs arranged in horseshoe fashion in the large room. My boss roughly ordered me to report to the big boss.

As a lad of only eighteen years, I had never been treated so callously. My first impression was to escape. But, I walked over to the big boss' desk and stood there. After a few moments that seemed to be a lifetime, the boss peered over the rims of his glasses and said, "Mr. Smith?"

No one had ever addressed me as "Mr." I felt that title should be reserved for people with age or status or importance, but not for some young lad. I replied, "Yes, sir."

The boss continued, "Do you remember the suggestion you dropped into the suggestion box earlier in the summer about how we can improve our record keeping?"

"Yes, sir," I answered.

"Well, we've talked it over. We decided it's a good idea. We're putting it into practice. So, we are giving you this cash award."

What a happy relief! Not only was I relieved that I was not being prosecuted for some unknown violation, but I had just asked the Lord for help. Now, early Monday morning help had arrived. When I looked at the amount of the award, it was only about $25. I instantly bowed my head and said in my heart, "Lord, thank you for your quick answer to my prayers. Lord, You know I appreciate this. It will help. But, Lord, it is not nearly enough to get me back in school. Yet, I trust You to help me."

Thursday afternoon brought another surprise. Everyone working at the construction site was notified that the E. I. DuPont de Nemours and Company was building that plant for the United States government at a cost of one dollar. (The government would pay all salaries and expenses, but the DuPont Company would only earn one dollar of profit for the entire project.)

The message went on to say the project was behind schedule. They hated to inform the workers, but the DuPont Company was required to fulfill its contract by a certain date. In order to finish the job in a timely way, everyone would be required to work an additional two hours per day, Monday through Friday. Two hours each day! Five days each week! That's ten hours of overtime! Time-and-a-half pay for ten hours! That's fifteen hours of extra pay per week!

I again bowed my head and prayed, "Almighty Father in heaven, thank You Lord! With this overtime for the remainder of the summer I'll have more than enough money to get back into college any maybe even some for next year. Thank You, Lord, for keeping Your Word to me."

Let me ask you a question. Was this just some strange set of coincidences? Or, did the Lord keep His promise when I asked and trusted God to stand behind His Word?

Although I rejoiced in these answers to my prayers, still, I was puzzled by the amazing promise of Malachi 3:10. What could be a blessing so tremendous, so big, **"that there shall not be room enough to receive it?"** Certainly, the Lord was not speaking of money—was He? Nonetheless, I was determined to always give a tithe plus an offering of the first of everything I earned or received.

Snooks

My dad had two brothers. John died in Thalmann, Georgia, many years ago. The other, Troy G., or "Snooks," as he was called, worked as a conductor for the Seaboard Airline Railroad in Georgetown, South Carolina, about sixty miles north of Charleston. Snooks married Hazel, but they had no children.

Dad was a telegraph operator for the Seaboard Railroad for forty-three years before he passed away. Since Georgetown is not very far from Charleston, Uncle Snooks would frequently drive down to visit with my dad on week ends. They would drink wine together, tell jokes, and reminisce about the good old days.

Uncle Snooks could have been a great stand-up comic. He told many funny stories. He made people laugh wherever he went. He talked about a panhandler begging on the sidewalks of Georgetown. When the panhandler approached him, he said: "Get on the other side of the street, Mac! I'm working this side."

Every time Uncle Snooks came to visit with my dad, he would always spend time with me. He wanted to talk about Jesus. Each time, I showed him scriptures that give God's simple plan of salvation. Very simply the Bible tells us: (1) **"For all have sinned, and come short of the glory of God" (Romans 3:23**, KJV); (2) **"For the wages of sin is death; but the gift of God is eternal life through Jesus Christ our Lord" (Romans 6:23**, KJV).

Since every one of us has sinned and "come short of the glory of God," and the wages for our sin is death, how do we receive God's "gift" of "eternal life"? The answer: **"If you shall confess with your mouth the Lord Jesus, and shall believe in your heart that God has raised Him from the dead, you shall be saved. For with the heart man believes unto righteousness; and with the mouth confession is made unto salvation" (Romans 10:9–10**, KJV).

Time after time Uncle Snooks and I would have this conversation. Each time he tried to elevate me above Jesus. Each time I tried to help him understand that Jesus is our Savior and Lord; Jesus is the Son of the Almighty God. We must trust Him completely. He is our only hope. Every time I talked with Uncle Snooks, I tried to help him understand this simple truth. Every time he returned to Georgetown without *realizing* or understanding God.

The last time I saw Uncle Snooks alive, he was in Charleston, visiting with my dad. We had our conversation about the Lord Jesus. He still did not seem to understand.

However, a couple of days later, he called me on the telephone. He said when he was driving back to Georgetown that night; he drove by a small wooden church along the highway. A single bright light outside of the church lit up the building. He drove up into the churchyard, parked his car, and went inside. The outside light enabled him to see the empty pews and the pulpit at the front of the building. He walked down the aisle and kneeled in front of the platform near the pulpit. He confessed to God that he is a sinner and asked Jesus to come into his life and forgive him and help him to begin living his life for God. Uncle Snooks said God heard his prayer and answered. He said, "Now I understand! Now I am a child of God!" Charlene, the pretty girl I was to marry in June, never met him in person, but she was able to talk with him during this telephone call.

Not long afterwards, before he had the opportunity to return to Charleston, Uncle Snooks was driving his car with a friend to see the new home he was building across the river from Georgetown. As they turned left off of Highway 17, a man coming from Charleston, driving faster than 80 miles per hour, crashed head-on into his car. My uncle, his friend, and the driver of the speeding car were all killed.

Aunt Hazel asked me to say a few words at Uncle Snooks's funeral. When we arrived in Georgetown, my aunt said something had really happened in Snooks's life, since he last returned from Charleston. She said a poor neighbor did not have proper clothes to wear to church. She said, "Snooks got out not just a suit. He gave his best suit to the man." She said, "A little boy was working trying to fix his bicycle. Snooks went to the store and bought him a brand new bike." She said, "I cannot understand why he was doing these things."

When the Lord Jesus comes into your life, when you *realize* God, everything is made new. **"Therefore if any man be in Christ, he is a new creature: old things are passed away; behold, all things are become new"** (2 Corinthians 5:17, KJV) Snooks's behavior was reflecting his new walk with Christ. Snooks had realized God.

Chapter 6

You're in the Army Now

My pal, Marion, and I were the best of friends. We attended church together, sang in the youth choir, double dated, and enjoyed life. But, the Korean conflict was raging and young men were being drafted into military service.

We talked about how we should handle our military obligation. We decided upon two different paths. Marion wanted to "join the air force and see the world." I said, "Marion, if we join anything, it will be for four long years. If we let them draft us into the army, we can be out in two years and back on the beach."

But Marion's mind was made up. He enlisted in the U.S. Air Force without me. He performed his basic training somewhere out in Texas. After basic training, he was assigned to work in a boiler room on the air base at Sonderstrom, Greenland. He described Sonderstrom as a frozen base surrounded on three sides by frozen mountains and on the fourth side by a frozen ocean.

After several months of service, a boiler exploded, killing Marion's colleague. The air force transferred him to a desert base in one of the western states of America where he completed his four-year tour of duty.

More than a year after Marion joined the air force, I received a unique postcard in the mail. The message on the postcard began: "Greetings!" It said the president of the United States and my friends and neighbors had decided that I should be inducted into the military. This was a standard postcard that draftees received during the war years.

Reporting to the local draft board as directed by the postcard, I was bused along with twenty-four other young men to Columbia, South Carolina, for a pre-induction physical examination. I remembered a star guard on our high school football team. He had been rejected by the army because of flat feet. I also have very flat feet.

We stripped down to our shorts. The doctor, followed by two aides with clipboards, began examining us. When the doctor examined me, I pointed down to my feet and said, "Look, doctor, I have flat feet!" The doctor paused. Looking down and pointing with his finger, he counted, "One, two!" He said, "You are all right." Then he finished making his rounds.

The only one he rejected that day was a very large young fellow named Andy. Andy was so huge they could not weigh him on a single scale. A scale only weighed up to 300 pounds. The medics brought in a second scale and asked Andy to stand with one foot on each scale. They were trying to slide the indicators along the bars of the scales to weigh him, but Andy's weight kept shifting slightly back and forth. They were never able to get an accurate weight. Finally, they decided that if they could not weigh Andy, they probably could not clothe him either. They rejected him. They classified him as "4-F" and sent him back to Charleston to his great delight.

April 6, 1953, I reported to Fort Jackson, South Carolina, outside of Columbia. I was inducted into the U.S. Army for a period of two years. I began as a "private E-1." That is the lowest form of humanity in the military. Our first order of business was to get new clothing—colored olive drab. Some of the troops had problems getting proper sizes. I was six feet one inch tall and weighed 155 pounds. My clothes fit just fine, or as fine as Army clothes can fit.

One problem disturbed me. Combat boots were made of leather with the smooth side turned in and the rough, unfinished surface facing outward. We were told that we were required to "shine those boots until you can see your face in them." It seemed impossible at the time, but I soon learned that many seemingly impossible tasks were indeed possible with a lot of hard work. I guess this was an invaluable part of training, expecting to accomplish things no matter what! That training has served me well throughout my lifetime.

Our first week end at Fort Jackson they loaded us into the back of big army trucks and drove us out to a huge lake. The drill instructors began doing their job, preparing civilians from many walks of life for military service. Our tour could also include combat. War was raging in Korea, although they called it a "police action." They gave us wheelbarrows and shovels. We were ordered to bog out into a lake and shovel the mud from the bottom.

After an hour of shoveling, everyone was assembled on the bank of the lake. A request was made for volunteers who had experience driving trucks. How I wished that I could drive a big truck. Surely, driving a truck would be much easier than shoveling sticky mud. A number of experienced truckers were selected. Then, these "truck drivers" were given the job of pushing wheelbarrows full of mud out of the lake. Immediately, I was very happy that I was not a truck driver!

I was assigned to an infantry company. Our abode was like a half tent/half wooden structure. It was comprised of board siding, extending about four feet from the ground. Screen wire reached from the wooden siding to a canvass roof. We were alphabetically designated to sleep in bunks, which were stacked two high.

Never mind that the weather was still very cold in early April. The army does not operate with common sense. They had a certain date when they removed heat from the buildings. We had no warmth in our new "home." In the morning frost was everywhere. If you dressed in long underwear, you were comfortable during the cold morning hours. By the middle of the day, however, the sun brought intense heat. If you marched with all of your gear on your back, wearing long underwear, you sweltered.

The weather was a real dilemma. If you dressed for the morning cold, you were scorched by noon. If you dressed for the midday heat, you froze in the mornings. Unaccustomed to these conditions, I soon acquired a serious respiratory infection. I went on "sick call." The sergeant gave me two APC tablets and sent me back out for training. The trainees called those APC pills "all-purpose capsules." No matter what kind of problem you had, they gave you APC capsules. When the weekend came, I was running a fever and had severe chest congestion.

I went to the orderly room to get help. The NCO (non-commissioned officer) on duty reached for the APC bottle again. I realized that if I could not help myself, no one would help me. While the NCO was getting his APC bottle, I slumped back in my chair and began breathing deeply through the congestion in my chest, making a horrible, rasping sound.

Hearing and seeing this, the NCO quickly called the hospital for help. The hospital dispatched an ambulance. The NCO thought I was dying. He called the hospital two more times. They could not get the ambulance there quick enough for this young fellow in charge. In the hospital, a doctor told me I had pneumonia.

Just a few days later, after a series of penicillin shots in the rear, I was discharged from the hospital and sent back for basic training. Although I did not feel completely well, duty called. Since I missed a week's training with my unit, I was assigned to another outfit that was just beginning basic training. This time I was assigned to Battery C, Forty-third Field Artillery Battalion, in a barracks on "Tank Hill." Tank Hill is named because of a large water tank on top of the hill.

Although the barracks had no heat, they offered better protection from the unfriendly changes in the weather. There were four two-story barracks in the battery with an "orderly room" in the middle where the commanding officer, the first sergeant, and a clerk were located. At the end of the row was a kitchen and "mess hall" where we ate our meals. A "day room" with a pool table and chairs provided some entertainment. Each outfit consisted of 220 trainees.

Trainees were assigned turns performing "KP," or kitchen police. We assisted with food preparation and cleaning the mess hall. If a trainee caused a problem, he was given additional duties as KP. For big problems, the trainee was given a tablespoon and ordered to remove the grease from the grease trap, a large cistern that collected grease from the kitchen.

If a trainee caused an even bigger problem, he was given a shovel and ordered to dig a "six by." A "six by" is a hole six feet wide, six feet long, and six feet deep. The commanding officer fastidiously checked to insure that the precise measurements were exact. If a dimension was too short, more dirt had to be removed. If a dimension was too long, dirt had to be packed back on the sides of the hole to make the measurements exactly a six-foot cube. When the job was completed to the Commanding Officer's satisfaction, he kicked some leaves into the hole with his combat boots and ordered the trainee to refill the hole.

Although basic training was very rigorous, it was excellent exercise and sometimes almost fun. Our unit was a "light weapons" outfit. In addition to carrying an M-1 rifle, we learned how to fire and maintain Browning automatic rifles, machine guns, hand grenades, rifle grenades, two sizes of mortars, and even a flame thrower.

We also qualified with a .45-caliber pistol. The instructor explained why the army changed from .38 to .45 calibers after the Spanish American War. The Army discovered in guerilla warfare that you could empty your .38 revolver into a guerilla and he could still come and kill you before he died. With a .45-caliber pistol, one shot—even in the hand—would knock a man down.

Wherever our outfit went, we marched in cadence. The drill instructor (DI) marched with us counting cadence. To the command of "forward march" everyone started out on his left foot. At first we all counted out loud with the instructor: "one, two, three, four—one, two, three, four." Then the DI became creative. To the cadence of marching troops we would participate with him in reciting various rhymes, such as: "I don't know but I believe; I'll be home by Christmas Eve. Sound off—one, two; sound off—three, four; shake it on down now: one, two, three, four—one, two—three, four!"

Another of these marching cadence rhymes was "If I die in a combat zone, box me up and send me home." There were many other rhymes. Some were obscene. If not for the fact that people overseas were dying in a vicious conflict, basic training would have been something like football camp and preparation for the autumn football season.

We were required to "fix bayonets" and charge into dummies with wooden sticks affixed to them. The dummies appeared as enemy troops coming towards us with their bayonets in place. Thankfully, their bayonets were merely wooden sticks. At the command of the drill instructor we charged into the dummies. Parrying the wooden stick with an upward swing of our rifle, we brought the butt of the rifle down on the dummy's head. We lunged forward and upward with our bayonet into the dummy to lay open its midsection.

A drill instructor who had just returned from Korea told of how awful it is to use a bayonet live in combat and have a person's intestines erupt over you with a terrible stench. After we practiced this gory exercise until we had mastered the techniques, we stood at attention. The drill instructor shouted: "What is the spirit of the bayonet?" We shouted: "To kill! To kill! To kill!"

Can you imagine a tender-hearted young fellow undergoing such harsh training? How can a person who is basically a lover and not a fighter manage such a transformation? War was raging overseas. The techniques that we were learning were designed not only to kill, but to save our lives, as well as the lives of others. Virtually every unit departed for Korea immediately upon completion of basic training. I asked myself, "How can I kill someone in combat? How can I fulfill what is being required of me?"

That night after taps, slipping out of our barracks, I went up Tank Hill to a base chapel. The army always leaves the light on and the doors unlocked in the chapel. I walked to the front of the chapel, knelt down, and prayed to the Lord about my predicament.

Years earlier, when I reached nine years of age, I had been promoted from the primary department to the junior department in Sunday school. Our church at that time was the Hampton Park Baptist Church in Charleston, South Carolina. The church gave each child entering the junior department a brand new Bible. It was my first Bible. When I took the Bible home, my mother penciled on the front flyleaf: **"Psalm 50:15."** Mom did not preach to me or even mention what she had done.

When I found the inscription, I turned to the verse, which states: **"And call upon Me in the day of trouble; I will deliver** you, and you shall glorify Me" (**Psalm 50:15**, KJV). More than a half of a century has passed. Through the hard knocks of life, I have discovered that God keeps His promises. God has never disappointed me in all of these years. When I call upon the Lord, He hears, and He answers. Sometimes He answers, "No." Sometimes, "Yes." Sometimes, "Wait." God's promises are like blank checks. All you need to do is fill them out and cash them by faith. Even when we fail to understand God's answer, in time we look back and understand. Hindsight is always 20/20 vision.

The Ten Commandments admonish us: **"Thou shall not kill."** I learned that a more accurate translation of this commandment is: **"You shall not murder."** Fighting as a soldier in war is not the same as a street fight, where a person willfully and maliciously with premeditation murders someone.

People confuse the difference in a person who commits murder and a soldier who serves in the military or who serves the government as an executioner. These are as different as night and day. A great outcry is presently being made around the world against the death penalty. Do you know who originated the death penalty? God established the death penalty. **"Whoso sheds man's blood, by man shall his blood be shed; for in the image of God made He man"** (**Genesis 9:6**, KJV). Who repealed the death penalty? Those that have fallen away from God's word and think they are nicer and smarter than God.

People rationalize and say that Jesus and the New Testament changed that. Now, we are supposed to love and forgive. The Lord Jesus indeed commands us to love one another; to **"bless them that curse you and pray for**

them that despitefully use you." On a personal level every one of us must be willing to forgive our fellow man—even of murder.

However, in the New Testament we read: **"Let every soul be subject unto the higher powers. For there is no power but of God: the powers that be are ordained of God. Whosoever therefore resists the power, resists the ordinance of God: and they that resist shall receive to themselves damnation. For rulers are not a terror to good works, but to the evil. Will you then not be afraid of the power? Do that which is good, and you shall have praise of the same. For <u>he is the minister of God to you for good</u>. But if you do that which is evil, be afraid; for <u>he bears not the sword in vain:</u> for he is <u>the minister of God, a revenger to execute wrath</u> upon him that does evil"** (**Romans 13:1–4**, KJV).

Hence, the New Testament describes governmental authority as a **"minister of God"** who **"bears not the sword in vain: for he is the minister of God, a revenger to execute wrath upon him that does evil."** When the Apostle Paul was inspired to write these words, he was not speaking of our merciful system of justice today with trials by jury and countless legal appeals. Paul was writing about the merciless system of Rome—the same legal system that crucified Christ Jesus.

The Bible, therefore, teaches believers to love and forgive. The Bible also teaches that the government is **"the minister of God, a revenger to execute wrath upon him that does evil."** What then is the position of a believer who has been inducted into government service? Jesus teaches that we must **"render unto Caesar the things that are Caesar's and unto God the things that are God's."**

Another scripture also came to my mind: **"I will never leave you, nor forsake you"** (**Hebrews 13:5**, KJV). After crying out to God for His help and direction in my life, I left the chapel that night with an inner aura of peace and determination. I would go wherever I was sent and I would do whatever I was called to do to the best of my ability.

Regardless of how tough and unnecessary the drill instructors tried to be, each day was very special. They reminded me of when I entered the High School of Charleston as a freshman in September of 1946. Hazing of freshmen was a polished art by upperclassmen. The school had been an all-boys' school until the following year when a few girls began to be admitted.

Freshmen were required to run through a "belt line" and be paddled with belts, boards, fists, and whatever the upperclassmen could find. They shaved the hair of many freshmen. Most had their faces painted with lipstick. A couple of small boys were tied to the flagpole rope and hoisted up the flagpole.

In my case, I had an older brother who was a rough, tough tackle on the football team. Because my big brother was around, the upperclassmen realized that I was his younger brother. They treated me with all due respect. After crying out to God for help in my time of need that night in the army, I discovered **"there is a friend that sticks closer than a brother"** (**Proverbs 18:24**, KJV).

Even as an aged man (seventy-seven years at this writing), I still experience and am thankful for my **"friend that sticks closer than a brother."** This is why I am writing. If you are going through life and do not understand what it means to *realize God*, then you are missing the greatest blessings this life affords.

Never mind those science enthusiasts—atheists—smug in their own self-conceits. They do not have a clue regarding anything outside of their little test tubes. What (or, more appropriately, I should say "the One Who") I am talking about cannot be contained in a test tube the size of the universe. Yet He is small enough to live in a little child's heart. With all of the actual physical evidence of spiritual blessings that are manifested in people's lives, I find it difficult to understand why everyone does not *realize* God. How can anyone fail to reach out and grasp the incredible power that is offered to anyone who believes with faith?

Basic Training

The obstacle courses, the long marches, learning to assemble, disassemble, and shoot different weapons—I relished them all. Not only were they a joy, but these activities helped me to mature and grow. When we went to learn about the flame thrower, the cadre asked for a volunteer to demonstrate the weapon. I was surprised; I was the only volunteer.

Instead of using normal napalm, they used a much thinner flammable liquid. The flame thrower has two "triggers." The first trigger ignites an extremely hot blaze at the tip of the weapon. The second releases the combustible fluid that ignites as it passes out of the weapon, shooting a fiery stream many feet away. As I fired the flame thrower, I could feel the intense heat. The instructor said when napalm is used, the heat is not as noticeable.

One day while talking with the battery clerk, a corporal from Alabama, he said he was cumbered with too much typing. He could hardly perform his duties. While working as a carpenter clerk prior to entering the military, I perfected my typing skills. I volunteered to assist him in my spare time after training each day. Don't get the idea that I am a benevolent saint. Typing is a lot easier and cleaner than scrubbing and polishing the barracks, etc.

Working in the orderly room at the end of each day, I became acquainted with the commanding officer (CO), the executive officer (XO), the first sergeant, and the battery clerk. Towards the end of our sixteen weeks of basic training, we went on a field operation called *bivouac*. Bivouac is comprised of two weeks of pretending to be at war. We lived completely out in the field. We dug fox holes and went through virtually everything that could be encountered in a real battle.

Probably because I had volunteered to help the battery clerk, the CO assigned me to take care of the supply tent out in the bivouac area. Or, perhaps, my **"friend who sticks closer than a brother,"** the Almighty God, wanted me to be in the supply room. While the troops were sleeping on the ground and in fox holes, I was sleeping on my fold-up cot in the supply tent. Actually, I would have enjoyed being with the troops in the field and experiencing all of that training. Even as the supply clerk, I still participated in some activities, such as the infiltration course. We crawled across a field at night under live machine gun fire. Bright tracer bullets streamed overhead. If you stuck your head up too high, your training came to a permanent halt with machine gun bullets through the head.

Since my job was to take care of supplies and issue them as needed, there was not a great deal to do. With so much time on my hands, I swept the supply room, mopped the floor, and then arranged all of the equipment in neat rows similar to the displays in a supermarket.

One day the commander for our regiment, a colonel, was driving around in the bivouac area inspecting the troops. He and his driver stopped by my supply room. When the colonel entered the room, I snapped to attention and saluted him. He was very favorably impressed with the neat, clean display of rocket launchers, grenades, etc. After talking with me, he ordered his driver to write down my name, rank, serial number, and date of birth. He said, "We need such men here at Fort Jackson."

I thought about the words of King Solomon: **"Whatever your hand finds to do, do it with all your might"** (**Ecclesiastes 9:10**, KJV). Once again God's Word proved to be a definite asset in my life. When you have a relationship with the Lord, you should want to do whatever you do **"with all your might."** God always honors His Word.

During the two weeks of bivouac, we spent a weekend out in the field. We could not return to our barracks for Sunday chapel. Our commanding officer told me the chaplain could not come out to hold a Sunday worship service. He asked if I would be willing to conduct a worship service for our troops.

I happily volunteered. In our outfit we had four black fellows who enjoyed harmonizing, singing spirituals in the barracks while they cleaned and prepared for inspections. I invited them to sing some Gospel songs at our bivouac worship service on Sunday. They were happy to oblige.

On Sunday morning, all 220 men in our battery met together on the side of one of those lakes we had cleaned out when we first arrived at Fort Jackson. The quartet sang. I read the scripture in the third chapter of the Gospel of John and preached about being born again. I gave my testimony and told how God kept His promise of **John 3:16** in my life.

At the conclusion of the service, I invited anyone who wanted to receive Jesus as his personal Savior to come forward and pray with me. The response of those fellows was overwhelming. I could not count the number that came forward. That evening, they wanted to sit by the lake and talk more about Jesus. We read scriptures, talked about the Lord, and sang until late after darkness.

I suppose if such things happened today, the commanding officer, the chaplain, and I would all be in court somewhere, and those fellows who were preparing to go overseas to war and possibly die would go without **"the peace that passes understanding"** that God gives to those who trust in Him.

When we were on the hand/rifle grenade course, learning to use grenades, we had two accidents, almost simultaneously. When you throw a hand grenade, you grasp the grenade in your throwing hand, holding down the lever that activates the grenade. When you pull the pin out of the grenade, as long as you hold the handle down, the grenade should not explode. As you throw the grenade, the handle flips open and activates the grenade. Grenades are manufactured to explode a set number of seconds after the handle is released.

A young fellow carefully followed these instructions. However, immediately as he threw the grenade, it exploded and riddled his body with shrapnel. The base hospital dispatched an ambulance. While the ambulance was on the way, another young fellow was crouched, holding his rifle butt on the ground and leaning it towards the target. When he pulled the trigger to launch the grenade, the grenade exploded on the end of his rifle. The young fellow properly had his "steel pot" helmet on his head. The helmet deflected the shrapnel. He did not receive a scratch. However, his ears rang for a few days.

The ambulance rushed the trainee to the hospital. Each of his shrapnel wounds was carefully cleaned and stitched. He made a complete recovery. If you see him on the beach or at the swimming pool you will recognize him by the myriad of zipper-shaped scars across his body where he was sewn back together.

Graduation Day

Finally, our outfit had successfully completed sixteen full weeks of training. Towards the end of our training period, the fierce fighting in Korea had diminished. Finally, the war came to an end. Our outfit was perhaps the first in a long time that did not transfer directly to Korea.

We celebrated with a graduation. During the ceremony, I received a letter of commendation from the regimental commander. He designated me as the outstanding trainee of our battery. For sure, there were several men who deserved the honor more. However, my Heavenly Father has a way of reminding me that He does indeed love me with **"an everlasting love."**

Our commanding officer also told me I had three "holds" or opportunities to stay at Fort Jackson, rather than be transferred to another base. One hold was placed by the regimental commander, one was placed by the cadre who perform training, and the third was filed by our commanding officer. The CO said the choice was mine. I could choose any one of the three holds.

Life after Basic Training

Deep inside, I felt that I should stick with my outfit and become the battery clerk. The fellow from Alabama was finishing his tour of duty. Therefore, my first fifteen months in the army were spent at Fort Jackson, South Carolina, as the battery clerk. My commanding officer taught me how to shoot pool with him in the day room. Frequently, he would get me to leave my job and shoot pool. I think he enjoyed playing with me because, more times than not, he would win.

While stationed at Fort Jackson, I was only one hundred miles from home. When I was not assigned to work on weekends, I hitched a ride to Charleston. The bus took almost four hours to travel slightly more than one hundred miles. I could hitchhike in about two hours.

Prior to being inducted into the army, I met a young lady in church. I'll call her Sue. Sue was beautiful. Not only was she pleasing to the eyes, but we enjoyed doing things together. We both attended church together on Sundays. Every possible weekend, I returned home to Charleston.

One weekend I was designated as charge of quarters. I was required to be in the orderly room to take care of all problems until Sunday evening at 6:00 p.m. Around 5:30 p.m. on Sunday evening, Bill, a fellow cadre member from Mississippi, came into the orderly room. Bill said: "Smith! Let's go to Charleston." I replied: "I'm willing, if we have a way to get there."

Bill said to our friends standing around: "Watch me call his bluff. I have a car that we can use." I replied: "You're on!"

I called my girlfriend and told her about Bill. She recruited a girlfriend for him. We arrived in Charleston around 8:30 p.m. We picked up our dates and took them to dinner. Then we drove to the beach on the Isle of Palms, where there was music and lots of activities. Finally, in the wee hours of the morning, we dropped off our dates and headed back to Fort Jackson.

When we arrived at our outfit, everyone was lining up for breakfast at the mess hall. We enjoyed breakfast and then went to work. When you are young, you hardly notice that you did not get any sleep—especially for such a great cause.

The commanding officer and I were friends. I had learned to write all of the necessary reports that he was responsible for sending to Washington. He trusted me to take care of the administrative matters in the battery, thus relieving him of a great deal of responsibility.

The Winds of Change

After many months of serving at Fort Jackson, the army decided to stage special maneuvers in Georgia, South Carolina, and North Carolina called "Operation Flash Burn." I received orders to transfer to Augusta, Georgia. I was to join an outfit there and then travel to North Carolina for the maneuvers.

My commanding officer was not at all pleased. He had been living quite easily. Now, he would be faced with trying to break in a new clerk. The CO sent me to the hospital for a physical examination. After a thorough examination, the only health problem they could find was a small nasal polyp. The ear, nose, and throat (ENT) doctor said the polyp did not need to be removed.

My CO arranged to have his friend, a major who was in charge of the ENT clinic, order the captain to admit me for treatment and remove the polyp. The CO's strategy was to legitimately have my transfer orders rescinded.

In the hospital they discovered a mild lung infection and gave me a series of penicillin shots for a couple of weeks before scheduling surgery. On the morning of the surgery, the doctor gave me a local anesthetic and began to work on my nose. I noticed the doctor had his text book open. He would read his book and then chisel in my nose. Then he would read some more and then chisel away.

After finishing the cutting, he took long strips of gauze that appeared to be coated with cod liver oil or some lubricant. He carefully packed the strips deep into my nasal passages. A couple of days later, the doctor removed the strips of gauze from my nose and examined his work. He was not happy with the results, so he performed another operation. Again, he read his text and chiseled away.

At the conclusion of the operation he packed my nasal passages with the oily strips of gauze. A couple of days later, he removed the gauze. Now, I could breathe freely through both nostrils. That evening, I walked from my hospital ward through the corridors to the hospital theater.

Elizabeth Taylor was starring in the movie *Elephant Walk*. Sitting in the theater for some time, I realized I had been continuously swallowing. I took my tongue and touched some of the mucous on the back of my hand. I had been swallowing blood. No problem, I thought. I had lost a great deal of blood during the operation. What difference does a little loss of blood make?

After the movie, I walked by the library and stopped to look at some books. I casually mentioned to the librarian that I was swallowing a little blood. The librarian became very upset. She said I should immediately return to my ward and tell the nurse.

When I told the nurse, she, too, became very upset. She told me to get in bed and lie still, while she called the doctor. As I lay there in bed, suddenly, I became nauseous and vomited into a bed pan. When I saw the large amount of blood that I threw up, I also became a little concerned.

Although the nurse called the doctor around 8:00 p.m., the doctor did not arrive until after 11:00 p.m. A few days later, I learned from an aide in the doctor's office that the doctor was drunk and had to sober up before he could return to the hospital. I also learned that my nose doctor was actually a foot specialist. No wonder he had his text book open during the surgery!

I was not concerned. Once the doctor arrived, he would know what to do. He would replace those long strips of oily gauze into my nasal passages. This should stop the bleeding and everything would be fine. When the doctor arrived, he placed a cord in my nose and pulled it out of my mouth. Tying a wad of gauze on the cord, he pushed the gauze into my throat and pulled the cord in my nose to pull the gauze securely into the back of my nasal passage. Then he inserted the oily gauze strips in my nose and packed them firmly into my nasal passages. He tied the cord on a small stick to prevent the gauze in the back of my nasal passage from falling down into my throat. I wondered how he could ever get that wad of gauze from the back of my nasal passage.

After noting these procedures in his records, he was preparing to leave. I made a huge mistake. I asked him to take another look because it didn't feel right. When he looked into my mouth, he could see profuse bleeding. Removing the strips of gauze from the front of my nose, he said, "Son, this might hurt a little bit." He grasped the stick tied onto the cord and snatched and jerked that wad of gauze through my nasal passage and out of the front of my nose. When the gauze popped out of my nose, I was tensed and drawn into a tight ball of pain.

Then, the doctor ran a cord back through my nose and out of my mouth. This time, he tied a really big wad of gauze onto the cord and pulled it tightly to the back of my nasal passage. I almost choked at the size of the gauze as he pulled it into my throat. The wad of gauze was so big; a reflex action in my throat kept swallowing, trying to remove the gauze. Next, he replaced the oily strips of gauze in the front and tied the cord on another little stick to keep the ball of gauze from falling down into my throat.

After writing this new procedure into his records, he looked in my mouth and discovered the bleeding was still going full force. His methods had not worked. He shrugged his shoulders and left the hospital. I was placed in my first private room since entering the army. I had lost so much blood that the nurse began administering a blood transfusion.

An LPN (licensed practical nurse) came and sat by my bed. Every now and then she reached over, grabbed my wrist, and checked my pulse to see if I were still alive. Whereas, I thought that once the doctor arrived, everything would be all right, now I realized the doctor was not the one in charge. I had lost a considerable amount of blood and was still bleeding. If the bleeding did not stop, I could see myself being pushed down that long narrow green corridor that leads to the morgue.

Have you ever arrived at a point when you knew that today might be the last day of your life? Such a moment helps a person cut through all of the superficial thoughts and things that cloud our vision and enables us to see and think clearly about more important things, such as life or death.

As I lay there, reeling from the pain of that gauze being ripped through my nose, I wondered whether I would live or die. A couple of Bible verses filled my thoughts. I did not remember at the time exactly where the verses are found, but I remembered the words. Since that time, I discovered the verses are cited twice in the Bible. **"My son, despise not the chastening of the Lord; neither be weary of His correction; For whom the Lord loves He corrects; even as a father the son in whom he delights" (Proverbs 3:11–12 and Hebrews 12:5–6**, KJV).

Actually, the verses brought me great comfort. I prayed: "Lord, you must really love me dearly, because this is the grandest chastening I have experienced in my life." I understood this could possibly be my last night on earth. I knew God does indeed love me. I knew that I had invited the Lord Jesus to come into my heart and forgive my sins and be my Savior. I knew I would go to be with God. I was not afraid.

One overwhelming thought became very evident to me. I realized I might never again have the opportunity to tell someone about Jesus—to help bring a person to a saving knowledge of the Lord. I thought about people I had talked with in the past. I realized the gravity of such a moment. I knew that protocol and other politically correct notions of polite conversation are not nearly as important as doing everything within your power to help someone make the vital decision of *realizing* God in all of His fullness.

Within myself I decided if ever the opportunity presents itself, if I survive, I will do my very best to help anyone come to know the Lord Jesus as Savior. (Perhaps this is the reason why my wife and I are presently serving as pastor of the International Baptist Church Sofia. Perhaps it is also a deep motivation for writing this book.)

As dawn began to break, the bleeding slowed and finally stopped. When the day shift arrived, the new staff began to wash and clean the bed patients. When they wiped me off, they started the bleeding again. The doctor issued orders to not touch me or my bed.

My hospital stay lasted for a total of forty-eight days. After several days, the big wad of gauze in the back of my nasal passage came loose from the cord that held it in place. The wad fell down into my throat. I was able to cough it out of my mouth. What a blessed relief!

Finally, I was discharged. I returned to my outfit. Not long afterwards, with only nine months left in my enlistment, I was placed on orders to transfer to Germany. A friend at the personnel office told me, "They do not transfer a person overseas with less than ten months of service." My CO again sent me to the hospital to try to derail my orders. However, after the harrowing experience in the base hospital, I think the army wanted me to be as far away from Fort Jackson as possible.

How Long Is Forever?

After a brief period of leave, my transfer orders instructed me to catch a train in North Charleston and proceed to

Camp Kilmer, New Jersey. There, I would board a troop ship for Bremerhaven, Germany. When I showed the orders to my girlfriend, she decided we should become engaged. I told her that engagement is very serious. When a person is engaged, they are no longer permitted to date others. I explained while I am overseas, she should be able to date others instead of staying at home.

She cried. I got her a ring. We became engaged. She accompanied me to the train station. As I was preparing to board the train, she said a lot of nice things and concluded by saying: "I'll wait for you forever!" What a nice sendoff. No one had ever told me anything as nice as that in my life.

Something I considered to be significant: I, along with approximately 2,200 troops, set sail on June 10, 1954 for Southampton, England. From there we sailed to Bremerhaven, Germany. Why is this significant? I was born on June 10, 1932. On my twenty-second birthday the Lord gave me a free trip to Europe with all expenses paid.

Our ship, the USNS *Geiger*, was a cruise vessel that had been converted into a troop ship. Down below, hammocks were strung seven deep. Fitting more than two thousand troops into one ship does not leave much extra space. That evening we proceeded from Staten Island towards the Atlantic Ocean. Since my name begins with S, as in Smith, I was near the end of the alphabet. All of the hammocks were not occupied there, so I got into a bottom berth.

Lying in that hammock, I wondered what would be in store for us overseas. I thought about my girlfriend and the amazing sendoff. "I'll wait for you forever," she had said. As the ship left New York harbor and entered the ocean, it began to sway gently up and down. When I awakened in the wee hours of the morning, I felt like a pancake being flipped in a frying pan. The ship was violently crashing up and down. We encountered a storm in the Northeast Atlantic.

As a young boy, I spent many happy days in Charleston's harbor. Riding boats through the waves was a joy. When I dressed and went for breakfast ("chow," they call it), only about seven GIs were in the breakfast line. Standing in line for breakfast, the fellow in front of me suddenly threw up onto the back of the GI in front of him. When I saw and smelled this, I also began to feel somewhat queasy.

Finishing breakfast, I walked around the ship, exploring. Almost everyone was seasick. I was surprised to see that even the navy crewmembers were seasick. I thought sailors were immune to seasickness. People were throwing up all over the ship—including up and down the stairwells. Through a porthole in the upper deck I could see the bow of the ship crashing into large waves. White, turbulent waves were sweeping over the deck of the ship. The bow would go up on a big wave and then crash down into the sea. What an exciting ride! After about three days, the storm subsided and almost everyone became acclimated to the voyage.

I was enthralled by the beautiful, royal blue, clean water of the ocean. Around the shore the ocean is polluted and discolored with sediment. What a special treat to stand on deck near the bow of the ship and watch the flying fish jump out of the water and sail in the air away from the vessel as it pushed towards our destination.

How do you keep 2,200 men occupied for eight days while sailing across the Atlantic Ocean? The ship had a library where anyone could check out books. I volunteered to maintain the library. They organized a hillbilly band. With all of the innovation possible, the military tried to find things to interest everyone. In the mornings they announced a religious discussion would be held in a certain room. I went to these meetings so we could talk about Jesus. I guess a couple of dozen troops came to the meeting. I sat next to a man in a civilian suit.

People began talking about all kinds of religious stuff. When I had the opportunity to join in, I mentioned the blood of Jesus that was shed for our sins. It was as if no one heard me. Again, I talked about the redeeming blood of Jesus. I'm not sure what kinds of religions those folks were talking about, but they did not seem to know the Lord Jesus and His sacrifice on Mount Calvary. After a while, the man in civilian clothes next to me opened his Bible and pointed to a scripture: **"For Christ sent me not to baptize, but to preach the gospel; not with wisdom of words, lest the cross of Christ should be made of none effect. For the preaching of the cross is to them that perish foolishness; but unto us which are saved it is the power of God"** (1 Corinthians 1:17–18, KJV).

What an eye opener! I learned that many people are "religious," but they have not *realized* God. They have not received the grace and mercy that God offers through His only begotten Son, Christ Jesus. Since that time, I have also discovered that I have family members in Christ Jesus in countries around the world. I'm talking about people who have invited Jesus to come into their life to forgive them of their sins and be their personal Savior. I have friends in

Egypt, Jordan, Greece, Germany, Austria, France, the United Kingdom, Belgium, Holland, Romania, Bulgaria, virtually everywhere I have traveled. I also discovered religious people who do not even have a clue about God's cleansing power They have no indication of God's presence in their lives.

It is just as those verses describe: **"the preaching of the cross is to them that perish foolishness; but unto us which are saved it is the power of God."** Perhaps this is what the Apostle Paul meant by **"having a form of godliness but denying its power."**

After eight days at sea, our ship docked in Southampton, England. We were allowed to go ashore for twenty-four hours. We had to be back on board by 6:00 a.m. the next day. Many of us rushed down to the train station and boarded a train for London. I had a little booklet published by the Defense Department. It told about the people and customs of England. A small cartoon in the book said British men are often very reserved. The British fellow sitting next to me saw the cartoon and asked to borrow my book. He showed the cartoon to his friends. They had a big laugh. They must have been the exception, because they were not reserved at all.

What a happy time! We saw Big Ben, Westminster Abbey, the famous London Bridge, the Thames River, Buckingham Palace, the changing of the guards, the Tower of London—things that I had only read about and seen pictures in books. As night began to fall, we made our way to Piccadilly Circus, the main part of London. The lights there almost rival the lights of Times Square in New York.

As my two buddies and I were walking along, another GI approached us and said: "You fellows had better keep a lookout for your wallet; these girls will take everything you have." As he said this, three English girls passing by overheard him. One of the girls said, "He's right. You should be very careful in this city." My friends began to talk with them, and suddenly I realized that these girls had agreed for us to take them to see a movie.

I did not want that. I did not need that. I was engaged. I was no longer eligible. They insisted that we were merely going to see a movie, so we went to a theater where *Murders in the Rue Morgue* was playing. After a while, one of my friends left with his girl. Later, the other fellow left with his girl. What a mess! Now, I was left alone with this girl in the movie. I am engaged. I am no longer eligible for such as this!

We finished watching the movie. When it was over we went outside. The young lady was nice and understanding. She said that she had to get home, so she left. I was alone in Piccadilly Circus at night. I wandered around enjoying the flashing lights and looking into store windows. As I looked in the window of a shoe store, someone came and grabbed my right arm. I looked into the face of one of the prettiest young ladies I have ever seen.

She looked up into my eyes, smiled, and asked: "How would you like to 'shack up' with me tonight?" In all of my twenty-two years I had never even heard of such a thing. I explained about my fiancée. I told the girl about the Lord Jesus. I carefully outlined God's plan of salvation and how she could be born again. This young lady listened attentively to everything I said.

When I finished, she looked back into my eyes and said: "You still have not answered my question. How would you like to shack up with me tonight?" Then, I told her plainly; "Thank you, but no thanks. I cannot shack up with you tonight." With that the young lady said, "No hard feelings," and excused herself.

Walking away from this scene, somewhat bewildered, I came to a street corner with traffic signals. As I waited for the light to turn green, another lady approached me. She was nice looking, but not nearly as pretty as the previous little lady. However, this one was endowed with extremely large breasts. She grabbed one with both hands. Lifting it up in her dress, she said: "Come wiz me to zee hotel and you can see if it's real."

I thanked the lady for her kind offer and made my way on across the street. I began to wonder what was happening. I had been to New York, Miami, and Los Angeles and had never encountered anything like this. I made my way back to the train station and returned to our ship in Southampton.

At 6:00 a.m. we cast off on the final leg of our journey to Bremerhaven. As the troops were being transferred to many different cities across Germany, I stepped up to a desk and reported to a captain for my destination. The captain reared back in his seat and gleefully shouted: "Boy! Are you from Charleston?" Although he was just being playful, it was good to know I still had my Charleston accent.

My orders were to report to the Second Quartermaster Group in Kornwestheim, a suburb of Stuttgart. Riding all day on the train, I was thrilled to see Germany for the first time.

I saw a number of remnants and fortifications from World War II. Perhaps the most impressive sight was the way the German people planted virtually every available centimeter of soil with vegetable gardens. I remembered the "victory gardens" we planted in Charleston during the war.

Our quarters in Kornwestheim were the best I had seen since entering the army. I was stationed in Ludendorf Kaserne. *Kaserne* means barracks. The allies purposefully did not bomb this site so it could be used by our troops. The barracks were made of brick; they had hot and cold running water. Even the toilets flushed with hot water.

Because of my clerical experience, I was assigned to work in the personnel branch. I "cut" orders for personnel who were transferring or being detailed to another assignment.

Around the middle of July, about one month and a half after my sweetheart at home told me goodbye, "I'll wait for you forever," I received a letter from home. I guess she had waited the required amount of time, because she said the deal is off. Our engagement is finished. That is why I can now say from experience: How long does forever last? Exactly one month and a half!

Talking with my colleagues, I learned that three out of four of the fellows in our outfit had received similar "Dear John" letters. Some of the men would pool pictures of former sweethearts. When a Dear John letter arrived, the GI would send some of these photos with a note: "Thank you for your nice letter. However, I cannot remember exactly which one you are. Would you please pick out your photo and send it back so I can cancel you off of my list?"

The saddest Dear John letter of all was to the first sergeant. He had been overseas for two years and received a letter from the States. His wife said she was having another baby. My heart still aches for this man and his family.

On Sunday morning when I went to the morning chapel service, I showed my Dear John letter to the chaplain. The chaplain was a stout, black fellow. He took me aside and talked with me. He said: "Son, don't you fret over this letter." He continued, "The Lord has already picked out a splendid young lady for you. You just keep your faith in the Lord and you will see."

Actually, deep down in my heart, I knew that the young lady who had been my sweetheart was not the right one for me. We had some major differences. However, as a young novice, I thought we could perhaps work through our differences and make our lives work together. When I think back after all of those years, I can now see clearly how and why the Lord wanted me to wait for His choice and not my own.

Our base in Kornwestheim was surrounded by fields of sugar beets. The Germans used "honey wagons" to haul sewage to the fields to be sprayed on the crops as fertilizer. When the honey wagons were being used, they reminded me of home—the odor of mud at low tide or the paper mill and pungent factory odors.

The countryside came alive on weekends with Germans walking throughout the area. In the South where we live in the United States, people passing on the streets generally greet each other with a "Hello," "Hi," or "Howdy." In Germany the people greet each other with words that sound like "Crease Got!" I was told the interpretation is "Go with God!" and the reply, "God go with you!" What a nice way to honor the Lord!

Our base was surrounded by a chain-link fence with barbed wire on top. One day I was talking through the fence with a young girl. She was about my age. She told me that a fellow from our base fathered a child with her. Then, her fellow transferred back to the United States and she never heard from him again. She resorted to prostitution In order to survive and feed her child.

This young woman talked about the war. She said she was enjoying a peaceful Sunday evening at home when she heard bombs exploding in the distance. The sounds came closer and closer. Then, through tears, she said her home exploded. She saw a large wooden beam fall on her younger brother and crush him to death.

She said she believed that Adolf Hitler was a good leader. She said when he first came into power everyone had a good job and they enjoyed the good things of life. She blamed Hitler's top aides for causing death, destruction, and the war. I was surprised to hear her say: "If Hitler were to return today, I would still say, 'Heil Hitler!'"

Since she was struggling to keep herself and her child alive, I handed her a five deutsche mark coin through the fence. When she saw the money and realized that I did not want her services or anything in return, she cried.

One weekend I had the opportunity of visiting Dachau outside of Munich. Dachau was a concentration camp during World War II. Our tour guide was a former German soldier who had served in the German army. He told of how the allies came through the area during the closing days of the war. Some American GIs were talking about the atrocities at Dachau.

When he heard them talking about the horrible cruelty in this place, he accused them of lying. He said, "No such crimes were committed by the German army." He said the soldiers placed him in the back of their jeep and drove directly to Dachau. When he entered the place, he was astounded. He saw bodies stacked up along a wall like cord wood, waiting to be burned in the crematorium. He showed us where people were forced to stand in front of a brick wall to be gunned down. A "blood ditch," near the wall was covered with a grated wooden drain. The ditch was used to drain away blood from thousands who were shot.

He said on a clear day some would be hanged from the hanging tree. Later they might be shot to be sure they were dead. The hanging tree died from the tremendous number of bullets fired into it.

When prisoners arrived at Dachau, they were told they would receive a shower bath. Both men and women were ordered to take off all of their clothing and leave all personal items outside of the shower. After the people packed into the room, the doors were shut and locked. Water showers began wetting the people. Then, gas was pumped into the room killing them all. He said the poisonous gas attacked through wet skin, as well as by breathing. He said their clothes and items were cleaned and sold in places such as Spain.

Clergymen used large metal tongs, similar to ice tongs, to clasp a corpse in both ears. Bodies were dragged into an adjacent room. Doors to the crematorium were opened and metal stretchers pulled out. Two or three bodies were loaded onto a stretcher and pushed into the oven where they were cremated. He said people serving on the burning detail could only do this job for about a month before they had to be exterminated. Jewish rabbis were used first. When they ran out of rabbis, they used Catholic priests and then Protestant clergymen.

He said ashes were placed in a tin can, similar to a coffee can and mailed to the next of kin for a fee of thirty-five marks. Ashes indiscriminately placed in cans were not the exact ashes of a relative. If the relative failed to pay for the ashes, they were subject to a trip to Dachau.

After viewing these grisly sights, we visited long wooden shelters and saw where prisoners were kept prior to their execution. The exact number of thousands who were slaughtered at Dachau cannot be accurately determined. However, the number of buildings in the holding area suggests a tremendous loss of life. The stark reality of "man's inhumanity to man" still troubles my spirit until this day.

At the entrance to Dachau a bronze statue of an emaciated prisoner stands with the words written in German: "To remember the dead; to remind the living." In 1996 my wife and I concluded a period of service with the United States Customs Service in Bucharest, Romania. We took two weeks of annual leave and traveled around Europe before returning home to South Carolina.

When we arrived in Dachau, I was amazed at the bright, professional staff who told about the history of this concentration camp. I was astounded to hear them declare that the death equipment in the place was never used to kill anyone. The statue outside with the reminder was already obsolete. The dead were forgotten; the living were not reminded of anything.

During this trip we spent a night at Stuttgart. I took my wife on the train out to Kornwestheim and Ludendorf Kaserne, where I lived for nine months. The base was closed and deserted. A tall chain-link fence with barbed wire surrounded the former base. I pointed out where I had lived. I also showed my wife the chapel where, as I told her, "that prophet of God told me back in 1954 that I should wait for you because God had already picked you out for me."

That chaplain was right. God had indeed prepared a wonderful little bride for me. She has been my constant "helpmeet" for more than fifty years. I would not trade her for all of those I have seen or dated in my lifetime.

In the Sermon on the Mount, the Lord Jesus gives the key to success: **"But seek you first the kingdom of God and His righteousness, and all these things shall be added unto you"** (**Matthew 6:33**, KJV). When you *realize* God, when you seek God and His kingdom first, you have God's solemn promise that **"all these things will be added unto you."** This includes college, employment, home, food, and a loving mate—**"all these things"**!

The sad fact is that many have their vision clouded with so many notions, reasons, ideas, and facts that they fail to *realize* **"the sincere milk of God's Word."** **"No good thing will He withhold from them that walk uprightly"** (**Psalm 84:11**, KJV).

Sometimes many of God's children are destined for suffering and excruciating situations. I have learned that it is safer and better to be in a seemingly impossible situation with the knowledge that you are in God's presence, and in His watch and care, than to be in the middle of your bed and out of God's will for your life.

Chapter 7

Holy Land Bound

As soon as I arrived in Germany, I thought about how much closer Germany is to the Holy Land than the United States. I began to think about attempting to visit the land where Jesus walked and ministered to the people.

In those days an organized tour to Jerusalem cost approximately $1,500.00. As a corporal in the army, I earned about $121 per month, including my overseas pay. My starting pay in the army as a private E-1 was $68.00 per month. I had subscribed to a $50.00 savings bond each month at a cost of $37.50.

The grand total of my available cash was approximately $300.00. In my heart I believed the Lord wanted me to experience the Holy Land. The people at the American Express office in Stuttgart answered many of my questions. I could get a third-class ticket on a train, the Oriental Express, from Stuttgart to Athens for $25.00. From Piraeus, the seaport at Athens, I could book passage by ship to Alexandria, Egypt, for another $25.00. American Express said I could get a steamship ticket from Beirut, Lebanon, to Naples, Italy, via Alexandria and Syracuse, Sicily, for $37.00.

Another hurdle was getting thirty days of leave from the U.S. Army. Although a soldier accumulates thirty days of leave each year, the military normally will not grant thirty days leave at one time. Our commanding officer in the quartermaster group where I was stationed was a lieutenant colonel. I made an appointment and convinced him that the army should grant me thirty days leave so that I could travel alone to the Holy Land.

Finally, on a cold, wintry Monday morning in January of 1955, I boarded a train in Stuttgart, Germany. Trains in Europe were not like the coaches used in America. In America a passenger coach consists of a long, open car with an aisle down the middle and seats arranged by twos on either side of the isle. In Europe the coaches have compartments that seat about six people with a single aisle running down a side of the coach.

I found my third-class seat and put my duffel bag in the storage rack overhead. Third-class seats usually are hard wooden benches. I was happy to discover they had converted a second-class coach for third-class passengers. Another blessing: I was the only person in the entire car. Actually, I had an almost private compartment for most of the trip. I could even stretch out and sleep at night.

For two and one-half days I would be traveling on this train. As a young man I was thrilled to see the countryside; we traveled from Germany through Austria and into Yugoslavia. A sight still vividly imprinted in my mind is a guard with the government. He walked through the railroad car. He was tall, brown, and had a thick black moustache with whiskers. He wore a long, heavy, olive drab topcoat—the kind the military wears. Each time he passed by my compartment, he looked directly at me and scowled.

Years later, when I was working with the United States Customs Service, I used this man as an example of how we should not greet visitors to our country. Perhaps the man was actually a nice person, but his behavior left me with an indelible impression that I still associate with the former Yugoslav Republic. Border personnel should reflect favorably upon the great nation they serve.

Traveling a couple of days on the train, I thought about the thirty days that lay ahead. In my pocket I had a ticket on the ship across the Mediterranean Sea from Piraeus, Greece, to Alexandria, Egypt. I also had a return ticket on a ship from Beirut, Lebanon, to Naples, Italy. I was not sure how I would get to Cairo from Alexandria or how I would get from Cairo to Jerusalem. But I knew I must reach Beirut by a certain day in February in order to board a ship to Naples.

I thought about the money that remained of my original $300. My total cash on hand was down to $187, plus two ship tickets. Could I survive on this amount until I reached Beirut? What about hotels and food that would be necessary? I had packed some chocolate bars, chewing gum, and other such food items to help me survive. Now that I had started this trip, I realized that once I crossed the Mediterranean Sea, there could be no turning back. Reaching Beirut in a timely way for the return trip was mandatory.

Thinking about such vital matters, I asked myself how I became involved in such an adventure. The answer was very plain: I believed the Lord wanted me to have this experience of walking where His only begotten Son had walked. The Twenty-third Psalm came to my mind. I recited the first verse: **"The Lord is my shepherd, I shall not want..."** (KJV). Again, I recited that verse: **"THE LORD IS MY SHEPHERD! I shall not want."** For two and a half days this verse kept echoing in my heart. Understanding the reality of the verse, I relaxed and eagerly looked forward to each day of the journey. I knew that I was traveling in good hands. I had a Good Shepherd who was watching over me. **"The Lord is my shepherd, I shall not want."** This simple promise forged a solid bond between the Almighty God and His child.

As the train traveled through Yugoslavia, a man and his wife came on board. They sat in the compartment with me and spoke excellent English. They explained many things to me and pointed out sights along the way. When the train stopped at a station, the man left our coach and returned with a delicious cheese pie. I had never seen anything like it. He gave me a big slice comprised of thin slices of cheese prepared as a round pie. Not only was it delicious but very nutritious.

When we finally arrived in Athens, we were getting our baggage together to get off of the train. I looked around to say goodbye to my friends, but they were gone. **"Be not forgetful to entertain strangers for thereby some have entertained angels unawares" (Hebrews 13:2**, KJV). To this day I wonder if that couple was a bona fide couple. Or could they have been angels who had come to help me?

For a couple of days I thrilled at visiting places I had only read about and seen pictures of in school books. I thought about how the Apostle Paul walked through the Agora, or marketplace, and preached about Jesus from Mars Hill near the Acropolis. The temple of Zeus, the amphitheater, the

Parthenon, Athena Nike, the caryatids—what a wonderful experience to be there in person. I remembered studying about these places in school and in the Bible!

Time seemed to fly. I soon found myself in Piraeus preparing to board a ship for Alexandria. At the waterfront, an English movie company filmed a movie to be called *Doctor at Sea*. An extremely beautiful young actress in the cast became the famous Brigitte Bardot from France. The movie company shot scenes at the pier and on board the ship as we crossed the Mediterranean.

Since I was traveling in what I thought was "last class," I did not have contact with the movie personnel. I thought I had the lowest class available, but I discovered that there were some passengers who spent the night on the deck. Had I known, I could have traveled deck class, I would have conserved and been with them, but I had a room with a bunk, not to mention food.

When I learned that I was to be fed an evening meal, I sat at a table with a single plate in front of me along with some other passengers. I wondered what would be served for dinner. The waiter brought out a large round metal tray. It was packed with many different kinds of pickles. It was not exactly my idea of a great meal, but I ate plenty of pickles. Later, the waiter returned; he took away the tray of pickles and my plate. Then he brought a clean plate and another huge platter of food.

After we ate from this platter, the waiter again came and removed the platter and soiled plate. Then, he brought a clean plate and another platter of food. After all of the platters had been served, the meal was scrumptious. I only regretted that I had eaten so many pickles before I realized they only serve one course at a time and a clean plate with each course.

The next day when we arrived at Alexandria, a host of local people met our ship. Some were selling various items. Some offered to help with baggage. "Willie Hassan," a guide, offered to take me around to see the sights. I explained that as a soldier I did not have enough money to pay a guide. Willie insisted that he worked for a very meager amount and would not take "No" for an answer. Willie helped me to find a cheap hotel. He returned the next morning to show me the sights. We visited a huge stone column from the empire of Alexander the Great. We went through the catacombs. We toured the palace of former King Farouk of Egypt. We saw the Riviera along the coast. What a beautiful place!

As we toured around the city, Willie stopped at a tea shop for a cup of hot tea. The tea cost one piaster, or about three cents. When I looked at the tea cup I saw the lip prints of a thousand former clients encrusted in the sugar on the rim of the cup. Although I was frugal with my funds, I told Willie that, even if the tea costs ten piasters, we must go to a place where they wash their dishes and are sanitary.

Willie was happy to work for a minimal amount that I could afford. When it was time for me to head for Cairo, he offered to go with me and to continue to help me see the sights for his same low fee, but I declined his generous offer. He arranged a bus ride for me to Cairo.

The Cairo museum is perhaps the most amazing museum I have visited. At that time, hundreds of mummies were on display. (I remember reading in the news years later that when the late Anwar Sadat was in power, he took the mummies off of display because of Muslim beliefs.) I saw the golden burial mask of King Tutankhamen and the artifacts from his tomb. Huge statues of Pharaoh Ramses and many other Egyptian rulers along with countless artifacts overwhelmed me.

One exhibit was very impressive. It was a grave marker from a Christian who died in the first century. The Christian marker said, "You may take my body and spread it to the four corners of the earth. You may throw it into the sea or burn it in the fire." It read: "When the archangel shouts, and the trumpet of God sounds, and my Lord and Savior, Jesus Christ, returns to earth, my body will come alive and I will go to meet Him." What a powerful testimony of faith! Especially in a land where many believed they must be embalmed in order to reach the next world.

In Cairo I discovered the Sphinx and the great pyramids of Giza are situated at the edge of the city. I could visit them by a tram. I do not have words to describe the awe of seeing these tremendous pyramids, rising out of the sands of the Great Sahara Desert—one of the seven wonders of the ancient world! I walked all of the way around the great pyramid. I climbed up inside the passage way to the inner chamber or burial tomb. The passage way had been an air vent. In order to ascend to the inner chamber, you must crouch down and pull yourself up with handrails on each side.

In the 1950s people were allowed to climb the massive stones to the top of the great pyramid. However, a posted sign read: "You may climb the pyramid only with a guide."

I saw a group of "guides"—young fellows about fifteen or sixteen years of age. I asked how much it cost to go to the top. Quickly, they all agreed: "Five dollars and we'll take you right up." I looked up and thought. I would really like to go up, but I could not afford to spend five dollars for such a thing.

I thanked them for their offer and turned to walk away. Immediately, the price dropped to four dollars. Four dollars! That was 20 percent better, but still out of reach of my limited budget. I continued to walk away. The price dropped to three dollars. I stopped; looked; and then continued to walk. As I walked and considered each new offer, the price dropped from five dollars down to ten cents.

The guides were begging: "Please! Walk no further! Only ten cents!" Ten cents was easily within my budget. The necessity for a guide became evident when I realized that veering off course could be hazardous to your health. Stones at the bottom were about chest high. The closer we climbed to the top, the easier the climb became. Finally, we reached the top of the Great Pyramid, the Pyramid of Khufu or Cheops.

On top the pyramid is flat. I walked around the edge and gazed out over Egypt. On one side I saw the two smaller pyramids and the sands of the Great Sahara desert stretching out and disappearing into the horizon. On the other side I saw the sprawling city of Cairo. Down below I could see the Sphinx and people and camels; beyond this, the sparkling waters of the Nile River sliced through the landscape. I was amazed at how the parched dry sands of the Sahara turn green with growth and vegetation as they approach the

Nile River. After we climbed down, I felt somewhat guilty for the price of ten cents, so I gave the fellow around twenty-five cents in Egyptian piasters.

The flight from Cairo to Jerusalem cost $25. While I was waiting at the airport for my flight, I picked up a brochure for English-speaking tourists. The folder addressed the problem of affluent tourists visiting Egypt and upsetting the economy by paying camel jockeys more than a professional businessman or doctor could earn. The brochure said: "For example: If you would like to climb the Great Pyramid, you should only give the guide one piaster." One piaster! That was only three cents! I was still overcharged! And to think their first price was five dollars!

American Express could not tell me how to get a visa into Jordan. I discovered that visas sold almost like hotdogs at the border. A visa was no problem. American Express had told me to take a baptismal certificate to prove that I am a Christian. This was indeed a requirement in those days.

From Cairo, we flew over the Red Sea. I could see the Suez Canal connecting to the Mediterranean Sea. As we flew along, the pilot pointed out Mount Sinai. He said they believe this is where Moses received the Ten Commandments from God. (Since that time I have read of some archaeologists who discovered a mountain in Arabia. The top of the mountain is scorched black from some kind of fire activity. There is no scientific explanation for the burning that took place on top of this mountain. These archaeologists believe that this mountain in Arabia may actually be Mount Sinai. The Bible tells of God appearing to Moses and the Children of Israel on top of Mount Sinai with smoke and fire. How sad that nations cannot cooperate with each other in order to excavate and explore such places to learn more and understand.)

In order to skirt around Israel the airplane flew over the Gulf of Aquaba. Jordan, Arabia, Egypt, and Israel all converge at this gulf. Also, the continents of Africa and Asia come together here.

Flying along, I realized that the land below toward the Mediterranean Sea was the "wilderness" through which Moses led the Israelites out of slavery and bondage in Egypt. They traveled through this land for forty years before Joshua finally led them across the Jordan River into the Promised Land. Just a glimpse gives great insight of the harshness of their "wilderness wanderings."

As the airplane began to descend, I saw the Dead Sea, the lowest body of water in the world. I saw the Jordan River, snaking its way from the Sea of Galilee down to the Dead Sea. As we were approaching the landing strip, I saw the walls of Old Jerusalem. I saw Al Aqsa—the Dome of the Rock Mosque. I saw the Mount of Olives. What a thrill! I was about to reach my goal—a visit to the Holy Land! The land where Jesus walked and lived! (Airplanes are no longer allowed to land in Jerusalem. Flights to Israel today go through Tel Aviv).

Immediately after landing, I found a reasonably priced hotel and checked into a room. Since it was still early in the day, I decided to fulfill a promise I had made to a missionary friend back in Germany. An Assembly of God Missionary named Paul and his wife told me about their good friend Ayoub. Ayoub was born and raised in Jordan. An Assembly of God missionary led him to a life-changing experience with Jesus Christ. Ayoub had *realized* God. My friend in Germany made me promise that I would visit him and tell about the work in Germany. Also, I was instructed to bring back a report to Germany of what Brother Ayoub was accomplishing in Jordan.

Brother Ayoub lived in Es Salt near the capitol of Amman. I learned that the best way to travel in the Holy Land was by taxi. That sounds extravagant, but it was not as fancy as it sounds. A large American automobile would wait at a city until it had a full load. Then, it proceeded to another city. The cost was divided among the five or six passengers.

I was seated in the front with an Arab between me and the driver. Three Arabs were in the back seat. As we drove along, the men were discussing something in Arabic. The passenger next to me could speak English. He said, "They want to know where you are going and what you are doing in Jordan." I explained about my trip and my promise to speak with Brother Ayoub in Es Salt.

He said, "The Arabs hate Americans and the British." Then he added, "In 1946 when the United Nations established Israel as a nation, the Arabs were going to fight and kill the Jews. The ones they did not kill would be driven into the Mediterranean Sea and drowned." Then, he said, "The United Nations stepped in and protected the Jews. Primarily, they blame the British and the Americans for these actions of the United Nations."

He said, "After Israel became a nation in 1948, thousands of Arabic people were moved from their homes and land. They were placed in refugee camps with hardly enough food to survive. They also lacked proper housing; no jobs—nothing!" He said, "This is still a big problem today." (That was in 1955.)

The taxi pulled up at the bottom of a wide sandy road that led up a large hill. As he dropped me off, the driver said, "This is Es Salt on top of the hill." I stepped out into the hot parched sand and watched as the taxi drove off into the distance toward Amman, the capitol. I also looked up and realized that the sun was beginning to lower towards the horizon.

As I walked along the road up the hill into Es Salt, children began coming out of the houses. They followed along behind me. Soon, thirty to forty children gathered around. They followed me as if I were the Pied Piper. They tried to reach into my pockets. When I stopped and turned towards them, they backed off.

I spoke the name of the man I wanted to see, thinking that perhaps they would recognize the Arabic name. They just stared at me. Since Ayoub is a pastor, I said: "Church! Church!" One little fellow finally stepped forward and shook his head up and down in a "yes" motion. I said, "Church." He nodded agreement. Then he stuck out his hand for his fee.

I gave him a chocolate candy bar. He did not know what it was. He stuck out his hand again. I gave him a pack of Juicy Fruit chewing gum. Again, he did not know what it was. He stuck out his hand again. I gave him one piaster (about three cents). Although the chocolate bar and chewing gum were much more valuable, he proudly took the coin and the candy and motioned for me to follow him.

What a procession! A little boy was leading me with a large crowd of children following up the middle of the road into Es Salt. There was not a car in sight. We arrived at a place with a wall about ten feet tall. Over the wall I could see a small cross on top of a building. A huge green wooden double gate on the wall was shut and locked. On the other side of the gate I could hear people playing basketball.

I knocked on the big green gate. No one answered. I could hear the people running and bouncing the ball on the other side. I knocked and knocked. Then, I pounded on the gates. Finally, the gates were opened. Inside were a number of young people and two young men about my age. One was from Detroit, Michigan, and the other was from England. They explained that they were working with the refugee children. They had to play behind the big wall because local youth frequently caused serious problems. That is why they were in no hurry to see who was knocking.

I told them about keeping my promise to talk with Brother Ayoub. They said they knew him and would take me to see him but only upon one condition: I must agree to have dinner with them and spend the night. They explained that they were isolated from the world and wanted desperately to talk with someone who could tell them what was happening in the world and also just to visit with them. (With the sun already beginning to sink in the west, their words sounded like a sweet melody to me.)

After dinner, they assigned a young fellow to accompany me to Brother Ayoub's home. Arriving at the home a few blocks away, we discovered he was on a trip. He would return the next day. His wife said he would contact me when he returned.

On the way back to the refugee mission, an Arabic teenager about eighteen years of age stopped us. He said to me, "We do not like the British and we do not like the Americans. The quicker you get out of this country, the better off you will be." He continued, "Those children who were following you when you came into the city—they were not following you because you are some strange, foreign oddity. They were following you because they were seeking an opportunity to stone you."

I pulled out my passport, opened it to the Jordanian visa, and told the young fellow: "See here! Your own government welcomes me to the Jordan."

He replied: "We do not like our government either."

Although I am basically a lover and not a fighter, I decided that I must be somewhat tough. Since I was in a foreign land without anyone to help, I told the young hoodlum: "Listen to me! I came to this country to look around and see the sights. I will stay here until I have finished. When I am finished, then I will leave." When he realized that I would not be intimidated, the young fellow walked away.

That evening the two refugee workers and I talked about everything from politics to sports to just plain nonsense. Those fellows were really hungry for news and to talk with someone. Their dedication had isolated them from all current events.

The next day, Brother Ayoub came by, picked me up, and took me back to his home. I learned that he and his wife had ten children, including one that was fairly new. I told him about Brother Paul in Germany and the work that he was doing. I mentioned the splendid Gospel meetings that we were conducting in the U.S. Military Crossroads Chapel in Stuttgart. I told him of lives that were being changed as people believed in Jesus and accepted Him as their Lord and Savior.

Brother Ayoub started three churches in the surrounding area. He talked about how missionaries come from America and build a nice building. Then, they cannot understand why their churches are not filled. Brother Ayoub did not have the resources to build impressive buildings. He did know the language and the people. He went from door to door telling people the Good News of Jesus. All three of his churches were filled.

After a lengthy visit, I told Ayoub I must be getting back to Jerusalem where I had checked into a hotel. He looked into my eyes and said, "Brother, the Lord has sent you here, and I'll not let you get away. As long as you are in the Holy Land, you are going to stay with me. I have a small automobile the mission board gave me. I will take you around and show you all of the Bible sights."

I thanked him for the good offer, but I reminded him that he had ten children and three churches to take care of. I could not encroach upon his good nature.

Brother Ayoub looked back at me and let me know in no uncertain terms that he meant what he said. I would be staying with him as long as I was in the Holy Land. Since I could not refuse such a kind, sincere, yet demanding offer, I offered him the money that I was going to spend in the Holy

Land to cover his expenses for gas, etc. He would not touch the money or even consider my assisting with any expense.

We departed in his automobile for Jerusalem. He went into the hotel and retrieved my baggage. With his firm but gentle persuasion, he was able to talk the staff out of billing me for the night that my baggage had spent in my room there.

What a wonderful experience! We walked the *Via Dolorosa*, the traditional path that Jesus walked, carrying His cross on the way to Calvary to be crucified. We visited the Church of the Holy Sepulcher. Inside, a slab of rock was said to be the place where the body of Christ was washed before He was buried. Upstairs in the church, a large life-sized picture of Jesus hung on a cross, surrounded by all sorts of holy ornaments. The cross hung over a silver-covered hole in the floor. The hole was said to be the actual hole where the cross of Jesus was placed.

I asked how this could be, since the Bible says that Jesus was taken out of the city to be crucified. The man said the site was outside of the original walls, but the walls had been extended, and now Calvary is inside of the city.

About three floors beneath this hole in the floor, I was told that the original cross upon which Jesus had been crucified was dug up at this site. I asked myself, "How could the 'original hole' for the cross be three floors above where the cross was later dug up?"

Next, we walked out of the Old Damascus Gate of Jerusalem. A short walk from the city we saw a wall with a green door. Over the door was the inscription: "The Garden Tomb—the tomb wherein the body of our Lord was laid. I am the resurrection and the Life." A tomb had been hewn into the rock in the garden. Inside of the tomb an iron fence prevented me from standing on the place where they said the body of Jesus was placed. An old cross was etched on the wall. Outside of the tomb I could visualize how a big round rock slab could have been rolled over the door to seal off the tomb as the Bible describes.

To the right of the tomb at the edge of the garden, a small hill looms into the air. It is considered to be a part of Mount Moriah. On the side of the hill, a rock formation resembles a skull. General Gordon in the British Army discovered this place. It is called "Gordon's Calvary." I wanted to climb up on the hill but was told it is forbidden, because it is a Muslim graveyard.

As I thought of the description of Golgotha, the place of the skull, Calvary Hill, I felt as if I were standing on holy ground. During New Testament times, the ancient road from Jerusalem to Jericho and Damascus passed nearby. The Romans crucified people near such main roads as a warning to all who passed by. The site is far enough away from the city to prevent the stench from being a problem. Yet the hill is close enough to serve as a warning to all who passed by.

We visited the Dome of the Rock (Al Aqsa) Mosque. The mosque is built on the site where King Solomon's temple once stood. Usually, when you see a picture of Jerusalem, you see this golden dome. Inside, under the dome is a huge rock that is sacred to Muslims, Jews, and Christians. They call this Mount Moriah. They believe it is where Abraham sacrificed a ram in the place of his son, Isaac (Genesis

Chapter 22). The Muslims believe that a large hole in the rock was made by Mohammed's horse when he leaped up into heaven.

Just over the wall near the mosque is the valley of Kidron, mentioned in the Bible. An ancient monument in the valley is Absalom's (the son of David) tomb. Across Kidron brook at the base of the Mount of Olives is the Garden of Gethsemane. I was impressed by the very old olive trees and wondered if the trees could possibly be linked or related to the trees that were there in the time of Christ.

A beautiful church with a colorfully painted façade at the Garden of Gethsemane is called "the Church of Many Nations." A Russian Orthodox Church is also on the side of the Mount of Olives. We drove to the top of the Mount of Olives and had our picture made with Jerusalem in the background. What a wonderful view of Jerusalem from this site.

On the rear of the Mount of Olives we visited a church called "The Church of the Ascension." A single long candle was burning on a rock at the church. I was told that this stone marks the place where Jesus ascended up into heaven.

On another day we stopped at the Jordan River near where John the Baptist baptized Jesus. We visited Bethlehem and saw the place where Jesus was born. From Christmas displays with a wooden stable and manger I always visualized the place where Jesus was born as a small wooden barn behind an inn. Actually, the place where Jesus was born is now inside of the Church of the Nativity. Instead of a wooden building, the birthplace is something like a grotto in stone.

A large silver star on the floor with a hole in the middle enables people to come and kiss the rock where Jesus was born. While we were in this place, a group of priests came in with their long robes and incense burners on chains. They really smoked up the place. The space was small and smoke from the incense burners was so thick, it became difficult to breath.

We stopped at Bethany and saw the tomb of Lazarus (the brother of Mary and Martha), whom Jesus raised from the dead. We also saw Rachael's tomb and many other impressive Biblical places. We had traveled a long way from Bro. Ayoub's home. I wondered how we could travel that distance and return home after dark.

Brother Ayoub stopped in a village called Ramallah to visit some Christian friends. A man and his wife with a teenage daughter lived in a meager, but very well kept home. They invited us to eat dinner with them. We sat around their table and enjoyed a splendid meal. Then, these people invited us to spend the night and continue our journey the next day.

They were not merely being polite. They insisted that we stay with them. They were using the same high-pressure Arabic manners that Brother Ayoub used when he invited me to stay with him. Brother Ayoub agreed we would spend the night. The problem: they did not have a guest bedroom. The man and his wife insisted that we sleep in their bed and they would sleep on the floor. I told them I am a soldier. I am trained and accustomed to sleeping on the ground. Never mind that. Brother Ayoub and I were obliged to sleep in their bed while they slept on the floor. Although I am from the South, which is noted for its hospitality, I have never experienced anything like their kindness.

Once we were back in Es Salt, Brother Ayoub began taking me around with him to meet some of the members of his congregations. In the first home we entered the people offered us tea or coffee. They brought out coffee in very small cups that resembled a child's toys. The coffee was black and thick. Normally, I do not drink coffee, but I managed to sip through it.

As soon as we entered the next home, the people asked us if we would like to have tea or coffee. I began to say, "No, thank..." but Brother Ayoub touched me on the arm and I decided to try the tea. Later, he explained that when a person visits another, it is an insult not to offer something to drink. At the same time, it is an insult to refuse something to drink when it is offered. He said if you visit at meal time, the same code of ethics applies to food. I also learned in Ramallah that this code applies to their beds at bedtime. For the remaining visits I drank tea. It was not nearly as strong as that thick coffee.

Sunday morning we were up early getting the family ready for Sunday school and church. The first church we attended was near his home. The building was small, but it was packed with children in Sunday school. Each child had a Bible picture printed in English to illustrate the Bible story for the day.

The worship service looked very much like a typical service at home. People were seated in pews. When we sang hymns, I recognized the tunes and sang in English. Everyone else was singing in Arabic. As the offering plate was passed, I took the money I had budgeted to spend in the Holy Land and placed it in the plate. Since Brother Ayoub would not accept any of my money to help defray costs, I decided I should give the money to his church.

After the offering, someone sang some special music. Brother Ayoub then got up and said a few words. Looking down at me he said: "All right, Brother Ray, I have already introduced you. Come on up. You are preaching this morning. You preach and I will interpret."

What a surprise! A twenty-two-year-young novice suddenly learns he is to preach the Sunday morning sermon with no prior warning or preparation! Of course, I willingly got up and gave them my personal testimony. Reading from the third chapter of the Gospel of John, I explained how the Lord opened His Word to me as a young man and made me His child. In conclusion I tried to show how God's wonderful invitation is offered to: **"Whoever believes in Him should not perish but have everlasting life"** (**John 3:16**, KJV).

(Today, at age seventy-seven, as I write these words, I am in Sofia, Bulgaria, for the sole purpose of telling people that Jesus is Lord! And Jesus Saves!)

After the first church service Brother Ayoub and I drove to a second church. It was very much like the first, except, this time, when Brother Ayoub said, "All right, Brother Ray, I have already introduced you…" I was ready, even though I was no more prepared than before.

After the second worship service, we drove to downtown Zarka and parked. A large animal carcass hung in front of a store. It was so big; I thought it was a cow. Brother Ayoub spoke with a man in the store and pointed at the animal. The man took his knife and cut-off a piece of meat. We left the place and window shopped for almost an hour. When we returned to the store, the man had cooked the piece of meat. He served the meal on a large round flat piece of pita bread with vegetables. As we began to eat, I realized from the oily taste we were eating sheep. The meal was delicious. We did not need knives and forks. We tore pieces of the thin pita bread with vegetables and meat on it. When we finished, everything was gone. There was nothing left to clean up.

After lunch, we went to Brother Ayoub's third church. We worshipped as we had done in the previous two churches.

Finally, the day was drawing near when I should leave. I had a very important ship to catch in Beirut in order to return to my base in Germany. Brother Ayoub made an amazing proposal to me. He told me to stay with him and not return to Germany. He said he would teach me Arabic and we could preach the Gospel to the people of Jordan and lead many souls to Christ.

His proposal was not a light-hearted, polite request. He was speaking very forcefully as he had done on my first day with him, when he compelled me to stay in his home rather than return to the hotel in Jerusalem. I thanked him for his good offer. However, I explained I was obligated to return to my base. My answer was not good enough. He was ready to force me to stay and work with him.

Under other circumstances I would have gladly consented. As a soldier in the United States Army, if I failed to return to duty, I would be "AWOL" (absent without leave). Such a charge is a very serious offense. I explained to Brother Ayoub that as a Christian, I am obligated to "**render unto Caesar the things that are Caesar's.**"

Brother Ayoub understood. He arranged a "group taxi" to take me to Damascus, Syria. He told me to go to an English school there, where they would give me a room and meals. His friend, Brother Asa, would also show me the sights in Damascus before I departed for Beirut.

As I was about to enter the taxi to leave Jordan, Brother Ayoub reached into his coat pocket and pulled out the money I had placed in the offering plate in his church. He said, "Brother, you have a long way to go to get back to your base. Here! Take this money! You will need it!" Once again, his speech was forceful and very demanding.

He was right. I had a long way to go, and the $187 that I had counted on the Oriental Express on the way to Athens had dwindled considerably. I could certainly use some extra funds. However, I told him that the money he was trying to give away had been placed in the Lord's offering plate for use in the Lord's service. It did not belong to him. He could not give it away. Considering this statement, he reluctantly put the money back in his coat pocket. We waved goodbye as the taxi pulled off on the road to Damascus.

Just as Brother Ayoub said, when I found the English school, they already knew I was on the way. They treated me as if I were a part of their family. Brother Asa took me in tow and showed me the sights of Damascus. We went to the house of Ananias on Straight Street. In Bible times when the Apostle Paul was on the way to Damascus to persecute

Christians, the Lord spoke to him. He was struck blind. He was told to report to Ananias in order to receive his sight. Paul became an outstanding Christian and wrote much of the New Testament (Acts 9:1-21).

After Paul was converted, his former allies sought an opportunity to kill him. When the disciples learned about the plot, they helped Paul escape from Damascus by letting him down in a basket from a window on the wall (Acts 9:22-25). Brother Asa showed me a place on the Damascus wall directly over a main gate. He said this is the place where Paul was let down from a window to escape.

When I returned to the English school, I asked the elderly lady there about this place on the wall. She said twenty-five years ago when she first came to Damascus, there was no such place on the wall. Because so many tourists come there looking for the place, they built this "window" for the benefit of the tourists. I thought about the places I had seen in the Holy Land. I am sure that some of the sights were also manufactured. However, many were genuine. The Mount of Olives, the Garden of Gethsemane, the Sea of Galilee, the Jordan River, Golgotha, Kidron Brook and Valley, King David's tomb, etc.—these are very real.

While Brother Asa and I toured around Damascus, we visited the main part of the city on Straight Street. A covering erected high overhead gave protection from the sun and the rain. Shops of all kinds were clustered on both sides of the street. As we walked along, sales people would actually come out and grab me by the arm and pull me into their shops to try to sell their goods.

When they offered an item for sale, their asking price was exorbitant. This was the same tactic the guides used at the great pyramid. An unusual specialty in Damascus is cloth with gold interwoven in the fibers. Neckties made of this material are especially attractive. The salesmen would bargain with me over an item. I watched as the price dropped to an extremely low amount. My friend, Bro. Asa, could not understand how I could resist such great bargains. I did not explain the crucial state of my finances at this point of my journey. It is explained by the old adage "getting blood out of a turnip."

On the day of my departure, Brother Asa arranged a "group taxi" to take me to Beirut. I gave him the best tip I could afford and was on my way. The folks at the English school told me not to miss seeing the huge snow-capped mountain on the left as I departed from Syria. When I arrived at this point the mountain was obscured by clouds. I was told that Mount Hermon could possibly be the place where Jesus was transfigured before three of His disciples **(Matthew 17:1–9)**.

Beirut, Lebanon, appeared to be the most beautiful city in the world. When I went down on the pier to board the ship, the sun was sinking into the warm royal blue waters of the Mediterranean. The sky appeared in dazzling orange hues, as if a masterpiece painted by the Great Creator. Someone said in the desert areas, the evening skies are the most brilliant in the entire world. Looking back towards the City of Beirut, the green cedar trees and colorful buildings on the hillsides were topped in the distance by a white snow-capped mountain. That scene still lives in my memories as perhaps the most beautiful city I have seen.

Years later, when I saw the bombing and fighting in Beirut on television, my heart wanted to cry. How could they destroy and lay waste such a marvelous place?

As the ship pulled out of Beirut harbor, I was on board. We sailed to Alexandria, Egypt and stopped to lade and unlade cargo. Then, we were on our way to Syracuse, Sicily located just off of the "boot" of Italy. Again the ship stopped to lade and unlade. Several passengers and I took the opportunity for sightseeing around the city.

I wanted to see the active volcano as we sailed, but we passed through the Messina Strait at night when not much was visible. The next day the ship pulled into Naples Bay where I debarked. Checking my bag into a hotel, I set out for Mount Vesuvius and the ruins of Pompeii. When Mount Vesuvius erupted many years ago, Pompeii was totally covered by volcanic ash. Archaeologists dug the city out of the ashes.

A guide showed us the sights. He explained how sexual behavior had dominated the city. He opened a wooden box at the entrance to Pompeii. It contained an old painting from the ruins. In the picture a naked man called *Priapus* was holding a balance-type scale. Fruits and riches were on one side of the scale. On the other side of the scale was his big, uncircumcised penis. The guide pointed out that sex outweighed everything of value in ancient Pompeii. During his tour, the guide pointed out homes with many different sexual acts painted on the walls.

When I saw these things, I thought of Sodom and Gomorrah. Could God have destroyed the city of Pompeii for similar reasons? I also wonder if God is going to deal with the United States of America for the same reason. The Bible warns us: **"For to be carnally minded is death; but to be spiritually minded is life and peace"** (**Romans 8:6**, KJV).

Volcanic lava and ash in Pompeii had engulfed people, pets, and houses. When archaeologists discovered hollow places in the solidified lava, they pumped the spaces full with plaster. When the plaster hardened, they had an exact replica of the one who died such a horrible death. I saw plaster casts of people writhing in pain as lava covered them. I saw a plaster dog chained to a stake. The dog also reflected intense pain.

In downtown Naples, the Monument to Victor Emmanuelle II is still impressed upon my memory. After a quick tour of the city, I boarded a train to Rome. After Rome, I needed to find a way across the Alps to Germany. Perhaps I could catch a train or bus? Originally, I thought that once back in Europe, I might be able to hitchhike, if necessary, in order to return to my base.

Rome, Italy! A wonderful city! The Coliseum, the Fountain of Trevi, plus many other magnificent fountains, the Appian Way on which the Apostle Paul traveled when he entered Rome, the catacombs where early Christians hid for their lives, the Vatican, the Swiss Guards, St. Peter's Cathedral, the paintings of Michelangelo on the ceiling of the Sistine Chapel, the Arch of Titus named after the Roman emperor who laid siege on Jerusalem and completely destroyed the city around 70 AD—outstanding sights are endless.

While in Rome, I met an American service man. He asked, "What are you doing in Rome?" I told him about my trip and how I needed to get back to Kornwestheim, Germany, near Stuttgart. He told me about an American air base outside of the city. He suggested that I go there and see if they have a flight to Frankfurt. "As a soldier on active duty," he said, "you are eligible to catch a free 'hop.'"

I caught the bus to the air base. Sure enough, since I was a corporal on active duty with the U.S. Army, they booked me on a flight the next day—all of the way to Frankfurt, Germany, at no cost. The only stipulation was that I had to be in uniform. Fortunately, down in the bottom of my duffel bag, I had been carrying a "Class A" uniform for just such an occasion.

When the airplane took off the next day, we headed towards the high mountains. A problem developed with the plane, so we diverted to a small airbase in Chaumont, France. The air force provided a free night in France. They gave me a place to stay and fed me. After breakfast the next morning, we took off and flew on to Frankfurt.

Boarding a train in Frankfurt, I traveled to Stuttgart and then on to my base in Kornwestheim. As I carried my duffel bag into the Ludendorf Kaserne, I reached into my pocket. Thanks to the free "hop," I still had ten U.S. dollars remaining. Thinking back over the past thirty days and how the entire trip seemed to have been conducted by a master tour guide, I said: "THE LORD IS INDEED MY SHEPHERD! I SHALL NOT WANT!"

Afterthoughts

After returning to my base, I reflected upon the breathtaking things I had seen and done. In the past I thought that walking where Jesus walked and seeing the sights of the Holy Land would be a tremendous, spiritual experience. After I had my color slides developed, I relived my trip with my colleagues at our base and documented the past thirty days.

Although I was thrilled to see so many Bible places, I realized true spiritual experience does not come by physical means, including my actual presence in Bible lands. If you desire an amazing spiritual experience with the Lord Jesus, it comes by faith. **"Draw near to God, and He will draw near to you"** (**James 4:8**, KJV). When a person earnestly seeks God, reading His Word, believing, and searching **"with all your heart"** (**Jeremiah 29:13**, KVJ), then you find or *realize* God in all of His fullness. I would not trade the spiritual experience of faith for every trip and tour in the world.

Chapter 8

"Homecoming Day"

Luke 15:11–32 is very special to me. It shows a loving God who is merciful, compassionate, pardoning, and who welcomes us home. For forty years I worked with the United States Customs Service. During this time, I witnessed many heartwarming homecomings and happy reunions. Such events made my job a joy. I remember young troops returning from the fighting in Grenada in the Caribbean. When they got off of the airplane, some literally kissed the pavement under their feet. My heart was thrilled to see loved ones being reunited with scenes of joy, warmth, kisses, and embraces—happiness! These scenes were repeated in many ways at Charleston's waterfront and airport as people returned home from around the world.

When the first troops were returning home, during the war in Vietnam, I was assigned to perform the custom clearance on board the naval vessel USS *Manley*. In order to prevent detaining the troops after the ship arrived at the dock, I traveled on a navy launch and boarded the ship as it entered the mouth of Charleston's harbor from the Atlantic Ocean near Fort Sumter. As the ship traveled up the harbor to its berth at the naval base, I reviewed their documents and granted complete entrance rights from the U.S. Customs Service.

After clearing all of the declarations, the ship's captain invited me to go up on the bridge (the place where they steer or run the ship). What an impressive sight! Tugboats were shooting silvery streams of water high into the air to welcome home the troops. Crews of naval ships dressed in white, starched uniforms lined up like dominoes along the railings of the ships' decks. The pier was crowded with mothers and children. The U.S. Navy band played spirited marches and anthems. Coffee, soft drinks, and cookies were being served on the pier. Scores of colorful balloons rose into the air. What a tremendous welcome along with hugs and kisses from loved ones.

Although I had served in the United States Army during the Korean conflict, the Lord blessed me with an assignment in Europe, rather than war ravaged Korea. When my tour of duty was finished, I shall never forget the long trip home. In those days the military traveled by troop ships instead of on airplanes as they do today. Instead of an eight-hour flight across the Atlantic Ocean, we made an eight-day voyage from Bremerhaven, Germany, to New York. Then we flew to Fort Jackson, South Carolina, where I was discharged from the military. We had no such homecoming in the army.

Arriving home in Charleston, I remember seeing my beloved mother and dad for the first time in many months. The gray hairs on their heads seemed to have multiplied. What a joy it was to be welcomed home by them and my neighbors and friends.

These homecoming scenes, still vividly impressed in my mind, are very special to me. They are just a glimpse of a wonderful homecoming that is yet to take place. I am speaking about the great homecoming day when we gather around God's Great White Throne; that day when we see our Lord and Savior, Jesus Christ; the One who made it possible for us to be there—the One who shed His blood for our sins to reconcile us to God.

In **Luke 15:11–32** we read of a homecoming in God's Word. This homecoming is very important. The Father in the story represents the Almighty God and teaches us wonderful things about God's love for each of His children.

The scribes and Pharisees criticized Jesus because He received tax collectors and sinners who came to Him. Jesus even ate with them. In the Gospel of Luke Chapter 15, Jesus gives three parables to show God's great love. All three of these parables portray God's love for the lost.

In the first parable Jesus Christ is the Great Shepherd. We are His sheep. One of His one hundred sheep becomes lost. He is not satisfied with the ninety-nine sheep safely secured in His fold. He searches the open country until He finds His one lost sheep. **Verses 5–7: "And when He finds it, he joyfully puts it on His shoulders and goes home. Then He calls His friends and neighbors together and says, 'Rejoice with Me; I have found My lost sheep.' I tell you that in the same way there will be more rejoicing in heaven over one sinner who repents than over ninety-nine righteous persons who do not need to repent."**

The second parable is about a woman who loses one of her ten silver coins. She lights a lamp, sweeps the house, and carefully searches the house. **Verses 9–10: "When she finds it, she calls her friends and neighbors together and says, 'Rejoice with me; I have found my lost coin.' In the** same way, I tell you, there is rejoicing in the presence of the angels of God over one sinner who repents."

The third parable is known as the parable of **"The Prodigal Son"** or the parable of two lost sons. **"Jesus continued: 'There was a Man who had two sons' " (Luke 15:11)**. This home had to be a very beautiful home because it represents the home of the Heavenly Father. Therefore, the home has all of the love, joy, and comforts that are possible. The two sons are called the younger and the older. The Father represents God.

Verses 12–13: "The younger one said to his father, 'Father, give me my share of the estate.' So he divided his property between them. Not long after that, the younger son got together all he had, set off for a distant country, and there squandered his wealth in wild living." We have an expression, "Got it made!" I like the way my wife, Charlene, says it: "I never had it so good!"

In this home with the father and two sons, they enjoyed virtually everything their hearts could desire. They had wealth, food, clothes, shelter, love, joy, concern, fellowship, comfort—what else could one ask for? They really "never had it so good!" All of the good things they enjoyed were blessings they had not earned or deserved. **"Every good and perfect gift is from above, coming down from the Father of the heavenly lights, who does not change like shifting shadows" (James 1:17).** But the younger son was not satisfied. He asked his Father for his part of the inheritance He got his things together, and set out for a distant country.

Years ago I studied adolescent psychology in college. It seems that as children begin to grow up, they struggle between the need to stay at home where all of their needs are supplied and the need to launch out into the world and become independent. To those who have parented teen-aged children, you have probably recognized this struggle within your own children.

"After he had spent everything, there was a severe famine in that whole country, and he began to be in need. So he went and hired himself out to a citizen of that country, who sent him to his fields to feed pigs. He longed to fill his stomach with the pods that the pigs were eating, but no one gave him anything" (Luke 15:14–16).

Have you ever heard the expression, "The grass always looks greener on the other side of the fence"? That's the way it was with this young man. He thought the grass would be greener in some distant country away from his Father's house. I had a colleague in America who accepted a job with the United States Customs Service in an outlying station in the Caribbean area. After he worked there for awhile, he wrote a letter and said the grass always looks greener on the other side of the fence, but when you cross the fence, you discover that the grass is not nearly as green as it appeared. We also have a saying for this: "There is no place like home!"

The young man in this scripture made the same discovery. He thought being away from his Father in a foreign land would be better than living at home. He set out with his inheritance and wasted his life away in wild living. The Bible does not list the things that he did. When we think of "wild living," we can make our own list.

As long as he had plenty of money, he had plenty of so-called friends. When his money ran out, so did his friends. If you must buy your friends, then they are not friends at all. King Solomon said: **"A friend loves at all times" (Proverbs 17:17).** We should beware of friends who lead us away from our Father. One of the greatest dangers young people face today are "friends" who influence us to leave our moral values, our beliefs, and our good friends and family. The phrase **"No one gave him anything"** describes the kind of friends he had.

Then, a great famine came. He neither had money nor even a friend to help. Finally, he was able to get a job feeding pigs. He was forced to eat with the pigs in order to survive. Eating pork is forbidden in the Law of Moses. To drop so low in life that you must live and eat with the pigs is perhaps as low as an Israelite could sink.

For many years I taught a young man in Sunday school. The young fellow attended church regularly. He had great potential for being an outstanding Christian, but he never could get interested in applying himself and using his talents for the Lord. Many times we talked about serving God, but he always stopped short.

As the years went by he married a pretty young lady and started a family. They moved into a home in another neighborhood. After several years, I discovered that this young man and his wife were both actively involved in working for the Lord with the children in their church. They had begun a very successful puppet ministry.

When I saw this young fellow, I said, "For so many years we talked about your potential to become an invaluable asset in the Lord's service, but you refused. Please help me understand what happened. How did you finally become such an outstanding Christian worker? I would really like to know. This may be the key to helping others find their place in life." My friend thought for a moment and then he answered, "Well, I guess I just made up my mind."

This is what the young man did in the pigpen where he began eating with the pigs. **"When he came to his senses, he said, 'How many of my Father's hired men have food to spare, and here I am starving to death! I will set out and go back to my Father and say to Him: "Father, I have sinned against heaven and against You. I am no longer worthy to be called Your son, make me like one of Your hired men" (Luke 15:17–19).**

Sin gives us a distorted view of life. Perhaps the greatest blessing of being a failure is the stark reality of life that we learn from it. When everything and everyone around us turn their backs upon us and we are left with nothing but memories, we can see and understand very clearly. We realize who is for us and who is against us. We realize what is good and what is not good. At this stage of total bankruptcy we suddenly realize what should have been evident before we arrived at this point. Failure also has a way of making us humble. Humility is good because God promises: **"whoever humbles himself will be exalted" (Matthew 23:12).**

This is the key to finding peace with God. We too must humble ourselves. We too must come to our senses; we too must make a decision; we too must go back to our Heavenly Father. This is what my young friend did. He came to his senses and decided that he would just make up his mind and return to his Heavenly Father and serve Him. The younger son in our story **"came to his senses"** and decided to **"set out and go back to my Father."**

"So he got up and went to his Father. But while he was still a long way off, his Father saw him and was filled with compassion for him; He ran to His son, threw His arms around him and kissed him. The son said to Him, 'Father, I have sinned against heaven and against you. I am no longer worthy to be called your son" (Luke 15:20).

I believe the younger son practiced his speech all of the way home. When he reached the very bottom of life, living in the pigpen with the pigs, he realized that his Father's servants were enjoying a much better life than he had. He would return to his Father and say, **"Father, I have sinned against heaven and against You. I am no longer worthy to be called Your son; make me like one of Your hired men."**

However, **"While he was still a long way off, his Father saw him."** His Father was keeping a watchful eye on that road from the day His dear son left home. He watched with anticipation, longing for the time when His son would return. When the Father saw him, never mind that the son was in rags; never mind the stench of the pigpen; never mind that he had no shoes; the Father **"was filled with compassion for him; <u>He ran to His son</u>, threw His arms around him and kissed him"** (emphasis added).

Then the son began his speech that he had been practicing: **"Father, I have sinned against heaven and against you. I am no longer worthy to be called your son"** (21). But his Father would not hear of it! **"The Father said to His servants: 'Quick! Bring the best robe and put it on him. Put a** ring on his finger and sandals on his feet. Bring the fattened calf and kill it. Let's have a feast and celebrate. For this son of mine was dead and is alive again! He was lost and is found.' So they began to celebrate" (Luke 15:22–23).

What a great celebration! Singing! Dancing! The very best of foods! Do you know why I like this story? Jesus says: **"In the same way, I tell you, there is rejoicing in the presence of the angels of God over one sinner who repents" (Luke 15:10).** Today, if you are willing and will come home to God, you can cause the angels of God in heaven to rejoice! Talk about "happy hour!" This is the real happy hour when one person will invite Jesus to save them from their sins!

Why do I belabor you with this story? I remember so well when I was that prodigal son. I remember when I made up my mind to come home to God. I remember the joy that changed my life forever when I asked God to forgive my sins and make me his child. I have seen so many brothers and sisters in Christ around the world whose lives were changed by making a similar decision. I know that God will welcome you when you "come to your senses and decide to return to your Heavenly Father."

We call this story the parable of the prodigal son. But, there is another prodigal son: **"Meanwhile, the older son was in the field. When he came near the house, he heard music and dancing. So he called one of the servants and asked him what was going on. 'Your brother has come,' he replied, 'and your Father has killed the fattened calf because He has him back safe and sound.' The older brother became angry and refused to go in"** (Luke 15:25–28).

We mentioned a part of **Matthew 23:12,** where Jesus said: **"whoever humbles himself will be exalted."** The part of the verse that we omitted applies here: **"For whoever exalts himself will be humbled."**

"So his Father went out and pleaded with him, but he answered his Father, 'Look! All these years I've been slaving for You and never disobeyed Your orders. Yet you never gave me even a young goat so I could celebrate with my friends. But when this son of Yours who has squandered Your property with prostitutes comes home, You kill the fattened calf for him!' " (Luke 15:28–30)

Have you ever seen people who don't appreciate the blessings they have? Those who constantly complain? They destroy the happiness and joy of living by their constant self-righteousness and pride. Many Christians have not left home today. They remain in the church, but they don't understand how blessed we are. They are like the older son; they destroy their joy by constantly complaining.

But again, the Father comes out in love and compassion: **" 'My son,' the Father said, 'you are always with Me, and everything I have is yours. But we had to celebrate and be glad, because this brother of yours was dead and is alive again; he was lost and is found' " (Luke 15:31–32).**

We have spoken of the younger son and the older son, but the Father has another Son. The younger son hurt his Father by leaving home and going to a far country. The older son could not enjoy the fellowship of his own home. The third Son left His Father's home and came to a far country to **"seek and to save the lost."** He came to give His life's blood on the Cross of Calvary to pay the debt we owe for our sins. This Son is the blessed Lord Jesus, the only perfect Son, the only Son who is worthy, the Christ, the Messiah, the one who is telling this parable. He gives us His Word: **"I tell you the truth, whoever hears My word and believes Him who sent Me has eternal life and will not be condemned; he has crossed over from death to life" (John 5:24).**

Do you know why I love this scripture? I love this scripture because <u>it is the only place I can find in the Bible where God ran</u>. Why did God run? To welcome home His lost son. This is so very important. When I was that lost prodigal son; when I came to my senses; when I decided to come home to God, I discovered that God was ready to run to meet me. Just as God ran to meet His prodigal son in this parable, He ran to meet me. God will also run to meet you!

If you have never received Jesus Christ as your personal Savior in faith, you are not God's Son. If you are willing to believe in Christ Jesus; that He died for your sins and arose from the dead; if you will invite Him into your life; then God is ready to run to meet you to welcome you into His kingdom as His son. As we read in the two earlier parables: **"I tell you that in the same way there will be more rejoicing in heaven over one sinner who repents than over ninety-nine righteous persons who do not need to repent" (Luke 15:7). "In the same way, I tell you, there is rejoicing in the presence of the angels of God over one sinner who repents" (Luke 15:10).**

Today we are living in the day of God's grace. Our Heavenly Father is still standing, gazing down the road of life. God is looking for His lost child to come home. Are you that lost child? Are you the one the Lord is seeking to find?

If you are willing to come home to God, then God is ready to run to meet you, to welcome you and receive you. I love these words of Jesus: **"Whoever comes to Me I will never drive away" (John 6:37).**

Chapter 9

My Greatest Mistake

After finishing my tour of duty and returning home, I was much more mature in many ways. Instead of seeking "my one and only," I enjoyed dating girls simply for the enjoyment of companionship. Large girls, small girls, tall girls, short girls, educated girls, not so educated, beautiful girls (I dated one classical young lady who had won several beauty contests—what a good looker!), and girls not quite so beautiful.

Each of these dates taught me important lessons about life. One of the most important lessons is, as the old saying expresses it, "beauty is only skin deep." I say this not taking anything away from beautiful girls. I learned that the happiest, most pleasant dates were usually the ones who are not as physically attractive.

Perhaps they are like Avis; they "try harder." I especially remember one little chubby girl. She was older than I. However, she and her mother prepared some of the best foods I have eaten. There was no pretense. We just enjoyed doing things together and making the most of every opportunity.

During those years, the Citadel, the College of Charleston, and the Medical University of South Carolina were Charleston's three colleges. The Baptist Student Union (BSU) provided fellowship and activities for students of like faith in each school. Although each college had a BSU organization, we frequently conducted joint meetings. Students at the Citadel military college were almost prisoners. Seldom could they attend the joint sessions. At these meetings, I met and dated several nursing students who were about my age. From a strictly rational approach, any one of these girls would have been an ideal choice as a lifetime mate. Although these girls were quality, outstanding, and very nice-looking dates, they appeared to be too rigid and "set in their ways." A date, even though fun, seemed to conform to strict traditional expectations.

After establishing what I thought was a mutually close rapport and relationship, I would sometimes say something stupid in jest. I would call and arrange a date. Then I would say something such as, "I'll pick you up at seven; if I'm not there by midnight, just go on to bed." Invariably, this invoked a serious lecture and reprimand.

In college I met a cute young lady who reminded me of my Dear John letter girlfriend. We dated and did a lot of happy things together. However, deep down in my heart, I understood that our differences were as broad as with my previous serious girlfriend. But I kept dating her and trying to learn.

One evening, she called me on the telephone and asked me to please come to see her at her home. She lived with her parents, just as I lived with mine. When I went to see her, she broke off our relationship. I said, "You called me to come all of the way over here to tell me this? You could just as easily have said this in the hallway at school."

I never called her again. I still do not understand her big production.

For the past couple of years as I dated a variety of girls, one pretty little nurse seemed to be very special. She believed that God had called her to be a foreign missionary. My best friend said her face looked like Elizabeth Taylor's. Her beautiful appearance complemented her sincere dedication as a Christian.

Since I was not sure of exactly what God wanted me to do, I thought perhaps assisting this young lady in her calling would be a pleasing thing in God's sight. Although I did not receive a particular message from the Lord, I reasoned that this was a good way to serve the Lord. After all, God says: **"You are My witnesses!"** Wouldn't serving as a foreign missionary fulfill this command?

The year was 1957. June would bring graduation from the College of Charleston. My friend would also be graduating from the Medical University of South Carolina. It was time to begin making serious plans for life after college. I was amazed to hear her say that even though she believed God was calling her to be a foreign missionary, she could not leave her mother. Although I was not sure exactly what God had in store for me, I knew that being united to someone without enough maturity to leave home and become an adult was not for me.

Early that year, walking down Broad Street, I heard someone shouting my name from across the street. My friend from high school days, J. Carroll Brown, waved for me to come over and talk with him. Carroll told me, "I am the state probation and parole officer in Charleston." Then he asked, "What do you plan to do after graduation?"

When I could not give a definite answer, he suggested working in his field. He pointed out that my experience with youth in church, along with my education would be assets as a probation and parole officer. He asked me to go with him into the Post Office Building on the corner of Broad and Meeting streets to meet Mr. Simon Fogarty, the federal probation and parole officer.

Mr. Fogarty welcomed us into his office. He asked questions and agreed with Carroll that my youth work and personality would be assets in the job. Mr. Fogarty suggested that I attend Florida State University and obtain an MSW (master of social welfare) degree. He explained that this would equip me with the very best credentials and information needed in the work.

After praying about this new possibility for my life, I drove down to Tallahassee, Florida and spoke with the registrar about the possibility of attending FSU in the fall. The registrar said I needed to take a graduate entrance examination. He said they had recently administered this examination on the campus. He sat me down in a room and gave me the examination. When I finished taking the exam, he calculated my score. Then, the registrar offered me a $1,500 assistantship to attend the school. This along with my remaining two years of GI Bill eligibility would enable me to go to school there in the fall. He suggested that I might try to get a job during the summer with the Domestic Relations Court in Charleston. He explained this would give me a good background for the program.

Arriving back in Charleston, I made an appointment to speak with Judge Pierce, the head of the Domestic Relations Court. As I walked into the judge's office for the appointment, I was really impressed. The judge called me by my nickname, "City." He had seen me playing basketball for the College of Charleston and even remembered my name.

After explaining my purpose to the judge, he offered me a job with his court. He said I could work during the summer after graduation in June. Then I could attend Florida State University in the fall. He said I could return and work in his court between sessions at FSU.

In my heart I believed the Lord was directing my paths. Everything was falling into place as if a Master planner were taking care of each detail. Seeing my friend Carroll on Broad Street, talking with Mr. Fogarty, the good response at Florida State, and now a job with the Domestic Relations Court—surely the Lord had to be directing all of this.

During my final semester of college, our old friend Dr. Timothy Walton Callaway retired as pastor of the St. Andrews First Baptist Church. I was elected, along with some others, to serve on the "pulpit committee." Our job was to find a replacement pastor for the church. After much praying, listening to recommendations, and searching, we found a pastor who seemingly had the qualifications that we were seeking.

When the committee met with this pastor, I was somewhat disappointed with some of his responses to the committee's questions. All of his answers to major concerns, such as faith, Biblical beliefs, etc. were splendid. The small answers about personality and such were the things that disappointed me. Overall, the committee considered him to be the one they were seeking, so I did not object.

After the new pastor began to serve in our church, he asked me to help him establish a viable youth program. Of course, I would be happy to work with him. However, he did not want me to merely assist him. He wanted me to work full time. I explained that was impossible. I had already arranged to work full time with Judge Pierce in the Domestic Relations Court after graduation during the summer and to go to Florida State University in the fall.

The new pastor pointed out how important it is to keep young people out of jail rather than wait until they are in trouble to help them. His argument is true. Certainly, it is better to provide the means of keeping youth out of trouble and jail rather than after the fact. Yes. This is the Lord's work. Yes. This is the Lord's church. But, what about all of these plans that I had made?

After much harangue, I finally gave in. I told the preacher that I could cancel my job with the Domestic Relations Court and help him during the summer, but in the fall I should attend the program at Florida State University. The preacher was happy with this concession, but he was not satisfied. His next campaign was to argue for more time than only the summer months. He was talking about a full-time job.

Reluctantly, I finally agreed to work with him through the fall semester. I explained that my GI Bill educational benefits expired in February of 1958. I needed to get enrolled in college before then or lose these benefits. He still was not satisfied. This time I was adamant. I believed that this is what the Lord wanted me to do. I thought I could help this man with his program and also do what the Lord had placed in my heart.

When I began working with the new pastor in my new job, I assisted the youth in a youth choir, youth revival, Bible studies, socials, and other activities. But, I had been doing this in my spare time, even before the pastor arrived. My new duties consisted primarily of composing the church bulletin each week and doing "other duties as assigned."

After the new preacher had preached for several months, he alienated a number of members in the congregation. Abruptly, he took about half of the congregation, as many as would follow him, moved about a mile away, and started his own church. I was left as the sole staff member and thrust into the position of "interim pastor." As if things were not bad enough, I discovered that the master of social welfare program that I planned to attend only begins during the fall semester. Since I did not enroll for the fall semester, my GI benefits would expire before the following fall.

The title of this chapter is my *"greatest mistake."* Do you understand my greatest mistake? My greatest mistake was not in choosing to work with a church rather than go to school. My greatest mistake was not in doing one thing as opposed to another.

What was my greatest mistake? My greatest mistake: I knew and experienced God's guidance and direction in my life, then I chose to disobey God. I thought I could make God and the new preacher and church satisfied. I discovered that I had failed in all points.

I learned an invaluable lesson. I learned that when you feel or hear the still small voice of God in your heart; when you know God's Spirit is directing your paths, then, you should listen carefully and follow this dream above all else. Never mind, what father, mother, friends, pastor, or the entire world says. When your heart is in tune with the Lord, you must follow His calling, this dream, above everything and everyone.

Recovery

What do you do when you discover that you have made a gigantic error? An error so huge that you may never be able to recover from it? Several months later a new, very special girlfriend and I were in a supermarket. By chance my former girlfriend, the one who made a production of giving me the axe, saw me and asked about my status. I told her that I was in the store with my girlfriend. She was very curious. I told her that she did not know my friend, that she was not in college. She was extremely anxious to see who I was dating. With the stealth of an international spy, she set up surveillance until she could get a good look.

My new little girlfriend was young. She was ten years younger than I. How could a twenty-five-year-old man consider marrying a fifteen-year-old girl? Out of the question! She sang in our youth choir at church. One night we were having a youth revival. I invited a young nursing student to come and sing a solo. She was an outstanding vocalist and a student at the Medical University School of Nursing. When we came in the door of the church, I looked at the youth choir. My little fifteen-year-old friend began to cry.

I dated this little girl. She was a joy to be around. She was entirely flexible. I gave her my stupid approach. I said, "I'll pick you up at seven. However, if I'm not there by midnight, just go on to bed."

She replied, "No. I'll wait for you until around three or four in the morning. If you're not here by five then, I'll go on to bed." How can a fellow escape such an understanding, compassionate, love as this? A beautiful person with a sense of humor and a love that will not be extinguished. I told her that I was not sure of what I would do in life; perhaps become a foreign missionary to Africa. This marvelous little girl was ready to leave her mother and father and family and friends to go with me wherever the Lord might lead.

Someone told me that Shakespeare married a child of around nine years. They also cited several other notable people who married a much younger person. In order to even think of marrying such a young person, she must have legal parental consent. Her parents loved me. I loved them. June 21, 1958, a year after I graduated from the College of Charleston, we were married at the James Island Baptist Church on James Island, South Carolina.

Dr. Timothy Walton Callaway performed the wedding ceremony. My good friend the Rev. Robert P. (Bobby) Dukes sang at our wedding. William T. (Billy) Benke served as best man. As I stood there in front of the church and watched my little bride come down the aisle holding on to the arm of her dad, I saw the determined look on her face—a look of love and devotion. I knew she was the right choice—the one that prophet of God in Kornwestheim, Germany, told me to wait for back in 1954.

After the pastor, my new bride, and I had signed the three copies of the marriage licenses, Dr. Callaway gave the original to my bride. He said, "Here, this is yours in case he tries to get away!" After more than a half a century, she is still the apple of my eye. I mentioned these other girlfriends because I seriously considered each one of them. The Lord promises: **"Trust in the Lord with all your heart and lean not unto your own understanding. In all your ways acknowledge Him and He shall direct your paths" (Proverbs 3:5–6**, KJV). Do you see how God stands behind His Word? My primary concern was to trust the Lord and please Him in every way possible. The little girl I married is the very best choice I could have made. Now, I give God the credit and the glory for keeping His promise.

There is one strange fact that I do not understand. Perhaps it is coincidental. Each one of the three girls that I seriously considered marrying was born on November 25.

My bride and I discussed how I had failed to follow God's direction in my life in working with youth. Together, we tried to regain God's direction. I applied for a graduate program at the University of North Carolina in Chapel Hill, North Carolina. The program was similar to the one at Florida State. However, after seeming to be so promising, the university informed me that they had too many candidates from North Carolina. They regretted that they would not be able to accommodate me in their program.

Charlene and I visited the Connie Maxwell Children's Home, a ministry of Southern Baptists in Greenwood,

South Carolina. We thought perhaps we could become employed there and work with youth. The director of the home offered me a nice job. However, the job was basically administrative but not working with youth. I had an administrative job at the time with the Fort Sumter National Monument in Charleston's harbor. Our office was located in the U.S. Customhouse. We decided that we could do more youth work at church than we could employed at Connie Maxwell.

The more we tried, the more it became evident that the door of opportunity for youth work had slammed shut and would not reopen. When a job with the U.S. Customs Service became available, I transferred from the National Park Service to the Customs Service.

After our first son was born, we moved from the city of Charleston to North Charleston. We began attending the Pittman Street Baptist Church. The Rev. Harry P. Chaffin was pastor. In addition to being a splendid pastor and preacher, this man of God was also a very skilled counselor.

One day Brother. Harry was talking with me about my greatest mistake—failing to follow God's direction in my life. I explained to him how we had tried to recover from this mistake, but nothing seemed to work.

Brother Harry said, "Ray, you used to play basketball at the College of Charleston. What was the worst defeat you ever suffered in a game?"

I said, "Man! Do I remember that! We were playing the Stetson University Hatters in Deland, Florida. It was my sophomore year. I did not start in the game. I was sitting on the bench. When the opening buzzer sounded, before the sound finished echoing around in my ears, I looked up and the score was already nine to zero!"

How I remember that game! "Eel," one of our guards, was bringing the ball down the court (they called him eel because he was so slippery). He flipped a fancy behind the back pass to "Brown Fingers," a forward on the edge of the court. The pass missed Brown Fingers by about six feet. The ball bounded out of the open side door and into the darkness of night. They never could find that ball. They had to break out another game ball.

"When the final buzzer sounded, we lost the game 105 to 44. What a loss!"

Brother Harry asked, "Ray, when you were on court, warming up for the next game, what was the score on the score board?"

"Why, the score is always nothing to nothing at the beginning of a game," I replied.

"That is exactly the way life is," Brother Harry continued. "Every day when you wake up, the score for today is nothing to nothing. It does not matter whether you won or lost yesterday. You might have won a great victory, or, you may have suffered a humiliating defeat. The question is: 'What will you do in today's game of life?' "

What a great perspective! I thank the Lord for Brother Harry and for the many people that he helped to live their life to the full. This great Saint of God, not only touched many lives, but he also built several churches and buildings that are still a monument to his witness and service for the Lord Jesus. We thank the Lord for every member of his family.

Not only do I appreciate Brother Harry and his splendid family, but every morning I realize that today's score is zero to zero. What can I do today to get on the scoreboard for the Lord?

Footnote: My wife and I recently returned from the International Baptist Convention Summer Assembly in Interlaken, Switzerland. One of the principal speakers was Dr. Richard Blackaby, a giant of a Christian. After listening to Dr. Blackaby and re-thinking "my greatest mistake," I wonder if this entire event was perhaps God's way of helping me to join the Lord's agenda rather than my own. It is said that "God works in mysterious ways, His wonders to perform."

Had I attended Florida State University as I originally planned, I would not be married to my dear little bride of more than fifty years. Without a doubt my little bride has been a far greater asset than all of the degrees I could ever earn. I thank the Lord for **"directing my paths" (Proverbs 3:5-6)** even when my own understanding was inadequate.

Chapter 10

God Honors His Word Again and Again

Four years after we were married, Timmy was born. Tim only weighed a little over six pounds at birth, but his crib and other paraphernalia crowded us out of our apartment. We began looking for a home. As a Korean War veteran, I qualified for a GI Bill home loan. In those days, with only a $100 down payment, a veteran could buy a house.

My older brother's friend and neighbor, a naval captain, transferred to Norfolk. His wife and child still lived in their home in North Charleston. He built his home at a cost of $15,500. During the years they lived in North Charleston, he reduced the principle to $13,000. After transferring, he tried to sell his $2,500 equity. He dropped his offer down to $2,000; then to $1,500; and then to $1,000.

Since veterans could buy a home for only $100 down, equity sales suffered. After a couple of years of living in Norfolk by himself, the captain earnestly wanted to sell his house and move his family to Norfolk. He told my brother he could keep anything over $500 if he could sell his home for him.

My brother told me if I needed a home, just give the captain $500 and move in. What a blessing! A centrally located, three-bedroom, bath-and-a-half, brick veneer home on a nice lot with trees. Today the value of the home exceeds $150,000. It was our first home.

Although the house was not exactly what we wanted, we decided to live there until we could find our dream home. Then, we would move. After a couple of months in this neighborhood, we decided that we would rather have that house with our wonderful new neighbors than any other house on the market. Forty-eight years later we still thank the Lord for our home and our neighbors.

Four years after Timmy arrived, Jimmy was born. Two fine young sons! We were truly blessed! As a GS-9 customs inspector with the U.S. Customs Service, we had a nice home and about $1,000 in our savings account.

As I mentioned earlier, Charlene and I give a tithe and an offering of every cent we earn. Although we did not ask God for anything in return, we were aware of the blessings God promises to those who tithe: **"Bring you all the tithes into the storehouse, that there may be meat in my house and prove Me now herewith, says the Lord of hosts, if I will not open you the windows of heaven, and pour you out a blessing, that there shall not be room enough to receive it"** (**Malachi 3:10**, KJV).

Without question we were blessed. We could feel God's love and blessings in so many ways in our lives. Still, I wondered about a blessing so tremendous **"there shall not be room enough to receive it."** What blessing could possibly be so tremendous? I could not imagine such a thing.

The church we attended in North Charleston was struggling. The congregation had a nice brick Sunday school building on a large plot comprised of eight residential lots. But the church did not own the land. It leased the property for about $870 per year. We did not have a sanctuary building. Since the land belonged to a real estate company, the leasing agreement required the church to pay taxes for the property as well as the leasing fee.

I was elected to serve as chairman of the finance committee. Immediately, we devised a promotional plan to raise money to purchase the land and save the leasing fee and property taxes. At the time, the eight residential lots were valued at $2,000 each or a total of $16,000 for the entire plot. (You must understand that these property values were in the middle of the last century).

We prepared a large white chart with 160 squares. Each square was divided into one hundred smaller squares. Hence, the value of each smaller square was $1. Each of the 160 larger squares was valued at $100. People were encouraged to sign-up for a large square and buy a "lot" of church property. If a person gave $100, their large lot was colored green and they were given a certificate of ownership. As they contributed towards the purchase of a lot, a smaller square was colored green for each dollar they contributed.

Although the congregation was small and no one in our church earned a great deal of money, during the first year, we rejoiced as our chart began to turn green. Donations totaled more than $10,000 of the $16,000 needed to buy the land

When the congregation realized how much money we had given during that year, someone said, "We don't need the land! We need a sanctuary!" But, $10,000 was not nearly enough to build a sanctuary, and no bank would loan us the amount necessary to hire a contractor to build a church. The people talked and prayed about their dreams. Finally, we decided to launch out on "the faith plan."

Under the faith plan we would raise as much money as we could and do as much work on the new sanctuary as we could. The work we could not do would be contracted to professionals. The faith plan was under way.

The pastor obtained a copy of an architect's plans (with the architect's permission) of a church in Scranton, South Carolina. With minimal revisions, the drawings were exactly what we needed and wanted.

Charlene and I talked about the "faith plan" and how the Lord had blessed us with a fine home, two splendid sons, $1,000 in savings, and a good job. We decided to withdraw our savings and put the entire $1,000 as an offering into the faith fund for a new church building to honor the Lord.

Shortly after our donation, the U.S. Customs Service promoted me from GS-9 to GS-11. Along with the overtime that I worked, the raise amounted to more than $1,000 per year. Through the Lord's faithfulness, our offering was returned within that first year and during the years that followed our offering was returned more than thirty-fold. Now that I am retired, the added salary also resulted in a ten-fold higher retirement annuity. What a great blessing! However, it was not so much blessing that we did not have room enough to receive it.

Another interesting "coincidence" that year, I was blessed with a special award from the United States Customs

Service. I had submitted an essay in the U.S. Customs Service National Lawyer's Association Essay Contest. I had no legal training, and was not a lawyer.

In my essay I told how the Customs Service should modernize many laborious features of the Tariff Act of 1930 to allow for a flat rate of duty to be assessed on crewmembers and passengers baggage declarations. At that time the law required each item upon which duty was to be assessed must be classified according to the Tariff Schedules of the United States Annotated. The rate of duty for each particular item should be levied according to the tariff schedules, regardless of how trivial the item might be.

In my essay I outlined how a flat rate of duty would yield virtually the same amount of money within seconds of calculating rather than minutes. I also recommended a monetary limit to the flat rate of duty to close a loophole for those who might try to use this special flat rate to circumvent the tariff schedules. A number of other similar recommendations were included in my essay.

My essay won first prize in the national contest. The prize was not a great deal of money. I did not think it was much of an accomplishment until the regional counsel in Miami wrote a letter asking for a copy of the essay. He told me that first prize in the contest was a coveted prize among customs lawyers and the competition was extremely keen. During the passing months, I saw every one of my ideas in the essay adopted on a national basis by the Customs Service. Then, I realized how much God had blessed me with this award. What a blessing! But, it was still not so big that we did not have room enough to receive it.

God blessed us abundantly in so many ways. Yet, I wondered what kind of blessing could be so big **"that there shall not be room enough to receive it."** Since we were blessed beyond measure, I saw no need to ask God for such a tremendous blessing.

Our "faith plan" at church extended over a three-year period. We raised all of the money we could and did all of the work we could on our new sanctuary. With the promotion on my job, Charlene and I accumulated about $2,000 in our savings account. We again prayed for the needs of our church. Once again, we decided to place our entire savings into the building program as an offering to the Lord.

In early January of 1969 our telephone rang. A lady in the church where I had met Charlene told about a baby girl who had just been born in the Medical University of South Carolina Hospital. The baby's mother was only fifteen years of age. The mother, along with her parents, loved this baby with a supreme love. They agreed that the baby should have a normal mother and father and not a fifteen-year-old mother with no husband. They also agreed that the baby should be reared in a Christian home.

Many single mothers of high school age claim to love their baby and will not allow the child to be adopted. They keep a child who will grow up without knowing the parental love of a loving father and mother. Often, because of the lack of education, and having a child out of wedlock, the single mother and her child are consigned to a bleak future.

The lady on the telephone asked if I knew a Christian family in our church who might be interested in adopting this little baby. Although I had never thought of it, at once

I knew someone who was interested. I told the lady that I would call her back. I spoke with my wife, Charlene. I told her of the conversation. I asked her if she knew any Christian family that might be interested in adopting a newborn little girl. Immediately, Charlene said, "Yes! I do! I want to adopt her!" My wife had thought of the same family I did.

When our two sons Timmy (age six) and Jimmy (age three) returned from school and day care, we asked them what they thought about adopting a baby sister who was just born. They both agreed a baby sister would be great!

I called the lady and told her of our plans. She suggested that I call the pastor of the church. After speaking with the pastor, I called my former schoolmate lawyer friend who now had his own practice to assist with the legal proceedings.

A humorous thing happened on the day that we received our daughter. The baby's natural grandmother called me at work. She asked, "Where can we meet you to give you the baby?"

I was working at the U.S. Customhouse, a very prominent landmark in Charleston, with plenty of parking around the building. I suggested meeting her there. The grandmother, however, did not know the location of the Customhouse. At that time Carroll's Fish Market was located across Market Street from the Customhouse. This was a familiar landmark, so we agreed to meet there.

I quickly called Charlene at home. She hurried downtown. There in the parking lot in front of Carroll's Fish Market, we received our daughter. The natural grandmother and grandfather brought their granddaughter from their daughter in the Medical University Hospital to surrender the child to her new parents. When we received our adopted daughter, the scene that day was filled with true love, human compassion, and sacrifice. A young mother and her parents were more concerned about the welfare of their little child than they were about their own feelings. They were willing to do whatever it took to insure the future of this little girl.

Today, our hearts are still warmed by the selfless feelings of this new mother and her parents for their child. I think of the words of the Lord Jesus: **"Greater love has no man than this, that a man lay down his life for his friends" (John 15:13, KJV).**

When our daughter was growing up, sometimes we would drive into the city. We usually concluded our visit by driving around Charleston's famous battery. Driving down East Bay Street, we passed by the Customhouse and Carroll's Fish Market. We would tell our precious daughter in jest, "That's where we got you—at Carroll's Fish Market."

When our first child was about to be born, we decided if the child were a boy, we would honor our former pastor who married us by naming our child "Timothy Callaway Smith." If the child were a girl, Charlene always loved the name "Sherri Ann." Timmy was born.

When our second child was nearing birth, we decide if the child were a boy we would honor both of our fathers and name him "James Patrick Smith." If the child were a girl, then Charlene would get her wish and Sherri Ann would be our daughter. Jimmy was born.

Now, finally, "Sherri Ann Smith" was born and coming to live at our house. What a wonderful experience of love! Although our baby daughter weighed only eight pounds and two ounces at birth, there was more love than I could possibly handle. I watched my wife. She could not contain all of the love that came along with our new little daughter. The same was true of our sons. Having a special little sister was more joy than they could imagine.

The adoption of our daughter brought very special insight. Probably from stories such as the stepchild in Cinderella, I thought adopted children were not the same as regular children. We discovered that there is virtually no difference. The same deep love, emotion, and sensitive feelings are the same. If any child has an advantage, it is the adopted child. Charlene says in addition to the great love, she was not required to carry her around for nine months.

I observed our neighbors. They, too, were caught-up in the love and blessing of our new daughter in the neighborhood. Our entire church family relished the joy and happiness of this new birth. Even at work, my colleagues shared in the joy and thrill of our new little daughter.

Suddenly, I realized the answer to my question. "That's it! That's it!" I shouted. This is the blessing that God promised. This is the blessing that is so big **"there shall not be room enough to receive it."**

At this writing our new little baby girl is now forty-one years of age. She has given birth to twin boys. Our happiness and overwhelming joy continues to multiply with two fine ten-year-old grandsons.

We conclude the Lord is faithful who promised: ***"prove me now herewith, says the Lord of hosts, if I will not open you the windows of heaven, and pour you out a blessing, that there shall not be room enough to receive it"* (Malachi 3:10**, KJV).

Living Life to the Full

Some time afterwards, while shaving and preparing for work, I looked in the mirror. Although my face was smiling, my eyes were not. Have you ever noticed how your eyes usually reflect deep inner truths? We caught many violators trying to clear through customs because eyes do not go along with fabricated stories

Although we were blessed in virtually every way, inside I was becoming unhappy and miserable. An even greater problem: I did not have a clue about why I was not overjoyed. Jesus gives a wonderful promise: **"The thief comes only to steal and kill and destroy; I have come that they may have life, and have it to the full" (John 10:10).** In the King James Version, it reads: **"I am come that they might have life, and that they might have it more abundantly."**

I did not have **"life to the full"** or **"life more abundantly."** Since the Lord promised to give us life in fullest measure, I began to pray specifically about my problem. I prayed: "Lord, You promised to give me life to the full, life more abundantly. Yet, I find myself most miserable. Therefore, I am praying that You **'restore unto me the joy of my salvation.'** I am asking You to keep Your promise in Your Word." Then I added: "Lord, I will ask at least three times each day:

in the morning when I wake up, in the middle of the day when I pause for lunch, and at night before I go to bed. I shall continue to ask, to seek, and to knock until You answer and restore the joy I have known.

After several days of praying this prayer, my thoughts turned to a situation on my job. I worked as a customs inspector. My big boss was the collector of customs. In those days the Customs Service reorganized and changed his title to district director of customs. At the customhouse we also had a separate customs enforcement agency.

One night I was working at the Charleston International Airport. A new agent in charge of the enforcement agency came into my office. He introduced himself and began to talk with me. He said he had transferred from Miami. While in Miami he went into his office and found one of his agents with his feet propped up on his desk, reading a racing/gambling sheet, and smoking a Cuban cigar. He said, "I told that agent to put out that Cuban cigar, throw away that racing sheet, and put his feet on the floor before someone accuses him of being a customs inspector." Then he laughed vigorously at his joke.

Do you see the problem? His story was a direct insult to me and my colleagues. Part of his premium pay depended upon performing additional hours of service each week. Instead of doing something to benefit the customs service, each evening he would come by my office with similar conversations.

He asked if all of the military aircraft arriving in Charleston gave a twenty-four-hour notice of their arrival. I told him that although Charleston is a landing rights airport with such a requirement, we are talking about the U.S. Air Force, not privately owned aircraft. No! None of them gave such a notice. He said he wanted a list of the aircraft that failed to give the proper notice so that he could seize every one of them. I handed him our log sheets with all of the military arrivals for the past month and told him, "Good luck."

Can you see what an obnoxious person this man was? Tiring of his nonsense, I began to do other duties to avoid listening to him. The Holy Spirit helped me to understand my problem:

Jesus said: **"You have heard that it was said, 'Love your neighbors and hate your enemy. But I tell you: Love your enemies and pray for those who persecute you, that you may be sons of your Father in heaven. He causes His sun to rise on the evil and the good, and sends rain on the righteous and the unrighteous. If you love those who love you, what reward will you get? Are not even the tax collectors doing that? And if you greet only your brothers, what are you doing more than others? Do not even pagans do that? Be perfect, therefore, as your heavenly Father is perfect"** (Matthew 5:43–48).

These words from the Lord convicted my heart. I understood why I lost the joy of my salvation. Immediately, I began praying for this man. I asked the Lord to forgive me as I forgave him. I began to try to help him. Instead of trying to avoid him, I eagerly looked forward to seeing and talking with him. When he began his ugly stories, I responded with good, positive words of kindness. The more he tried to be unruly, the more I tried to show him genuine concern and pray for him.

I don't think my words changed this man at all. After several months, he transferred to an office on the west coast. In the customs news I read where he had a serious altercation with the district director. He transferred to one of the New England states. Later, I read of similar serious problems that he was having in his new assignment.

Although I could not help this man, I began to notice the smile came back into my eyes. When I changed my attitude from dislike to love, God's love again began to flow in my own life.

When I was a child, I thought the Lord gave us this scripture to love your enemies so that we can be a witness for Him. I have since discovered that the Lord gives us these verses because when we hold a grudge, when we dislike someone, when we fail to love, we poison ourselves from within. Show me someone who is harboring ill will towards another and I'll show you a most miserable person.

Paul writes: **"Therefore each of you must put off falsehood and speak truthfully to his neighbor, for we are members of one body. In your anger do not sin. Do not let the sun go down while you are still angry, and do not give the devil a foothold"** (Ephesians 4:25–28).

Insomnia

Have you ever tried to sleep at night and sleep would not come? Do you sometimes wake up hours before time to get up for work and cannot get back to sleep? God gives us a promise to relieve this problem.

As with many other situations, failure to live a normal, healthy lifestyle can affect our bodies. Foods with caffeine or grease can stimulate us or give us indigestion. Such factors can affect our ability to rest. Sometimes we face serious problems, causing our minds to feel as if they are running very fast and cannot slow down.

As a Christian you should take care of your body. **"Don't you know that you yourselves are God's temple and that God's Spirit lives in you? If anyone destroys God's temple, God will destroy him; for God's temple is sacred and you are that temple"** (1 Corinthians 3:16–17).

However, times come when we must rest, and for whatever the reason or reasons, we cannot sleep. Listen to God's promise: **"Thou will keep him in perfect peace, whose mind is stayed on thee; because he trusts in thee. Trust you in the Lord for ever; for in the Lord JEHOVAH is everlasting strength"** (**Isaiah 26:3–4**, KJV).

Memorize these verses so that when the need arises, you will not need to get out of bed to read them. Then, when you cannot sleep or when your mind seems to be running away, recite this promise as you pray. Then, with all of your heart, trust the Lord to keep his promise in your life. Fix your thoughts on the Lord Jesus; only allow yourself to think of Him

Some of God's promises are provisional. God makes a promise, but God also expects us to do something. In this case the provision is: **"whose mind is stayed on thee."** When we finish our prayer, we must take command of our thoughts and only allow ourselves to think about Jesus. Think of how he fed the five thousand with the five loaves and two fish.

Think of Jesus calming the winds and the waves merely by commanding them: **"Peace, be still!"** Then Jesus said to His disciples: **"Oh you of little faith."** Think of Jesus loving the little children, breaking bread, and restoring sight to the blind.

Although it may take a while to master this technique, you can do it. Jesus commands you: **"Do not let your hearts be troubled. Trust in God; trust also in Me" (John 14:1).** Jesus commands us to take charge of our thoughts." When you are obedient to God's promise, you will discover that God will **"keep him in perfect peace, whose mind is stayed on thee; because he trusts in thee."**

When you awaken early in the morning and cannot get back to sleep, do not get out of bed. Also, do not fret. Take this special time to recite **Isaiah 26:3–4** in your heart. Then, do as the verse commands. Fix your thoughts upon the Lord. Only allow yourself to think about the Master and His great love. Use this precious time to have fellowship with God. More times than not, your thoughts of fellowship with God will be interrupted by returning to a sound sleep because you have attained **"perfect peace."** If you do not go back to sleep, consider how special this time is with God when everything is quiet and you are not being interrupted as you communicate with the Master.

Soaring Like an Eagle

Have you ever seen an eagle with giant, outstretched wings soaring high in the air? After retiring, we traveled in our old motor home to Alaska. We heartily recommend this trip to any who can arrange to go there. In early May of

1997 we traveled to Oklahoma City and saw the University of California, Los Angeles, girls' fast-pitch softball team win the college national championship. Then, we turned north to Omaha, Nebraska, and saw the Louisiana State University baseball team win the boys' College World Series.

From there we traveled through Canada, up the Alaskan highway, and spent the summer touring Alaska. God must have loved these northlands. Snow-capped mountains, Mount McKinley, the tallest mountain on our continent, pristine lakes, glaciers, herds of caribou, buffalo, elk, moose, mountain goats, giant crabs, shrimp, halibut, and vegetables, whales, sharks, grizzly bears, schools of salmon—great spectacles of nature!

In the city of Haynes we saw more American bald eagles than in our lifetime. In the fall Haynes celebrates American eagles with a special festival. Watching eagles catching salmon and eating them is almost as impressive as seeing them soaring high overhead with outstretched wings.

As a child, my parents took us to Grant's Park in Atlanta. Walking through a tunnel we came up on a platform in the middle of a building called the *Cyclorama*. German artists created a painting of the Battle of Atlanta during the War Between the States. The great circular painting covers the entire inside wall of the building. Between the platform in the center and the wall, artists placed lifelike replicas of people, twisted railroad tracks, burning buildings, etc. It is as if you are standing in the center of the Battle of Atlanta.

I mention this because of one special detail that really impressed me as a child. Painted high overhead is an eagle with outstretched wings, soaring high above the battle.

Down beneath the eagle a fierce war is raging. The eagle merely soars above the strife and only sees it with his eyes. In those days I thought of how wonderful it would be to be able to soar like an eagle above the problems and strife of the world.

Listen to God's promise in **Isaiah 40:28–31: "Do you not know? Have you not heard? The Lord is the everlasting God, the Creator of the ends of the earth. He will not grow tired or weary, and His understanding no one can fathom. He gives strength to the weary and increases the power of the weak. Even youths grow tired and weary, and young men stumble and fall: but those who hope in the Lord will renew their strength. They will soar on wings like eagles; they will run and not grow weary, they will walk and not be faint."**

Many times during my life, I have placed my finger upon these verses and prayed. I asked the Lord to please keep His wonderful promise in my life. At age seventy-eight the Lord has not disappointed me yet. When I wait upon the Lord and wholeheartedly trust Him, God's steadfast mercy never fails. How I wish everyone would simply take God at His Word and learn to trust Him implicitly. Soaring on wings like eagles is wonderful. Your feet need not leave the ground, but your faith can soar with angels.

Chapter 11

College

When I graduated from college in 1957, I was fed up with school. I was disappointed with what I considered to be unnecessary practices. For example, I was considered to be a "jock." I enjoyed playing basketball on the school's basketball team. Although the student body was small at that time (around two hundred students, including boys and girls), the school took great pride in being rated very highly academically. Being a "jock" or athlete was more than frowned upon.

On the first day in the freshman chemistry class, a large crowd of students gathered, waiting to begin. The professor came to begin his lecture. He explained: "Every year this class begins with the same orientation lecture." He said, "A student is only required to sit through this orientation once." Then he said, "If you are repeating this class and have heard my orientation lecture, take your books and leave." Then he emphatically demanded: "Yes! Take your books and leave!"

At this command about three-fourths of the students picked up their books and walked out of the classroom. The remaining few students sat there trembling in their seats, wondering what kind of class flunks 75 percent of its students.

When I was a sophomore, our basketball team had a scheduled game with Armstrong College in Savannah, Georgia. Since Armstrong College is only a little over one hundred miles from Charleston, our team planned to ride to Savannah on the team bus, play a night game, and then return to Charleston after the game.

The chemistry professor scheduled a major examination on the morning after our game. The team members went to the professor and explained our predicament. We asked if the examination could be scheduled at another time. Actually, I think the professor knew our schedule very well and purposefully planned his examination on the day after our trip. He would not change the date.

During my years at the college, although I majored in English and minored in the social sciences, I completed all of the educational teaching requirements, including the National Teachers Examination (NTE). I was certified by the State of South Carolina as a secondary school teacher. In education courses we learned that when so many students are unable to successfully complete a class, something is dreadfully wrong with the teaching.

Speaking of the National Teachers Examination (NTE), our school viewed with great pride the fact that every student at the college who had ever taken the NTE made a grade of A. Perhaps my friends and I gave them a scare, but we still managed to maintain their tradition.

At the end of the semester my grade in chemistry was slightly lower than an A. As I entered the final examination, I thought with a high score on the final examination I could receive an A for the course. When the class arrived for the final examination, the professor gave a list of only seven questions. Glancing over the questions, I was shocked to see that one seventh of the examination consisted of writing the chemical formula for sugar, DDT, and bleaching powder.

What a cheap shot! No amount of learning or reasoning could deduce such formulae. The only way a person would know such facts is by rote memorization. In education classes we learned that the poorest type of teaching relies upon rote memory. Now, instead of hoping to receive an A, I began hoping to maintain my B average.

In the final examination for physical education, one of the questions on the final examination was to write the formal name of the local municipal swimming pool where swimming classes were held. I knew the answer to this question. As a child, I learned to swim there. It was named "the George P. Burgess Memorial Swimming Pool." However, I learned this fact prior to entering the college, not in physical education.

As I entered the final examination in a history class, the professor stated he was fed up with the grief the college administration was causing him. He did not want to give an examination, but he was required to do so. Therefore, he presented five questions. He said we should write a one sentence answer for each question and turn in our papers. He said he did not have time to read the papers and grade them. Therefore, whatever grade average we had coming into the examination would be our final grade for the semester. Since I had a solid B average, his decision was fine with me.

However, my good friend Joan only had a 68 percent average. Joan had studied until late at night every night for the past month in hopes of bringing her grade up to at least 70 percent, a passing grade. Joan explained her plight to the professor. She spent the full three hours writing all of the information she had learned in her examination booklets. After she completed the examination, the professor was true to his word. He would not even look at Joan's answers. She received a failing grade of 68 percent.

My friend, Len, was a 220-pound forward on our basketball team. His history professor's pet peeve was tardiness. If you were not seated in class when the second bell rang, the doors were locked. Both of the tall green doors to the class were shut and locked. Len knocked loudly on the doors. Inside of the class, the students were seated and the professor was standing in front of the classroom. No one moved to open the door. Len reared back and kicked the doors open. Both doors slammed against the walls. Len stood there with his books under one arm and said: "Man, what's your game?" Angrily, the professor pointed to the door with his right arm raised and shouted: "Out! Out! Out!" As the professor was shouting, the second bell rang. Although the professor would not let Len in the class that day, he was glad to let the matter pass without any further action.

In the freshman mathematics class the professor would go down each row and ask a question. If you answered correctly, you were still "in." If you did not answer correctly, you were excluded from the remainder of the class. You were not required to leave, but for all practical purposes you were finished for the day.

College

In the English composition class, we learned to write many different kinds of articles, from news reporting to fiction. This professor believed that any good writer must wrestle with each word that he writes. Our first assignment was to write a history paper. In order to try to begin the class with a favorable impression, I went to the library and painstakingly researched my topic. Carefully and precisely I completed my work. My corrected paper looked as if a tornado had blitzed across it with a red pen. The professor disagreed with the facts, dates, and just about everything I had written. I could have taken him to the library and proved that every detail on my paper could be substantiated by very reliable resources. However, I chose to remain silent.

Some weeks later I was in the hallway downstairs, waiting for the bell to ring, signaling the time for class. The professor passed by as I was walking up the stairs. He asked how I had enjoyed the assignment. I answered truthfully. I told him I really enjoyed the assignment. Not only was it a joy to write, but the subject matter was interesting and the words just seemed to flow. When I received this paper back, my grade was C-minus.

The next week I made it a point to be in the hallway to wait for the professor's arrival. Again, we were walking up the stairs together to the class. Again, he asked me how I had enjoyed the assignment. This time, I lied. Although there was no difference in writing this assignment and the previous one, I told the professor that I really had to struggle with this assignment. I told him each word was almost like a wrestling match. When I received this paper back, my grade was A-plus.

I suppose all of this contributes towards obtaining an education. Being educated does not merely consist of learning facts. Dealing with people and learning to handle the unexpected probably is more important than subject matter. Perhaps these lessons on life and reality were the most important things that I learned in college. Nonetheless, after receiving a bachelor of science degree, I felt that if I never saw the inside of a college classroom again, it would be soon enough.

Ten Years Later

Ten years later, however, things were different. I had married a very special wife. We had two sons, and I was employed as a senior customs inspector. Although I enjoyed my work, I felt as if I needed more mental stimulation. I read in the local newspaper that the University of South Carolina was opening a limited graduate school program in Charleston. The first course offered was creative writing, taught by Charleston author Richard Coleman.

Instead of attending class one hour a day for three days during the week, as in college, the class would last for three hours on one evening. I enrolled. What a happy surprise! The class was unlike any I had taken in college. It was fun to write the different assignments and then read and discuss each person's writings. What a joy to listen to a successful author tell of his works, techniques, and experiences. I decided to enroll in the school and pursue a master of education degree in the field of guidance and counseling.

— College —

Each semester I took a course. I looked forward to the splendid things I was learning while continuing to do my job with the Customs Service. After completing more than half of the master's program, the University of South Carolina made a sad announcement. Disappointed with local participation, it decided to close the Charleston graduate school.

At the same time, the Citadel military college announced the commencement of its new master of arts in teaching program. I went to the registrar of the Citadel and told him that I would like to transfer my semester hour credits from the University of South Carolina to the Citadel. The registrar said he regretted to inform me the Citadel could only accept six graduate credits from another school.

I also learned that graduate credits expire in seven years if a person fails to obtain a degree. After a semester passed, I developed a course of action. Arranging with my boss, I agreed to work each Saturday and take Tuesday as my regular off day. Customs assigned two inspectors to work from Tuesday through Saturday. My colleagues were happy to have someone volunteer to work every Saturday. I also requested to take four hours of annual leave on Monday afternoon for a full semester.

With this schedule I could leave Charleston at noon on Monday, drive to the University of South Carolina campus in Columbia, and take an evening course. Then, I could spend the night and take two more courses on Tuesday. I could also take two courses at the Citadel and transfer the credits to USC. I needed five courses to graduate.

How could I afford to commute to Columbia each week and spend the night in a motel? With two small children and a wife, I had vital family expenses. I only used two of the four years of my GI Bill eligibility I had earned during my years in the army. However, after I graduated from college, I failed to use the remaining two years in a timely manner. I read that the Veteran's Administration (VA) could reinstate eligibility under certain extenuating circumstances.

I wrote to the VA and explained my extenuating circumstances. I asked if I could be reinstated for a semester. The VA responded that my Korean conflict benefits had completely expired. However, since I served from January through March of the year 1955, I was also a Vietnam veteran and was entitled to one semester of further education. In church we sing a song called "The Doxology." In the words of the song, I "praised God from whom all blessing flow."

In June of 1972 I walked across the stage at the University of South Carolina in Columbia and received a master of education degree in the field of guidance and counseling. What a happy sense of accomplishment, not to mention all of the wonderful things I learned, plus all of the splendid students and professors with whom I had interacted.

Chapter 12

Amazing Trip

My good friend Bob told me his girlfriend's mother lived in North Carolina. She had friends in a church in Philadelphia. The church established a mission in Torremolinas, Spain. The mission planned to celebrate the completion of its first year. It arranged with a Spanish tourist agency for a flight from JFK Airport to Madrid, a connecting flight to Malaga, and a bus ride to a splendid hotel on the front beach of the Mediterranean Sea. Six nights in the hotel included an American-type breakfast. The whole package cost only $215.

I told my friend Bob I did not see how I could go, since I had a wife and three small children. Bob spoke with my wife. Charlene insisted that I should go on this trip. I wish my whole family could have gone with me. Later I learned Charlene knew I had been studying and working very hard for several years in order to complete all of the requirements for a master's degree. Now that I had graduated, she believed the week with Bob and my old high school friend Henry would be good for me. (Did I ever tell you that my little bride has always been an outstanding, understanding, precious lady from the time that I first met her until now—more than fifty years after we were married?)

Bob, Henry, and I drove to Greensboro, North Carolina, in our second car. We picked up Bob's girlfriend's mother, a school teacher, and a young girl. Reaching Philadelphia late in the evening, some friends in the local church agreed to take care of our car. We loaded onto a special bus for JFK Airport and our flight to Madrid.

As we were driving along in the bus, they began singing hymns of praise to the Lord. Suddenly, I understood. It was as if the Lord were communing with my soul. **"But You are holy, O You that inhabit the praises of Israel"** (Psalm 22:3, KJV). When God's people praise the Lord, God lives in the praises of His people. I had been rushed and busy for so long, now I felt as if I were being ushered along on angel's wings. I began to look forward to the coming week.

Each day in Torremolinas we enjoyed meeting and singing praises with God's people in the mission church. The ones on the program who preached were certainly inspired by the Lord. Each message uplifted our spirits. In the afternoons the Spanish people shut down everything for a siesta. Late in the evening, the stores and everyone began again with renewed vigor. One afternoon we made a trip to Barcelona and saw the architecture and artwork of the Moors when they were dominant in Spain.

Another day, we traveled to the bottom of Spain. We caught a ferry and traveled by the Rock of Gibraltar, crossed the Strait of Gibraltar, and visited Morocco and the Casablanca in North Africa. One afternoon we attended a bullfight in Malaga. I was surprised at how the people cheered as the poor bull was slowly aggravated, wounded, and finally killed. The toreador cut off and held up, what I was told, was a piece of the bull's ear. When he presented the ear to an old lady in the crowd, she reacted as if she had been honored as queen for the day.

Outside of the bullfighting arena stands a bronze statue of Alexander Fleming, the discoverer of penicillin. The Spanish people honored Fleming because penicillin saved the lives of countless bull fighters who had been gored by bulls.

This wonderful week of meeting new people, seeing new places, and singing and worshiping together seemed to fly by. At our final meeting, just before we were to board a bus to travel to the airport in Malaga, the speaker said, "The Lord has blessed me with a special gift of healing." He said, "Although the Lord can heal any problem, God has given me especial success in the healing of back and leg disorders." He said, "I will be happy to pray for anyone before we board our bus. However, I would like to begin praying for anyone with a back or leg problem."

Three or four people came forward for prayer. The worst problem was an old fellow who was born with one leg three inches shorter than the other. Before the leader prayed he said, "All of you in the back of the auditorium, please come forward and form a circle around those who came for prayer." He said, "Please pray with me." Since I was not a regular part of this group, I usually sat on the back row. The speaker insisted that all of us in the back should come forward.

I came forward along with many others. In the front of the church, the pulpit and speakers were elevated on a stage about a couple of feet higher than the floor. As the people began to move to the front of the church, some of us stepped up on the platform. The speaker put a fold-up chair on the floor right in front of where I was standing. I could have reached down and touched the person who sat in the chair. I mention this because I had an extremely good vantage point.

A slightly limping old fellow came forward. The speaker told him to sit up straight in the chair and extend both of his legs as far as he could out front. Plainly, one leg was at least three inches shorter than the other. From my vantage point and as a trained observer in the custom service, I carefully watched each move. I was very alert for any sign of wrongdoing or fraud. Actually, there was little to be gained by deception, since we were about to depart for home as soon as the meeting was finished.

The speaker got down on his hands and knees in front of the man in the chair. He reached out and took the heels of the man's shoes in his hands. Then, he asked everyone to pray with him for the man's healing. As the speaker and the other folks began to pray, I carefully watched. There was no hip movement. I saw the man's short leg begin to move slowly forward until it stopped even with the other leg.

The man in the chair was overwhelmed. The folks up close who could see what had happened began praising the Lord and thanking God for His love and mercy. Everyone joined together in one accord, praising the Lord. Although not many had been interested in being prayed for, suddenly, folks with all sorts of problems were asking for prayers.

Those of us, who left Torremolinas that day, were sure we had been standing on "holy ground." To this day that week is still very precious to me. We boarded our bus to the airport. Soon we were in the air and on the way from Malaga to Madrid.

In Madrid we had several hours to wait before boarding our flight back to JFK. Bob, Henry, and I scouted around the airport looking in the shops and exhibits in the terminal. We found a nice place to sit down and wait for our flight. We kept a close watch on the clock. One hour before takeoff we made out way back to the Iberia Airlines boarding gate. When we asked the airlines agent about our flight, she pointed out of the window and said, "That is it taking off now!"

We looked and saw our plane rise from the runway and head towards JFK Airport—without us. What could possibly have gone wrong? We were exactly an hour early at the gate. The problem: Daylight Savings Time! The clocks were exactly an hour off.

Later we learned from our colleagues that they had been looking for us on the airplane. The captain of the aircraft called back to the terminal. He told our friends that we "had been 'arrested' at the gate." Translating from one language to another sometimes causes confusion. What the captain was saying is that we were stopped at the gate. "Stopped" and "arrested" convey two entirely different meanings to Americans.

Was this a catastrophe? Our friends were all on board the aircraft heading home and the three of us were stranded in Spain. Every word in the Bible is inspired by God. A verse that has proven its worth time and again: **"And we know that all things work together for good to them that love**

God, to them who are the called according to His purpose" (Romans 8:28, KJV).

How could any good possibly come out of this mess? The three ladies that we brought with us would not be able to return to North Carolina immediately upon arrival. They spent the night with friends from the church and enjoyed a very special time of fellowship. Bob, Henry, and I received a bonus: an extra night in Spain. I had tried to find a model sailing ship in Torremolinas to take to my wife, but the tourists had purchased all of these nice souvenirs. In Madrid I found two excellent ships and was able to buy both of them for my Charlene. In the evening we attended a special performance; we enjoyed seeing outstanding flamenco dancers.

The next day we boarded the flight to JFK, met our friends at the airport in New York, and proceeded home via Greensboro. Everyone agreed that the missed flight worked together for good to all of us. Even my wife was well pleased with the two splendid sailing ships that we found in Madrid. When you *realize* God, life becomes wonderful—when you fail, botch up, and even miss your flight, God still makes it **"work together for good."**

# Chapter 13

Christmas 1964

My mother and dad were very special people. They loved each other, and they loved their six children. When I was a child, many modern conveniences had not been invented yet. On hot days in church, our air conditioning consisted of a cardboard fan mounted on a large Popsicle stick. If you could find a seat between two ladies, they both fanned so rapidly you could enjoy the nice breeze as they fanned away.

Our home in those days was heated by a small pot-bellied, coal-burning heater. In the winter Dad would get up early in the morning in the freezing cold. He would stoke the stove with crumpled newspaper, small pieces of "fat-lighter" kindling wood, and place coal on top. Then, he would strike a match and light the fire.

When it was time for the children to get up and get ready for school, Dad had that pot-bellied stove red hot. The red heat extended up the metal stove pipe into the ceiling. I feared that such heat would set the house on fire. Although our home was somewhat cold, you could stand in front of that heater and warm every part of your body. You merely had to keep turning around slowly as if on a spit.

I dreaded the time when I would grow up and be responsible for getting up early in the icy cold to start a fire for my future family. What a blessing when electric, gas, and oil heaters were invented along with thermostats that can easily be regulated to keep the entire house warm. Modern generations do not realize how blessed we are.

At home we did not have a refrigerator. We had an ice box. An ice box looked like a small refrigerator, except it did not have electrical wires and could not freeze ice or even keep milk cool. The ice man would come down the street with an insulated horse-drawn wagon. For five cents the ice man sold a fairly large block of ice with a piece of twine tied around it so you could carry it into your home and place it in your ice box. If you had milk or perishables, you placed them as close to the ice as possible. When the ice melted, all of the cooling power of your ice box was gone.

In those days the milkman delivered milk directly to your home. Each morning the milkman deposited quarts of milk in glass bottles on the front porch. The milk was not homogenized. About three or four inches of cream rose to the top of the jar. We had a small angle-shaped aluminum tube that we dropped down into the jar of milk. The cream siphoned into a bowl for whipping into butter or for use as pure cream.

Almost everyone kept chickens in their back yard in order to have fresh eggs. Whenever Mom wanted to prepare fried chicken, Dad would take his axe and chop off a chicken's head. All of the feathers had to be plucked and the innards removed so that Mom could prepare the family dinner. Nothing was wasted. The back, the wings, the neck, even the feet—everything was fried.

One day Mom and I were the only ones at home. Mom wanted a chicken to prepare for supper (we didn't use the word "dinner" much in those days except maybe for Sunday). Mom would not think of killing a chicken, so I was assigned to the task. I tried to hold the chicken with its neck on a block, so that I could cut of its head with the axe as my Dad did. The axe was heavy in my right hand, especially with my left hand holding the chicken. The chicken kept drawing its head back so I could not get a good chop with the axe.

I realized that my Dad's method would not work for me. Reluctantly, I grabbed the chicken by the neck and swung it around, as I had seen my neighbors do. I wrung the head off of my first chicken. When a chicken gets its head chopped off (or wrung), a reflex action causes the dead bird to hop and flop vigorously around the yard for several moments until it finally quits. What an ordeal! Especially for a tender-hearted young fellow.

With six children plus Mom and Dad, we needed a lot of pieces of chicken. Everyone loved to receive their favorite part. There were drumsticks, thighs, wishbone, breast, wings, back, neck, gizzard, etc. As a child I could not understand Mom and Dad. Their favorite parts were the neck, the back, the liver, the heart, the gizzard, and parts that didn't have much meat substance.

After growing a little older and somewhat wiser, I realized that Mom and Dad loved each one of us so much, they wanted their children to have the very best that they could give. Not only was this true about chicken, but in virtually everything, Mom and Dad's love was demonstrated to us in so many ways.

They would take us swimming at the beach, crabbing and fishing in the Stono River, and sometimes to the airport on Sunday afternoon to see the airplanes landing and taking off. After work, my dad would take me to Adgers Wharf downtown. Portuguese fishing and shrimp trawlers tied up there after a day of trawling in the ocean. I walked along the sandy riverbank picking up little rounded black "good-luck" rocks and shells while Dad negotiated for some fish for supper.

The greatest desire of my heart as a child was watching the airplanes at the airport and the ships in the seaport. Think of it! I became a United States Customs inspector, a job I enjoyed for forty years. In my wonderful job I was paid to board the ships and airplanes that arrived in Charleston from overseas. Not only was I paid, but I spoke personally with each captain of the ship. He depended upon me to grant clearance from the Customs Service so that he could lade and unlade cargo in our port.

Dad's joy in life was smoking a pipe with *Granger* tobacco. Tobacco was sold in a small pocket-sized can. The danger of smoking and breathing secondhand smoke was not condemned by the Surgeon General in those days. Movies glorified smoking. But my Dad would never smoke his pipe in our home. Even in the icy winter, he would go outside and sit in his car and smoke so that he would not inflict the smoke upon his family.

Every now and then my dad and his brother, Uncle Snooks, would drink wine and laugh and talk together.

— Christmas 1964 —

Although Dad enjoyed a bottle of wine, when money was scarce he would not touch a drop of alcohol. Only when bills were paid and we had plenty of food and other necessities would he consider his wine.

When I was very small, both Mom and Dad would take us to church on Sundays. Dad even named my younger brother "Luther" after the Rev. Luther Knight, a splendid pastor at our church. A faction within the church, however, was constantly stirring up some sort of strife. During the years of our church, every pastor that served there was forced to leave except one. He died before they could evict him.

Because of this trouble by folks who should have been reflecting the love of Jesus, my dad quit attending church. Mom, however, took her children to church every Sunday.

Finally, the Christmas season of 1964 arrived. Dad had completed forty-three years with the railroad as a telegraph operator. Dad began attending church again. As a young Christian, I was concerned about my Dad's relationship with the Lord. Was he a born-again, saved believer? What was his status with the Lord Jesus? On Christmas Eve we visited with Mom and Dad. Our first little son, Timmy, was over one year of age. Dad thrilled at entertaining him.

I never saw my dad eat a meal, no matter how small, without pausing to verbally thank the Lord for his food. Mouthing words and having a genuine inner relationship with God are two different matters. When we had time together, I asked my dad about his relationship with Jesus. He said he believed that Jesus is the Christ, God's Messiah. He believed that Jesus died for his sins on the Cross of Calvary. He believed that Jesus arose from the dead and ascended up into heaven and is coming again. His testimony sounded so good to me.

Christmas evening, Dad's esophagus hemorrhaged. He was rushed to Roper Hospital. We picked up Mother and brought her to our home so that we could help her get to the hospital. Dad's condition deteriorated. He lapsed into a serious coma. The doctors said the coma could be fatal if he did not soon recover.

A couple of nights later, in the darkness, our telephone rang. The nurse at the hospital said Dad's vital signs were failing fast. She said Dad only had about an hour and a half left to live. "If you want to see Mr. Smith while he is still alive, you should come quickly to the hospital."

Mother and I dressed quickly and rushed to the hospital. I stood at the foot of Dad's hospital bed. Mother was standing near the head of the bed. Dad was still in a coma. He was breathing deep, gasping breaths. A couple of tubes were inserted into his nose.

I watched in awe. Each breath seemed as if it might be his last. My dear mother's face reflected the agony and stress of the moment. Mom's six children were all married and gone. All she had left in the world was Dad, and now it seemed that he, too, would be gone.

Bowing my head, I prayed within my heart: "Lord Jesus, you promised when you left the earth you would send 'the Great Comforter,' the Holy Spirit. Please, Lord. Now is the time. This is the place. How we need you! Lord, we need your love and compassion. Please, please help."

Mom and I stood vigil all night long until the sun came up the next day. Dad was still alive. After surviving this crisis and contrary to all expectations, Dad unexpectedly came out of the coma. He began to regain his strength. The doctors said, "The only thing that saved him was his strong heart." They decided they would discharge him in a few days and let him return home to regain his strength. Then, they would readmit him to the hospital and correct the problem in his esophagus with surgery.

Mother told me about a strange thing that happened that night in the hospital. She said when everything seemed so bleak, when all hope was gone, suddenly she felt as if a great arm came and hugged her and said, "It's all right! It's all right!" Mom said she relaxed, because she knew that no matter what happened, the Lord would provide.

Each day after work, I went down to visit with my dad. Each day in the hospital someone would come and divert me to another room to another patient. They wanted me to talk with their family member or friend and pray with them. For several nights I was able to witness to someone about the Lord and pray with them in addition to visiting with my dad.

Finally, on a Sunday evening I went to visit Dad. It was the first time that I went to the hospital when someone did not come to ask me to come visit their room. Dad and I talked for a long time. Dad told me things about when he was living in Thalmann, Georgia, with his parents. He told me in great detail about his brothers, John and "Snooks," and his sisters, Myrtle and Josephine, and his dad. He said my great grandmother's name was Higgenbotham. She came over from Ireland to North Carolina before moving south to Georgia. He told me so many things; I wish I could have recorded them.

Around dawn on Monday morning, my younger brother, Luther, had spent the night with Dad. Luther said, "Suddenly, Dad drew a deep breath and he was gone." The doctors and nurses came running and tried to revive him. They said, "His heart is what saved him, but now he has suffered a massive heart attack and is gone."

Again, we received a call at home; this time, from my brother. Mom and I quickly dressed and rushed to the hospital. Those special people at Roper Hospital knew and understood such a situation. They quickly and efficiently handled all of the necessary business.

While Dad's body was en route to Stuhr's Funeral Home, Mom and I headed for the car. As we walked across the parking, my pastor, Harry P. Chaffin, arrived. He was walking towards the hospital. Charlene had called him. He had come.

When I saw Brother Harry, I asked myself, "What will he say? What can he say? At a time like this, when my dear mother has lost her faithful life's companion and I have lost my father, what can he possibly say to us?"

Brother Harry gave my mother a big, long bear hug. Then he shook my hand and hugged me. He just stood there. He did not say a word. I thought to myself: "That is the best possible thing he could say—nothing! Words can be so hollow; so empty. Especially at a time like this! But, love, friendship, compassion, and support speak louder than all of the words in the world."

The next big hurdle: to arrange the funeral. Mother asked that my brothers and I go to the funeral home to make the final arrangements. We met with the late Mr. Harry Stuhr, the owner. I was pleasantly surprised by Mr. Stuhr's approach.

In his funeral home he has many different kinds of caskets and supplies. Prices range from reasonable to extremely expensive. Mr. Stuhr said, "I understand how much you all loved your father." He said, "I know how you want to do the best you can for him. However, let me caution you. You each have a family to provide for." He said, "Any arrangements that you make should be made with this fact in mind." He said, "Tomorrow, your dad will still be gone, but you must continue to live and take care of your loved ones."

I was very impressed with Mr. Harry Stuhr. I had heard of undertakers trying to take advantage of someone in such a time of grief. However, Mr. Stuhr was exactly the opposite. He was trying to talk us into arranging a lower-priced funeral.

One of the things I had dreaded was the inevitable time when I would lose my father or my mother in death. Now that Dad was gone, it seemed as if I grew stronger, as if a portion of Dad's spirit had come into my life. I thank the Lord for all of the good years He gave us with our mother and dad. Over many years their example of honesty and integrity and faith coupled with an unfailing, selfless love for each other and for their children gives a child a strong foundation upon which to build a life.

As the weeks went by, I began to wonder about my dad's salvation. For so long he had not attended church.

He never served as a deacon or taught a Sunday school class. As such thoughts of doubt raced through my mind, I became overwhelmed by a very strong Spirit. It was as if the Lord were chastising me and reminding me: **"If you shall confess with your mouth the Lord Jesus, and believe in your heart that God has raised Him from the dead, you shall be saved. For with the heart man believes unto righteousness; and with the mouth confession is made unto salvation"** (**Romans 10:9–10**, KJV).

The simplicity of the Gospel, the Good News of Jesus, became very clear to me. My Dad had made a profession of faith. He believed in his heart that God the Father raised His Son, Jesus, from the dead. The Apostle John said: **"He that has the Son has life, and he that has not the Son of God has not life"** (**1 John 5:12**, KJV).

"He saved us, not because of righteous things we had done, but because of His mercy. He saved us through the washing of rebirth and renewal by the Holy Spirit, whom He poured out on us generously through Jesus Christ our Savior, so that having been justified by His grace, we might become heirs having the hope of eternal life" (Titus 3:5–7).

I am confident in God's word; one day I will see my dad again when the Lord Jesus comes to claim His believers, just as God's Word promises. Not only that, but I know I shall see every other believer who has received the Lord Jesus in faith—all those who have *realized* God.

Chapter 14

Strength in Weakness

Union Pier, situated behind the United States Customhouse in Charleston, South Carolina, is a relatively small pier used for receiving "break-bulk" cargo. Break-bulk is cargo that is not shipped in huge ocean containers. Break-bulk cargo usually is lifted from the ship on pallets and stored on the floor of a warehouse.

Importers and customhouse brokers file formal entries ensuring payment of duty for importations. When I received an entry on the pier, I would physically examine the merchandise and ensure that the tariff description of the merchandise matched the actual shipment.

Although some days were very busy, there were other days when not much was happening. Twice each day a messenger brought entries and messages from the customhouse. One day, I received a notice from the regional commissioner of customs in Miami of a special government-wide opportunity. It was called "Education for Public Management (EPM)." The United States government had a program for sending select employees to a university for ten months of study. The regional commissioner said he would like to receive some strong applications from our region.

I carefully examined the notice. Nine major universities across the United States participated. However, the government wanted employees in grades GS-13 through GS-15. The notice said possibly they might accept a GS-12 employee. A small note said under exceptional circumstances they might even consider a GS-11. My problem: I was a meager GS-11. However, I was not an exceptional circumstance. Consequently, I threw the message aside and went about my normal routine.

Several days passed with no new ships at Union Pier. All of my work was caught up. There was little to do. Seeing the notice from the regional commissioner, I decided to send him a "strong application." The principal part of the application was a statement of why the government should send the applicant to such a comprehensive program of study.

While attending graduate school at the University of South Carolina, I learned that everyone who obtains a doctor of philosophy degree (PhD) must perform an original, unique research project. Each student must write a dissertation on his study along with his findings. Such students discover new and improved means of accomplishing almost everything. However, after the person's goals are achieved, often this new knowledge is not put into practice. Such studies have revealed more effective means of motivating people, of increasing production, of cutting costs, of enhancing an organization.

In my application for the EPM program, I proposed to research the research. I explained that someone from our organization needed to examine these studies that had proven to be effective and then return to the organization and initiate them. I proposed to try the ideas locally and have them assessed by operations officers from the regional office. When these new methods had been tried and proven, then they could be implemented on a regional or national scale throughout the customs service.

In addition to stating the reason why the government should send me to college, I was also required to list my number one, number two, and number three choices from nine major universities. When I looked at the list of schools, I saw the University of Southern California. Watching football, baseball, basketball, and other sports events on television, I always admired the school's team spirit. Even the school colors appealed to me, since in my high school days at the High School of Charleston, our colors were garnet and gold. I also loved Florida State University, with similar colors. At the College of Charleston our colors were maroon and white.

Although USC was my personal first choice, I decided that I should read all of the literature concerning the nine colleges and pick the three schools that would be in the best interest of the government, especially since the government would be paying all expenses.

I learned that Harvard has the best research library in the United States, but I never cared to go to Harvard or to live in that cold climate. Since my project primarily involved research, I listed Harvard as my number one choice. As I remember, my information cited Cornell as a great research source. Therefore, I listed Cornell as my second choice. Choice number three was a toss-up. I could find no compelling reason for choice number three.

My first thoughts were that I could put my own personal choice of USC as number three. But then I thought about the government and the costs involved. Indiana University was one of the nine schools. It is much closer to Charleston than USC, so I listed it as choice number three to save on transportation costs.

I carefully typed my application on crisp, clean, appropriate government stationary. In those days we had no computers, so I carefully typed the application without strikeovers or erasures.

A couple of weeks later, I received a telephone call from our district director. He said, "The regional commissioner is on the phone. He needs a memorandum nominating you for the program." I told the district director: "Tell the commissioner the letter is on the way."

I again took a crisp, clean, government memorandum form and typed a letter from the regional commissioner to the Civil Service Commission, nominating me for the program. Instead of folding the memo and placing it in a regular envelope, I used a larger manila envelope so that the memo would appear with no creases, strikeovers, or erasures.

After putting the memo in the mail, I went home that evening and told my wife, "If the regional commissioner signs that memo, we are on our way to college again." A few days later I received a telephone call from the U.S. Customs Service training officer in Washington, D.C. He explained, ""The Civil Service Commission frequently deals directly with applicants to their program. They bypass the employee's agency. My job is to stay informed about such matters." He asked, "If you hear anything about your application, please give me a call and let me know." I was happy to oblige. I also realized that my application was indeed being considered, even though I did not have all of the necessary qualifications.

In my heart I began to ponder the seriousness of what I was doing. Along with the application for the program, I was required to sign a statement that I would work in any location and do any assignment that was necessary to further the customs mission.

In 1970 I had volunteered to teach during the summer at the U.S. Customs Service Academy, located at Hofstra University on Long Island, New York. That summer a ranking official from Customs Headquarters in Washington, D.C., offered me the opportunity of a lifetime. I could go to Washington as a GS-12. The following year I would become a GS-13 and the next year a GS-14. The position was called "operations officer." Today it is called management analyst.

For a couple of nights I lay awake rehearsing the advantages and disadvantages of such a move. For me personally, it would be almost instant success in my work. That is, if you consider success as being promotions, responsibility, and pay. I considered success as caring for my three children and bringing them up to be responsible adults, along with all that is involved in what we refer to as family values.

In 1960 my first boss with Customs and I had talked about such allegiances. He was perhaps one of the best supervisors I have experienced, even though he was a sort of an agnostic. As he described it, to him Customs was like a pure, unblemished gem more valuable than anything. He cherished his service to Customs above all other considerations.

I explained to him that my viewpoint was somewhat different. My "pearl of great price" is the Lord Jesus Christ. He ranks above all else. Because the Lord has blessed me with a splendid wife and home and children, my devotion is to the Lord and to my family. Since the Lord and my family mean so much, I will excel in all of my work and in everything I do so that I can be a blessing for them.

Taking my children away from two sets of grandparents, friends, family, church, schools, family doctors, etc., in 1970 and rearing them in a high drug area without local support caused me to decide against such an instantly successful move. Now, I was faced with even more uncertainty. I did not know what I would be doing or where I would be doing it. But, what an opportunity to attend a wonderful university with all expenses paid!

Do you understand my title for this section, "Strength in Weakness"? What a tremendous responsibility it would be for me to take my wife and three children away from grandparents, friends, church family, schools, etc., and move them, first to California, 2,300 miles away, and after that, who knows where? Do you see how I was somewhat skeptical and wondering about our future?

In the Bible I read: **"Have not I commanded you? Be strong and of a good courage; do not be afraid, neither be dismayed; for the Lord your God is with you wherever you go" (Joshua 1:9**, KJV). What a blessed promise from God! Immediately, I committed my life, my family, my future to God. I realized that God was promising me His protection. All I had to do was be strong and courageous. God would personally take care of everything else. In the truth of this verse I and my family began eagerly looking forward to whatever the future held in store for us.

(Since that time, I have mentioned this verse to several other believers who were facing a gigantic move with similar uncertainty. Every one of these believers took time to contact me later to tell me they also received undreamed-of strength from God in a time when they needed it the most.)

A few days later I received a telephone call from a Mrs. Gibson with the Civil Service Commission. She used very ladylike terms and carefully worded phrases to tell me that Harvard was not the place for me. Personally, I did not care to go there either. Then, she said: "Have you ever considered the University of Southern California?"

I told her that USC was really my personal first choice. Then, I explained that I had decided upon the three schools listed on my application because I thought they would be the most advantageous for the U.S. government. Mrs. Gibson said, "Young man, you wait right there by the telephone, and I will call you back in a few minutes."

In a few minutes she called back and told me that I had an appointment with Dr. David Mars in the School of Public Administration at the University of Southern California in Los Angeles. I was to fly to California in early August and arrange my schedule of courses for the fall semester. We should also find an apartment. Then, I was to return to Charleston and finally report to USC in September for ten months of graduate school. What a blessing! A lowly GS-11 was selected for such a marvelous educational opportunity. To this day, the thought of God's love in so many ways overwhelms me.

Instead of flying to California, I took the option of driving our family vehicle and applying for mileage instead of purchasing airplane tickets. The government allows this option, provided the costs do not exceed regular airfare tickets. By driving our station wagon, we were able to take our children and make a semi vacation out of the trip. Our dear friend Fran also needed to go to California. Her husband was serving in the military in Vietnam. He was to meet her in Hawaii for "R and R" (Rest and Relaxation leave).

After dropping Fran off at the Los Angeles International Airport for her flight to Hawaii, I met with Dr. Mars and arranged my schedule for the fall semester. Dr. Mars said I could merely audit all of the courses and just relax and learn. That way, I would not be responsible for taking tests and examinations. At the end of the course I would receive a certificate from the Civil Service Commission stating that I had successfully completed their Education for Public Management Program at USC.

I told Dr. Mars that I wanted to formally apply as a regular graduate student and work towards earning a master's degree in public administration. The College of Charleston and the University of South Carolina sent transcripts of my studies. I began the school year as a regular graduate student.

Leaving Dr. Mars's office, our next job was to find a place to live. We looked in the newspapers; we drove around; we looked at many places. Nothing seemed to meet our needs. Since I had three young, school-aged children, I knew I had to find a place where they could attend school while I was attending college.

As we drove around the Los Angeles area, we listened to a Christian radio station. Bill Glass, a former Cleveland

Browns professional football player, had become an evangelist. He would be speaking on Sunday morning at the Redondo Beach Baptist Church. During the week, he would be conducting an evangelistic crusade at the El Camino College football stadium.

Since we were strangers in the area, we decided to find that church and attend there on Sunday morning. On Sunday the children attended Sunday school classes for their age group. Charlene was in the ladies class; the men's class welcomed me. The men wanted to know why we left South Carolina and came all of the way to the West Coast. I told them of my schooling opportunity at Southern Cal. I also mentioned our plight of trying to find a place to live.

Mr. Mitch, the Sunday school teacher, told me he had some ideas. I should get with him immediately after church. During the time of worship, I met Bill Glass. I am six feet one inch tall, but I had to look up at him. He shook my hand. I felt as if his hand could have encircled mine twice. When he spoke, his voice was as strong and powerful as his big frame.

One of the things he said really impressed me. He said, "When I traveled with the football team, my colleagues read all sorts of mysteries and novels. However, I never did get much out of those stories." He said, "I would read the first few pages and learn the plot. Then, skipping over the middle of the book, I turned to the back to see what happened."

He continued, "One day I decided to try this technique with the Bible. I made a wonderful discovery: If you are a Christian, if you have placed your faith in the Lord Jesus

Christ and asked Him to forgive you of your sins and save you, then you are a winner." He said, "I have already read the back of the book. In the end the Bible says everyone with faith in Christ Jesus will be victorious."

After the service, Mr. Mitch, with his family in his car, led us to the corner of Torrance Boulevard and Anza Avenue. Apartment buildings lined both sides of the boulevard as far as I could see down the street. I went inside the apartment where I had parked our car. Although the lady manager had a vacancy, it was promised to someone. She said, "Call back after 2:00 p.m. on Monday. If those folks do not rent by that time, the apartment is yours." We rented that three-bedroom apartment. It also included a nice family swimming pool.

Victor Elementary School was adjacent to our apartment. All three of our children could attend school without having to cross a street. Obliquely across the intersection from our apartment was the Anza Avenue Baptist Church. The Rev. Clarence Scott from Texas was the pastor at that time. Those folks in the church became as dear to us as our own precious family back in South Carolina.

How can we explain all of our sudden good fortune? Jesus gives us a clue: **"But seek you first the kingdom of God, and His righteousness, and all these things shall be added unto you" (Matthew 6:33**, KJV). If you have *realized* God, then you will understand. If not, this probably sounds like foolishness to you.

During the ten months that followed, the folks in that church grew closer and closer to each one in our family. Brother Aaron invited me to go with him to speak with the prisoners about Jesus. Brother Aaron's son and I even sang a duet to the prisoners. Aaron said, "Every time I have visited this jail for the past nineteen years, some prisoners have decided to invite the Lord Jesus into their life to be their Savior. Usually," he said, "several prisoners received Jesus, but always someone comes to Christ." During the months that I accompanied him, his good record remained intact.

Since I was a student at USC, my wife and I qualified for student tickets to all of the sporting events. We did not miss a home football game. Charlene and I sat in the student section; we were able to get tickets for our three children in the end zone seating. The arrangement was good, because we could see our children from our seats and keep a watchful eye on them.

During the basketball season, we were able to get seats behind the basketball goal. After watching the game, we drove home. At 11:00 p.m. a local television station broadcast a replay of the game. Our children were thrilled to see themselves on television every time the teams came towards our end of the court.

Under the agreement between the government and the school, I was allowed to take any courses I desired. I earned forty graduate credits and two undergraduate credits. I also took five managerial seminars and received a certificate of completion for each one.

I learned that an educator from Boston University was on loan to the school; he was teaching a course titled "Conflict and Violence in Urban America." Conflict and violence are appropriate studies for an enforcement officer. However, I wanted to take the class because of the professor's reputation as an educator. In the first day of class he said: "My theory of education is that everyone in this class receives a grade of A unless, during the course of the semester, you can prove that you do not deserve it."

What a professor! Virtually all of my former teachers took a completely opposite viewpoint. The usual viewpoint is that you are stupid and know nothing at all, unless during the course of the semester you can prove otherwise. Our first assignment was to write a brief paper on conflict and violence. We could write about any type of conflict and violence we desired.

I decided to write the "true" story of how the American War Between the States came to an end. I told of how the great General Robert E. Lee was holding up in Appomattox Courthouse in Virginia. General Lee contemplated the last final battle of the war. The next day Lee would lead valiant Southerners against the Yankees. The Yankees that were not killed would be driven back into the sea and drowned. Realizing that the war would finally be ended, a small, whiskery runt came into the room. When General Lee saw the "boy," he decided it must be the shine boy. Lee took off his boots and gave them to him along with his sword to be shined. After all, the commanding general should look his best on the day when the war would finally end.

The whiskery little runt dropped the boots and ran out on the front porch holding General Lee's sword high in the air with both hands. He shouted: "General Lee has surrendered! General Lee has surrendered! He has given me his sword!" That little runt was none other than General Ulysses S. Grant, the head of the Union Army. What a sad mistake!

But General Lee, being a true Southern gentleman, could not go back upon his word, even though it was a mistake, so the war came to an end that day.

At our next class the professor was giving back the papers we had submitted. He showed me my paper graded with an A. Then he asked if he could please keep the paper. I was honored that he was not only a great educator but, evidently, also had a keen sense of humor as well.

During the Christmas break, the USC Student Travel Bureau chartered an entire airplane for a trip to Hawaii. For only a nominal sum we were able to fly to Hawaii the week before Christmas and spend six nights in the hotel. My wife, three children, my little widowed mother, and I were all able to make the trip.

Charlene and I received student tickets for all of the Southern Cal home football games. Student seating at football games is determined by a lottery. Twice, we were seated in the giant card section where students hold up various colored cards to present messages that cover almost the entire student section. We were also able to get tickets for our children to all of the football and basketball games. In addition to traveling to Hawaii the week before Christmas with the Student Travel Bureau, we had tickets for the family, including Momma Ruby (my mother) for good seats in the stands at Pasadena for the annual Rose Parade. After the parade we made our way to the Rose Bowl, where we saw our team, the USC Trojans, beat the Ohio State Buckeyes, 18 to 17. Southern Cal won the UPI National Championship with a two-point conversion in the last minute of play.

The Notre Dame football game that year was a classic. Notre Dame came to Los Angeles as the defending national champion from the previous season. Methodically, the Irish scored twenty-four points. Shortly before halftime, USC scored its only touchdown of the first half. Because they were so far behind, USC attempted a two-point conversion and failed. The halftime score was 24 to 6. The Irish were so confident, their cheerleaders were actually cheering for USC to beat Ohio State in the upcoming Rose Bowl. I think they thought that if USC beat Ohio State and the Irish could beat Miami, they would repeat as national champions again. I never saw an opposing team cheering for their opponent while the game was still in progress. It reminds me of a scripture: **"Pride goes before destruction, and an haughty spirit before a fall" (Proverbs 16:18**, KJV).

During halftime, I climbed the stairs to the top of the stadium so that I could photograph the Los Angeles skyline. I decided to wait at the top of the stadium to take a panoramic photo of the entire stadium during the kickoff for the second half. Anthony Davis, the Southern Cal tailback, received the kickoff two yards deep in the end zone. He ran straight down the sideline 102 yards and scored. I took photos. Thirteen seconds had ticked off of the clock and our team was already on the scoreboard again.

That football game seemed to be two entirely different games. Whereas Notre Dame led 24 to 6 at halftime, the final score was 55 to 24 in favor of Southern Cal. Later, I talked with friends back in Charleston; some left the game on television after the first half to go fishing; they decided the game was finished.

During the spring break we drove to Las Vegas and saw Elvis Presley live on stage at the Hilton Hotel about a year before he passed away.

When the school year ended, I was one of 3,500 students that received a degree from the university. My degree was master of public administration in the field of government affairs. What a difference! From thirty-five students in my graduating class at the College of Charleston in 1957 to 3,500 at Southern Cal in 1975! When I received my degree the professor said I had now graduated from USC from coast to coast (the University of South Carolina and the University of Southern California).

Our year at the University of Southern California fulfilled the dreams of each one in our family. In addition to the school experience we visited Hollywood, Beverly Hills, Universal Studios, Knott's Berry Farm, Disneyland (about once each month), the great white steamer to Catalina Island, Big Bear Mountain, the Mojave Desert, San Clemente, where President Nixon lived, the rose garden with more than 1,500 rose bushes in full color, the Berea Tar Pits, San Diego and the world's largest zoo, Tijuana, Mexico, Sea World, Busch Gardens, etc.

Our son, Tim, had a reading problem. When he should have been studying phonics in his school in North Charleston, the school changed to a new program that eliminated phonics. They gave the students cards with words on them to study. After a couple of years, the school realized that phonics was the proper answer and not words written on cards. However, the damage had been done. Tim missed two vital years of learning phonics.

His new school in California had a special remedial reading program. It was equipped to help students at any level. During our year in Torrance, with its superb curriculum, Tim was able to master the skills he had missed at home.

As we were preparing to return to Charleston, South Carolina, and my regular job as a customs inspector, our church friends must have been glad to see us leave. They staged three different farewell parties. At the first party they prepared a sheet cake with white icing and light blue writing. In the icing on the cake they had drawn an outline of the United States. They placed a small toy automobile on the left side at Los Angeles. On the right side of the cake Charleston was highlighted. Across the entire cake, they had written a Bible verse: **"Have not I commanded you? Be strong and of a good courage. Do not be afraid; neither be dismayed; for the Lord your God is with you wherever you go"** (**Joshua 1:9**, KJV). This was the verse that turned my weakness to strength when we were planning to go away to school. This promise from God empowered me to go without fear wherever our path might lead.

Now, in my heart it seemed as if God were reminding me: "Didn't I tell you? Don't you see and understand? Whereas you were filled with fear and doubt, when you trusted Me, you and your entire family have enjoyed the best year of your lives—just as I promised in My Word. And now, I will continue to be with you wherever you go if you will trust in Me." Life is wonderful when you *realize* God.

Chapter 15

The Desires of Your Heart

We designed our trip home into a family vacation. Leaving Los Angeles, we drove up Highway 1 to San Francisco. What a magnificent, scenic drive. Waves dashed on the craggy rocks along the Pacific coastline. We turned onto an eighteen-mile circular drive that passed along the coast where sea lions and seals were basking and barking on the rocks off shore.

Driving around San Francisco, we passed over the Golden Gate Bridge. We saw Alcatraz in the harbor. We watched the cable cars clanging up and down the hills. After a seafood meal at San Francisco Bay, we headed north.

Stopping near Bakersfield, we marveled at the giant redwood trees. These trees are many centuries old. Park rangers told of a lower segment of a tree that was shipped to Philadelphia for a science exposition near the end of the nineteenth century. Since the slice of the tree was so tremendous, it could not be shipped across the country. They sawed it into fifteen pieces and reassembled it at the exposition. The exhibit was thrown out. No one believed that a tree of such size existed. A hollow log on the ground was so huge that a man on horseback could ride through it. Cars once drove through a tree in the road. However, a storm toppled it in the 1950s.

Driving north, we were awed by snow-capped Mount Shasta in Oregon. For a family from Charleston, South Carolina, where we seldom see snow, such wintry beauty is overwhelming—especially in midsummer.

In the state of Washington we drove to Mount Rainier. The pretty, young National Park Service official at the entrance to the park told us of Paradise Inn six thousand feet up the side of the mountain. With ten feet of snow on the ground a heavy snow was falling. What a spectacle for the middle of summer. It was July 26, 1975. We spent two nights in the lodge. Snow was up to the window sill of our first-floor room where we stayed.

Our children thrilled at making a snowman and throwing snowballs. For a few brief minutes the clouds cleared and we could see the majestic snow covered peak of Mount Rainier. Although I had a fear of heights and never considered being a mountain climber, as we gazed at the beauty of that moment, the centers of the bottoms of my feet tickled with the urge to climb to the top. The mountain top seemed to be beckoning to climb up.

Descending from Mount Rainier, we began making our way back toward the east to Charleston. We saw a young fellow along the highway selling freshly picked cherries. At thirty cents per pound, we bought enough cherries to fill our cooler. After washing the cherries, Tim, Jim, and Sherri tossed cherry seeds along the highway all of the way back to the Mississippi River.

Perhaps you've heard of Johnny Appleseed, who went around planting apple seeds. If you drive out west and see cherry trees along the roadside, you can understand that Tim, Jim, and Sherri Cherryseed passed that way.

Not long after we returned home in North Charleston, we received a letter from our good friends Shirley and Claudio. Shirley's letter was short and to the point. "Good news!" she wrote. Hank's wife contacted him and said, "Why don't we get our family back together?" Then she wrote: "Psalm 37:3–4."

Hank was a young man and a member of the Anza Avenue Baptist Church where we attended while living in Torrance, California. Hank had a wife and three small daughters. Before we arrived in California, his wife decided to take their three girls and leave. Hank's heart was broken. He loved his wife and he loved his three daughters, perhaps more than anything in the world.

Since he was left alone, he devoted himself to loving and serving the Lord Jesus. He would take his spacious van and gather children in the area and bring them to church. Not only did he teach them the love of Jesus from the Scriptures, but he took them on camping trips on Big Bear Mountain. He took them on cookouts at Redondo Beach. Hank's sole delight was in the Lord and serving Him with all of his heart.

The verses that Shirley mentioned: **"Trust in the Lord, and do good; so shall you dwell in the land, and truly you shall be fed. (4) Delight yourself in the Lord; and He shall give you the desires of your heart"** (**Psalm 37:3–4**, KJV).

Shirley was telling us that Hank had realized the benefits of these verses. He trusted in the Lord; he did good deeds;

he delighted himself in the Lord above everything and everyone. Now, Shirley pointed out that God was giving him **"the desires of your heart."**

When I read Shirley's letter and this scripture, I felt as if these words slapped me in the face. Suddenly, I remembered the many deep desires of my heart; things I had only dreamed about became a reality during our year in California.

I not only attended but graduated from a major university. Money was not a problem. In addition to my regular salary, all of the school's expenses were paid in full. The school my son attended had a wonderful remedial reading program for children. We not only attended a football bowl game, but we attended the "granddaddy" of them all—the Rose Bowl. Our college football team won the UPI national championship. We participated in the gigantic card displays during the football season. We spent a week on Waikiki Beach in the winter when the United States was enduring cold weather. We cruised to Catalina Island on the great white steamer.

Why am I telling about all of these strange desires of the heart? When I read this verse that our friend Shirley mentioned in her letter about our friend Hank, suddenly, I realized that God had already kept this promise, to us. **"Delight yourself in the Lord, and He shall give you the desires of your heart" (Psalm 37:4**, KJV).

All of these peculiar desires of my heart—things that I would never ask for; things that a person would not even attempt to fulfill; these impossible desires that a person only dreams about—God had given us every one of them, plus many other blessings that we had not even imagined.

Do you understand what I am trying to say about *realizing God?* God keeps His promises. We might be slack concerning the promises we make: **"The Lord is not slack concerning his promise, as some men count slackness; but is longsuffering to us, not willing that any should perish, but that all should come to repentance"** (**2 Peter 3:9**, KJV).

The Almighty God freely offers His love to each person in the entire world. Each one of us has the opportunity to receive God's love in our life. We also have the right to turn our back upon God and reject His everlasting love. Jesus tells us: **"Enter in at the strait gate; for wide is the gate, and broad is the way, that leads to destruction, and many there be which go in thereat: Because strait is the gate, and narrow is the way, which leads to life, and few there be that find it"** (**Matthew 7:13–14**, KJV).

What is this narrow way that **"leads to life"**? **"Jesus said to him, 'I am the way the truth, and the life; no man comes to the Father, but by Me' "** (**John 14:6**, KJV). How can we *realize* God? By coming to Jesus Christ. Each one who comes to Christ with all of his heart; each one who invites the Lord Jesus to come into his life and forgive his sins and save him, passes from death into life! He receives a second birth "of the Spirit." He becomes an immediate part of Christ's body of believers. Suddenly, God's spiritual existence becomes reality. We begin experiencing the power of God in our life in many different ways.

Have you *realized* God? If not, these words will seem to you as foolishness. If you have *realized* God, your inner spirit is celebrating the blood of Jesus Christ that was shed for your sins. If you **"delight yourself in the Lord"** then **"He will give you the desires of your heart."**

After you trust the Lord to keep his promise of salvation, as His child, you can then trust the Lord to keep His other wonderful promises in your life. You can begin a beautiful close personal relationship with the Almighty God and His Son, Jesus Christ.

Retirement

Although I had refused a great opportunity to be promoted in my younger days, our children were married and gone. As we thought of survival after retirement, we realized that I should seek a higher paid job because our civil service retirement in those days was based upon the average of our highest three years of pay.

Our chief customs inspector developed a heart problem. After undergoing open heart surgery, he was absent for almost two years. During his absence, I was assigned to perform his duties. While serving as the acting chief inspector, I received the highest appraisal ("outstanding") for my services. Although the chief finally was able to return to work for a couple of hours every other day, Two years passed before he was able to return to his job.

However, he had suffered a mild stroke during his operation. The stroke caused a peculiar vision problem; the chief said his vision looked as if he was viewing the world through a "fish-eye" lens. He finally decided to retire because of his problems.

When his position was declared vacant, I, along with several others, applied for the position. My application reflected two master's degrees, one in government affairs. I had experience teaching and training customs inspectors in the National Customs Academy at Hofstra University on Long Island. I also had two years of practical experience in the vacancy with an outstanding performance appraisal.

When the boss made his selection, he chose a friend who had virtually none of these qualifications. At first, I was somewhat concerned. What did I lack? What had I done wrong? When I have problems, I look to the Lord and to His word. **Psalm 75:6–7: "For promotion comes neither from the east, nor from the west, nor from the south, (7) But God is the judge; he puts down one, and sets up another" (KJV).** When I read this Scripture, I said, "Lord, I do not understand, but I trust You and Your word. I shall happily live my life knowing that You are in charge."

This happened in the spring of the year. Around September, I was invited by the Customs Office of International Affairs in Washington to participate with a customs training group for two weeks in Athens, Greece. During the second week of the course, I had my wife to fly to Athens and join with me. She was welcomed by the Greek customs officers to join with us for dinner each evening as well as on various sight-seeing trips.

At the conclusion of the two weeks in Athens, I had a couple of weeks of annual leave approved. Instead of returning directly home to Charleston, my wife and I traveled to Egypt. We visited the Sphinx and pyramids; we went to Luxor and Karnak. We visited King Tut's tomb in the Valley of the Dead. Then we flew to Tel Aviv, rented a car, and traveled in the Holy Land. We returned to Athens and visited Rome, Paris, and London, and flew home from Frankfurt, Germany.

The supervisor in Washington who invited me to participate in this amazing assignment told me, "If you were the chief inspector, we would not have invited you to participate in this program. We wanted a journeyman senior inspector for the job." I asked my wife, "Which would you rather have—the job of chief inspector or the great assignment and trip we were able to make overseas?" My wife said, "It is no contest! The trip overseas was much better for us. It was the trip of a lifetime!"

Do you see how God works through these circumstances in our lives to accomplish His purpose? God continuously promises us blessings, guidance, and help. In addition, the Customs Service invited me to teach courses in Lisbon, Portugal, in Belize, Central America, in Paramaribo, Surinam, in Dakar, Senegal, and a month in Cairo, Egypt. Later I served in Romania during the embargo against Serbia.

Other things happened that helped me to understand what a blessing it was that I did not get the chief's job. Customs inspectors in those days worked under the Overtime Act of 1911. In the early days, customs worked similar to the post office and other government agencies; that is, they worked from 8 a.m. to 5 p.m. They enjoyed Sundays and holidays off, just as other government employees.

Shipping company representatives went to Congress and requested that the Congress authorize customs inspectors to work overtime on nights, weekends, and holidays.

Congress in those days was sensitive to the needs of our citizens. Congress told the shipping interests that the US Government would not spend the people's tax money so that the shipping interests could make more money for themselves.

The shipping companies agreed. They told Congress that if the Congress would pass an act, authorizing customs inspectors to work these hours, then the shipping companies would pay all of the costs involved. Congress then passed the Overtime Act of 1911. This act provided pay that was similar to the overtime enjoyed by waterfront union workers. It included such things as a guaranteed eight hours of pay for all holiday or Sunday work. It also provided liberal payments for inspectors who would be called out during the night; such callouts required the inspector to travel at his own expense from his home to many varied waterfront sites. Callouts also involved much loss of sleep.

Under this overtime system, my personal salary was about as good as if I had been promoted. The chief inspector worked overtime along with the inspectors. However, the Customs Service decided to eliminate chief inspectors from the overtime system. When this change was effected, I earned more than the chief inspector. The chief suffered a serious loss when he was removed from the overtime list.

The problem I faced was nearing retirement age without achieving a larger base salary. Overtime pay was wonderful, but it did not contribute even one penny towards retirement.

The General Accounting Office (GAO) in Washington began a serious attempt to change the Overtime Act of

1911. Even though the benefits were similar to other waterfront agency pay, the GAO was determined to revise the law. It solicited information from anyone who cared to comment on its study.

I typed a letter stating my viewpoint. I mentioned that a customs callout at night frequently involved the inspector traveling many miles to an outlying pier or terminal. Such travel was expensive and time consuming. I said the reason why so many customs inspectors are very old is because they cannot afford to retire. When an inspector retires, he loses all of his overtime pay and only retains a percentage of his base pay for retirement. Therefore, it is better to work until you die than to retire and take such a tremendous loss of salary.

My suggestion was that they should incorporate overtime benefits into the retirement system. My letter to the Congress was in true government fashion. I was required to submit seven copies of the letter.

Several weeks later, someone in the Congress sent me a copy of the *Congressional Record*. There was my complete letter in print in their publication. The happiness came when they decided that $12,000 of an inspector's overtime pay should be included along with his regular retirement benefits as well as the Thrift Plan for savings. (The Thrift Plan was similar to a 401(k) tax free savings plan).

The beauty of the new overtime law was it took effect exactly three years before I would reach sixty-five years of age, the year I retired. Therefore, my retirement salary incorporated $12,000 in overtime for three years in order to compute my three-year high salary for retirement purposes.

Because of this vital change, my wife and I have been able to be completely self-supporting as we serve as the Lord's missionaries to Bulgaria. Can you see and understand the truth of Romans 8:28? **"And we know that all things work together for good to them that love God, to them who are the called according to His purpose."**

Chapter 16

Becoming a Missionary

During the fall of the year 1999, Charlene and I attended the quarterly senior banquet of the Charleston Baptist Association at the Fort Johnson Baptist Church on James Island. At a cost of only four dollars, we enjoyed a full meal with a salad, dessert, and iced tea, plus an entertaining and informative program.

The principal speaker was a petite woman with an accordion almost as big as she is. Although small, she sang with luster and spoke with determination. As she sang hymns of praise to God, I felt as if I were intruding upon a very special private love affair between this woman and her Savior.

The little lady told of how, at age sixty-two, she believed God called her to minister to the orphans of Romania. She said she contacted the foreign mission board of her church. She was told that at her age, because she was single and a woman, they could not send her on such a mission overseas. Since she believed God had called her to this work, several churches banded together to send her overseas.

Working with the youth in Brasov, Romania, God laid His hand upon a number of youth and their families. The group continued to grow, and a Baptist church grew from her ministry. In all of my life I cannot remember such an amazing little lady who was so totally devoted to loving and serving the Lord. Charlene and I both were impressed by what we had seen and heard.

In February of 2000 we were delighted to learn that this little woman with her huge accordion would be speaking and singing at our church. Again, the woman sang, praised the Lord, and told of her work overseas. She told of how she packed as many as a dozen young people in her little automobile. She said, "The car is worn out and needs to be replaced." Then she added, "I am not worried about the problem because the Lord will provide." She told how much a brand new small car in Romania costs. Then, she said, "Perhaps one of you can help me obtain another car."

I thought within myself: "Lord, I am retired and on a fixed income. It would not be fair to take such an amount from the retirement fund I have provided for my wife." Then, within my heart I said: "Lord, if I had my job back, I could help this woman."

What an impossible thought! When I retired in 1997, the year I turned sixty-five, I had served the United States government for forty-one years and ten months. I was then approaching sixty-eight. I had been retired for three years. The Office of Personnel Management had completely closed out my civil service status. Getting rehired? Impossible! Who would even think of hiring such an old man?

Two weeks later, Charlene and I attended a party for one of my former colleagues, a customs inspector who was retiring. I had not returned to the office since I retired three years ago. I looked forward to seeing many of my former colleagues. When I entered the door of the sports bar in Mount Pleasant, my former boss saw me. He pointed his finger at me and said: "They're looking for you in Washington. They want you to go to Eastern Europe to help with a program there."

I told him, "I just might be interested. Who should I talk with?" He said, "'Call me at the office in the morning and I'll give you the name and telephone number of the man in charge."

The next morning, I got the information and called the International Affairs Office of the United States Customs Service in Washington, D.C. After working through the normal governmental red tape, I, a sixty-eight-year-old, "turned out to pasture for three years," former customs inspector was rehired by the U.S. government. I received a one year contract to go to Bulgaria to assist the Bulgarians in getting a large loan from the World Bank for the purpose of enhancing their border operations.

Do you know what makes this so significant? Just two weeks earlier, I said in my heart to God, "Lord, if I had my job back I could help this woman get a car." Charlene and I talked about these things. We decided that since the Lord was giving me a job again, we should not just give enough for a car. We should give enough money to get a van to help haul more of those children.

My new job was unlike any I had experienced. All of my former jobs were carefully described with a specified salary. My new job as a customs advisor required me to negotiate with a contracting officer to determine my salary.

Charlene and I discussed the amount that we should try to negotiate. We talked of my past salary. We agreed that my full salary, including the overtime that I was earning at the time when I retired would be appropriate. With this amount we knew we could survive nicely and also help the little missionary lady to get her van. We prayed about this and were sure that this was acceptable.

I called the customs negotiating officer in Washington. We began talking dollars and cents about my salary-to-be. When we reached the amount that Charlene and I had agreed upon, I relaxed, knowing that we would be able to accomplish our goal. But, the negotiating officer and I kept talking. Finally, he paused and said: "Ray, I'll tell you what. I will pay you the maximum amount that I am authorized to pay for this job."

The final amount of our salary included the amount that Charlene and I hoped to receive, plus exactly the amount that we had agreed upon to contribute towards the purchase of a van. We still wonder how much the Lord might have provided if we had agreed together to give a big school bus!

The Lord was not finished. Our assignment in Sofia, Bulgaria was one of those areas that included an accompanying tax-free cost of living allowance of 15 percent. This amount was enough to help pay our taxes on the money that we earned. When I retired, I was classified as a GS-12 step 8. When I was rehired, I was classified as a GS-14 step 6.

What does all of this have to do with becoming a missionary? After the first year, my contract was renewed for an additional year. During the two years that we were working in Sofia, we attended the International Baptist Church Sofia. For two years, we taught Sunday morning Bible studies. We were thrilled as our Bible study grew from ten or twelve to as many as one hundred. We rejoiced as we saw people from many nations profess their faith in Jesus Christ and be baptized.

People from countries around the world came to receive Jesus as their Lord and Savior. They came from Germany, Japan, Iran, Ethiopia, Nigeria, India, Bulgaria, Israel, and even the United States,

Our church does not own a church building. We rent the auditorium of the World Trade Center (called INTERPRED by the Bulgarians). When we baptized new believers, a group of cars traveled up the side of Mount Vitosha, a huge mountain adjacent to Sofia. It is covered with snow much of the year. In a frigid mountain stream flowing down the mountain these folks were baptized—totally immersed—in icy water. One August day we baptized eight people when the air temperature was around 50 degrees Fahrenheit.

Instead of bemoaning the icy water, these folks seemed to relish the fact that they were baptized in a natural, outdoor stream instead of in a warm, comfortable baptistery. One winter we baptized twenty-two people downtown in the Bulgarian Baptist church that had a baptistery. After twenty-two people emerged from the pool and made their way to the rear dressing room, water dripping from their wet robes leaked through the floor boards of the church. The water shorted out the electric keyboard, canceling the music for the remainder of the program.

A Dutch banker family united with our church. His family allowed us to use the swimming pool in their yard for baptisms. One day we baptized sixteen people in their pool.

— Realizing God *or* a form of godliness? —

The pool was warmer and safer than the creek on Mount Vitosha.

As we were approaching the end of our second year in Bulgaria, Charlene and I prayed about whether we should try to stay for another year or return home. Charlene said, "Why don't we pray about it and let the Lord decide." On a Monday evening we read our daily scripture together and bowed for prayer. We began praying that we were willing to stay for another year, or return home, or do whatever the Lord asked us to do.

Friday evening of that week around 4:00 p.m., I received a call from my two big bosses in Washington, D.C. It was 9:00 a.m. in Washington. They were just beginning their work day. They complimented me upon the good job that I had done with the team during the past two years. They remarked how we had already accomplished many of our three-year goals in the program.

They said approximately 150 applicants had applied to work in the program. Since we had already received two one-year contracts, they asked what we thought about sharing with one of these applicants. Charlene and I agreed that this was an answer to our prayer on Monday. We happily agreed to conclude our services in October at the end of our contract.

Sunday morning we arrived at the International Baptist Church Sofia around 9:30 a.m. for Sunday school. We talked with Pastor James Duke and told him we would be returning to America on October 8, 2002. When we announced we were leaving Bulgaria, Pastor Duke became ecstatic. I never saw such a happy man! News that we were leaving thrilled him! Then he explained.

He said, "I wanted so much to ask you, but could not because you were cumbered with a full-time job." Then he asked, "Would you please return to Sofia in January 2003 and preach for me until May so that my wife and I can have a furlough and take care of some important concerns?"

Our prayer on Monday had been: "Lord, we are willing to stay another year, or return home, or we will do whatever you ask of us." We both believed that God was working through all of these events to accomplish His will in our lives; therefore, we agreed to return and preach.

Pastor Duke, along with a visiting pastor from the United States organized an ordination council. They examined virtually everything I believed pertaining to the Lord, the Gospel, and the Bible. Then, a couple of weeks later, I was ordained to preach.

In January 2003 we returned to Sofia on a beautiful sunshiny Thursday. Sunday, we were greeted with about seven inches of snow. Five of the next seven Sundays were accompanied by new fallen snow and icy temperatures.

Since our church does not own a building, we rented a second floor apartment in a nearby apartment building. This was a perfect place to conduct prayer meetings, Bible studies, choir practice, etc. A couple of needy people could also live in the apartment.

In addition to our Sunday morning worship service, Charlene conducted a Bible study on Monday evenings in which she used the Bible to teach the English language.

Wednesday evenings we worshipped with a brief Bible study and a time of voluntary prayers. Thursdays we conducted a Bible study for the Iranian refugees. The Bible message was translated into Farsi for the Iranians. On Fridays we met with our praise team to practice music for the worship services.

Some of our people from various countries in Africa were destitute. We purchased wholesale foodstuffs and distributed care packages to them each week after prayer meeting. Those refuges seemed to have very little. Yet, they prayed as if they have a direct relationship with the Almighty God. It made me think of **James 2:5: "Has not God chosen those who are poor in the eyes of the world to be rich in faith and to inherit the kingdom He promised those who love Him?"**

I learned an invaluable lesson from these poor people. When we pray: "Give us this day, our daily bread" we rely upon our well-stocked pantry, the money we have in our pockets, our bank accounts, etc. When these poor people pray, the only hope they have is in God. They have absolutely nothing else. When you listen to their prayers, you hear a relationship with the Almighty that excels.

War was looming in Iraq. One Wednesday evening when our people arrived at the apartment for prayer meeting and worship, the police would no longer allow us to enter the building. We were told that a high-ranking Iraqi diplomat lived in the building, and under the new security system, we could no longer worship in the building. Consequently, we were obliged to get rid of our place of ministering to others during the week.

On the second Sunday of the month we have a roll call of nations to determine how many nations are represented in our worship service. We averaged having people from fifteen nations each month that we were there. During the four months that we were in Sofia, people from thirty-three nations worshipped with us.

When James and Audrey Duke returned from their furlough in May, we returned to our home in North Charleston, South Carolina.

Chapter 17

Clouds on the Horizon

After my final year with the U.S. Customs Service, my family physician performed a routine health examination. He administered a blood test. He said my "PSA" score of seven was a little high. I had never heard of PSA. He said PSA stands for *prostate specific antigen*. It is an indicator of possible prostate cancer. He said the score is not conclusive, but it could indicate a problem. He referred me to a urologist.

The urologist took eight biopsies of my prostate. The prostate gland is about the size of a walnut. Imagine how eight different samples from it would feel. Have you ever heard of the expression "feeling as if you were struck by birdshot?" The laboratory report for each of the samples was negative. The urologist then inserted a tube through my urethra and we both watched together on a television screen in his office at the inside of my bladder. The only problem visible in my bladder was an inner indication of outer small varicose veins that I inherited from my dad—a slight birth defect. (Dad had large, serious varicose veins in his legs that sometimes caused him severe pain.) Otherwise, the doctor said everything looked good.

A year later, the urologist made another PSA test. My score had dropped from seven to six. He said the scores can vary a couple of points, but this was not a significant change. Again, he took biopsies that resulted in negative findings. However, the prostate gland was somewhat enlarged. (I thought to myself, "With all of the biopsies that the man has taken, it is little wonder that the gland is enlarged?")

The next year my PSA score elevated to eight. The doctor was very alarmed. I wondered, what happened to last year's lecture that a couple of points did not matter? I guess if the couple of points change is lower it is not bad, but if the points are rising, this could be cause for excitement. Still the examination, biopsies, and laboratory report gave me a clean bill of health.

After my wife and I finished serving overseas for two years, we returned home in October of 2002. This time, when the laboratory report came back from the laboratory, the report showed one cancerous cell in only one of the eight biopsies. The urologist explained that prostate cancer usually grows at a slow pace. However, it still could spread and eventually cause suffering and death.

The urologist made a special appointment with my wife and me. He explained in detail the types of treatments that are available. He answered all of our questions. He also gave us a comprehensive book that covered the entire field of prostate cancer and problems. We thought of the radiation pellets that can be inserted into the prostate to destroy the cancer. We also examined in detail all of the types of surgery that are available.

I explained to the urologist that I was obligated to return to Bulgaria in January of 2003 and preach until May. I also told him that any surgery must be postponed until we returned. He agreed since the cancer sample was very small, and since prostate cancer is relatively slow growing. Six months should not be a problem. He administered a Loupron shot in my buttocks. He explained that the shot would shrink the prostate and make it more manageable for surgery. He said that I should have a second shot in four months. However, I could not receive the shot until after we returned from overseas in May.

Finally, we decided that our best course of action would be to simply do it the old-fashioned way. We decided to have an incision from the navel down and to remove the prostate gland along with its cancer. This procedure also enables the surgeon to check the nodes on both sides of the prostate to ensure that the cancer has not spread. After this procedure, the problem has been completely resolved.

When I looked at the copies of the vouchers I received from my two insurance companies, I discovered those shots cost almost $2,500 each!

For a number of years I had jested with my wife about her menopausal years and her hot flashes. I discovered the Loupron shot completely shut down my sex drive. In addition, I was now the one having the hot flashes. On our first Sunday back in Bulgaria, we were greeted with about seven inches of snow and below freezing temperatures. Actually, the hot flashes felt pretty good in this climate.

Chapter 18

Becoming a Pastor

Hardly a month had passed since we departed from Sofia for our home in North Charleston, South Carolina. Tommy, a deacon at the church where our children had grown up, called on the telephone. He said the pastor of the church had been there for seven years. He resigned and left the church. Tommy said, "While the pastor served, half of the congregation left the church. Now that he is gone, the other half of the people left." He said, "The church is in danger of closing. Please come and help us."

On our first Sunday back at Pittman Street Baptist Church, we counted a total of 21 people, including Charlene and me. This splendid church in North Charleston once averaged more than 155 in Sunday school. I preached there the last two Sundays in June.

I was scheduled for prostate surgery on July 2, 2003. Although we had been earnestly trying to help get the church back on a sound footing, my urologist/surgeon insisted that I should not preach for the entire month of July, after the operation.

When I returned to the pulpit in August, the church met for their regular monthly business meeting and elected me as their pastor. For two years we preached, worked, and tried to help the church to regain its spiritual impact in the community. Perhaps the greatest hindrance came from the feelings of those who had left the church for whatever reasons. Nonetheless, we slowly began to grow back in unison and in one spirit before God. Our people received a huge boost of confidence when we attended the Charleston Baptist Association's December Senior Banquet at the First Baptist Church of North Charleston.

Our seniors had more people at the meeting than any of the other sixty-seven churches in the association. We received a huge attendance trophy to take back to the church in honor of this achievement. In the spring we received a similar attendance trophy at another senior function for the Charleston Baptist Association at the annual meeting at the Bonnie Doone Plantation.

Attendance continued to grow from the twenties to the thirties to the forties to the fifties to the sixties. We were beginning to have seventies on Sundays, when an internal conflict developed. When the people departed from our church along with the former pastor, the children, youth, teachers, virtually the entire congregation, departed except for a handful of faithful believers.

We were basically a senior citizens' church. Something very beautiful resulted. Everyone within the church, without exception, loved the Lord Jesus. They loved the church. They loved each other. We had no dissension. Everyone was pulling together to try to accomplish the Lord's will for our church and for the community. We sing a hymn from our hymnbook that says: *"There's a sweet, sweet spirit in this place"* (*Doris Akers*). I have never experienced such a wonderful fellowship among God's people. However, I have read about such a church: **"And when the day of Pentecost was fully come, they were all with one accord in one place" Acts 2:1** (KJV). If you continue to read these verses, you see how God sent His Holy Spirit to these people and blessed them as well as those around them.

Ken was a member of our church. After graduating from the seminary he served as a pastor for nine years in Georgia. However, he developed a peculiar illness known as "*pseudo tumor.*" Although I had never heard of the problem, I learned that more than forty people were being treated for the illness at the local university medical hospital.

"*Pseudo*" means false. The brain perceives a false tumor and begins to manufacture fluids to counter the tumor. As fluids build up in the brain, the increased pressure causes severe, incapacitating headaches. Permanent loss of vision also occurs. Ken's problem became so severe, he was forced to leave the ministry. His wife struggled to provide for him and their two children.

In the hospital surgeons inserted a stent in the back of Ken's skull to relieve the pressure. However, after the surgery the stent was removed because of a staphylococcus infection. Tests revealed that Ken had suffered a 35 percent permanent loss of vision in one eye. When He recovered from the infection, surgeons again performed a similar operation on the opposite rear side of his head.

After the surgery, the doctor left the hospital. Ken began suffering from an internal hemorrhage. The doctor returned, removed the stint, and attempted to remove blood from the hemorrhage. Ken was partially paralyzed on one side and received extensive therapy for many weeks before he was able to return to church.

In past years Rick had been a member of our church. He was an outstanding athlete and graduate of the Citadel. He had a wife and children. However, Rick was diagnosed with leukemia (blood cancer). Doctors who were treating Rick could not control the problem. They recommended a bone marrow transplant and were seeking to find someone in his family who could be a bone marrow donor. His two brothers matched his blood type. Either one qualified as a donor.

Because Rick is an outstanding believer in Christ, and because of his outspoken witness for the Lord Jesus, I invited him to speak during the morning worship service in our church. What an inspiration! Despite his problems, Rick was an ideal witness for the Lord.

At the conclusion of the service I placed two fold-up chairs on the floor at the front of the church. I asked Rick and Ken to come and sit in the chairs. Then, I asked the congregation to come forward and reach out and touch both of these men and pray together that the Lord would bless them and heal them.

"Is any sick among you? Let him call for the elders of the church; and let them pray over him, anointing him with oil in the name of the Lord; And the prayer of faith shall save the sick, and the Lord shall raise him up; and if he has committed sins, they shall be forgiven him" James 5:14–15 (KJV).

The Lord heard and answered the obedient prayers of His people. At Rick's next doctor's appointment no leukemia could be found. Almost five years have now passed and the leukemia is still gone. Ken's headaches also disappeared. Although diagnosed with 35 percent permanent loss of vision in one eye, Ken's eye examination now revealed 20/25 vision.

When we simply take God at His Word with childlike faith, when we trust and obey, God hears and answers according to His will. The Lord offers blessings beyond measure to those who will receive His Son and believe in Him. God's power is still very much at work in those who simply trust Him in faith and ask for His blessings.

When it seemed that we were being blessed in virtually every possible way, my wife went to the doctor for her annual physical examination. Tests showed a problem with her pancreas. Her lymph nodes were also enlarged.

We made an appointment with Dr. Sam, a splendid Christian surgeon. After studying the laboratory x-rays and scans, his stark comments sounded very grim. He explained the methods of performing surgery and examining the pancreas and lymph nodes. Since we have several friends who died from pancreatic cancer, we knew full well the probabilities. However, the doctor ordered several other tests and conferred with other medical experts.

In addition, the doctor prayed. We also were praying along with the faithful members of our church. All of the new tests indicated that Charlene's pancreas as well as her lymph nodes were normal. No surgery or further action was required. Was this just a coincidence? We believe God still hears the cries of His people and answers their prayers as He promises in His Word.

I have been in churches in the past where they enjoyed a prayer breakfast for men, or a ladies prayer breakfast, or a youth prayer breakfast, etc. The folks at Pittman Street began a family prayer breakfast. Everyone is invited. The cost: nothing. The breakfast: bacon, eggs, sausage, grits, pancakes, biscuits, coffee, milk, juice. A sweet, sweet spirit permeated the breakfast crowd. I read in the scriptures where Jesus and the early followers met many times around a meal. We learned to appreciate the joy of fellowshipping and dining together in the Lord's Spirit. We thanked the Lord for Tommy, our five-star chef.

A problem in our church was the lack of children and youth. Whenever a couple or family would attend with a child or a young person, they looked around and did not see other children and youth. Consequently, they would not return. One family left our church along with two teen-aged sons. This family continued to mail their tithes and offerings to help us, but they took their boys to a church where they could be with other youth.

My wife and I attended a special retreat specifically for pastors. I posed the question of how to build a children's or youth program from zero. They advised me to hire a young ministerial student from a local college as "youth director." They said, to pay him (or her) a salary. They suggested working along with the student in order to build a program. I began searching for such a young person.

Also, I kept praying and searching for someone who loved the Lord and would come with their children or youth and help us to have a nucleus to build upon. Finally, a young couple came with a little daughter. They agreed to teach the children's class. I told them about the advice I had received to hire a youth director. They both agreed that they would take care of the children and the youth.

On the first Sunday when this couple began to help, eleven people attended the class from ages two to sixteen. Although this couple seemed to be highly dedicated and motivated, they arrived late for Sunday school virtually every week. A mother of one of the two would sit with the children each Sunday until they arrived to teach the class. Their idea was that at least four people from any age group should attend four Sundays in succession before they would establish a separate class.

Two or three youth who originally came, quit attending the class with the very small children. Some weeks later, a young mother came to our deacon leader. She told him she had talked with a couple of young people who said they would attend Sunday school if they had a separate class for their age group. She asked the deacon what he thought about her starting a youth class. The young couple who said they would teach the children and the youth was not present so that he could talk with them.

The following Sunday this young mother came to the pastor along with the deacon. Again, she told of these young people and offered to teach them. The young couple who were supposed to be working with the children and youth again was not present. We decided that it might be a good idea to try to establish a separate youth Sunday school class.

On the following Sunday morning the mother arrived along with three young people to begin a youth Sunday school class for young people. The mother of the little children's class arrived to teach the smaller children. She said her husband's softball team was short-handed so he would not be in church. When she discovered the mother with three youth in a Sunday school class, she began to raise unholy Cain. She telephoned her husband on the softball field. Although it was necessary for him to be there, he left the ball field to come to the church to stage a showdown meeting about who was in charge of the youth.

They wanted to fire the mother who volunteered to help. How could two people develop a program for all ages without additional help? They also refused help from another lady who had volunteered her services. (I think she wanted to try to teach in order to influence her sixteen-year-old son to join the class.) I don't know of any young person who would be willing to come four Sundays in a row and sit through an hour with my two five-year-old twin grandsons in the same room.

The young couple could not seem to understand. Jesus says: **"The harvest truly is plenteous, but the laborers are few; Pray you therefore the Lord of the harvest, that He will send forth laborers into His harvest" (Matthew 9:37–38**, KJV). We prayed for the Lord to send help to reach out to His people. Now that help is arriving, fire them? The couple and their daughter left the church along with her mother and dad.

However, that was not the end. After they left, they began mailing letters, not just to our members, but to others in the community, attempting to stir up further discontent. Normally, I try to shelter the congregation from such extraneous actions. However, in this case, I laid bare the entire situation before the church during the Wednesday evening prayer service in order to explain the matter from a Biblical perspective. Together, we prayed for them.

This event happened early in 2004. The sweet spirit that I mentioned earlier had dissipated. But, when the dissenters left, the same spirit of harmony, cooperation, and working together began to return.

Speaking of serving as pastor in a senior citizen church, during two years, I preached in seven funerals. I spent many hours in local hospitals with beloved friends and their families as they approached the end of their lives, as well as with some in other crises. Such trying times brought us closer to each other and closer to our Creator who loves and supplies our every need. Although I preached in seven funerals, we also baptized seven.

Chapter 19

Becoming Missionaries Again

For two years we preached at the Pittman Street Baptist Church without missing a Sunday, except for one weekend when we were stricken with a respiratory infection. Around the middle of May a former pastor of our church called on the phone. He had served twenty-four years in our church before retiring. Later, he became interim pastor of a church across the Ashley River in Charleston.

He called and said he had completed his tour as interim pastor. He asked if I would consider being listed as a reference on his resume. He explained that even though he was retired, he needed to supplement his income because of rising health insurance costs. I told him I would be honored and would give him the best of recommendations. He and his wife were both seminary graduates. They had served as missionaries in Brazil during the early years of their ministry.

After we talked for a while, I asked if he would please preach two Sundays in June at our church so we could attend the Southern Baptist Convention in Nashville, Tennessee. He was happy to oblige.

About three nights later, I awakened in the middle of the night. It was as if someone was talking with me. I knew that this dear man of God needed a church with just a limited income. I was preaching in a church that could offer such an opportunity. Our church is closer to his home than it is to ours. He is fully qualified in every way. I was a qualified customs inspector, filling in as the Lord had led us. I felt as if this voice were telling me plainly that I should surrender my work as a pastor to this beloved man of God.

I prayed about this situation. I believed the Lord led us to this church. Now, I felt just as strongly that the Lord wanted this pastor to take my place. When I went to him and asked him what he thought about taking over my job, at first he dismissed the matter. But, when I persisted, he talked with his wife and they both were amenable to serve.

At our Wednesday evening business meeting, the night before Charlene and I left for the Southern Baptist Convention in Nashville, upon our insistence, our church elected him as their pastor again.

What was happening in our lives? I was so sure that the Lord had led and opened the way for us to serve as pastor of this church. Although I did not understand, I now believed with certainty that we were doing exactly what the Lord wanted. I thought perhaps the Lord was answering my prayer and allowing me the liberty to teach the children. I set out with enthusiasm to establish a children's Sunday school.

Not long after I began to teach those little children, we received two e-mail letters from Sofia, Bulgaria. One message was from the deacons of the church. The other message was from James Duke, our pastor friend there. Both letters told of the intense pain and suffering of the pastor because of a serious back ailment. He needed to be relieved of his duties. The church needed an interim pastor for a year or two in order to give the pastor an opportunity to seek major back therapy in Texas.

My wife and I talked about the letters. We prayed about the situation. We now believed the Lord had sent the former pastor back to our church in order to make us available to return to Bulgaria. I showed the e-mail messages to our newly elected pastor and asked for his pastoral counseling. After reading both letters, he said, "Our church really needs your help, but when the Lord gives you such a call, you should be faithful to respond."

After talking with our pastor, I made an appointment with our former pastor at the North Charleston First Baptist Church. I requested some pastoral counseling. When I walked into his office, I gave him a copy of both letters from Bulgaria. He sat quietly and read both of the letters. When he finished reading, he looked up and said: "When are you leaving?"

We sent an e-mail to the church in Sofia and expressed our willingness to serve. They immediately accepted our offer. Then, we began the lengthy process of applying for and receiving a visa, so that we could return to Bulgaria. When I worked with the U.S. Customs Service, the government handled all of the necessary paperwork for getting visas, tickets, etc. The Customs Service obtained a year's visa within a week. It took us about two months to get a three-month visa.

While we were in the process of making arrangements to return to Sofia, we attended a pastor's conference in Savannah, Georgia. The four-day meeting sponsored by the South Carolina State Baptist Convention was designed to help pastors. It is called "Shepherding the Shepherds." We had a splendid room in the Marriott hotel fronting on the Savannah River. One night after all of the day's sessions were finished, Charlene and I were standing on the front porch of the room, looking out over the river into the darkness.

Suddenly, a brilliant, dazzling light burst out of the darkness above and fell straight down and disappeared as it neared the earth. We gasped in awe at the beautiful sight. Then we realized it was a falling star. The experience reminded me of a similar situation at the age of nine. I mentioned this earlier. It happened the night I helped my good friend, Jimmy, when his dad was sick.

You could call both of these incidents coincidences. However, both came at extremely spiritual moments in my life when I felt as if the Almighty God was dealing directly with me. No. I was not looking for a miraculous sign. God has already given me the only sign I need. God gave me (and you) **"the sign of the prophet Jonah. As Jonah was three days and three nights in the belly of the big fish, so the Son of Man must be three days and three nights in the heart of the earth."** I only wanted to do whatever God wants me to do.

Although God is not in the miraculous-sign business these days, to those who have a genuine faith in the Lord Jesus Christ, to those who have *realized* God, the Lord still responds to faith. I like the words of the hymn writer: **"And He walks with me and He talks with me and He tells me I am His own, and the joy we share as we tarry there, none other has ever known"** (C. Austin Miles, 1868–1946).

If you have not *realized God*, if you have not responded to God's invitation of love and received His only begotten Son into your life as your personal, intimate Savior, then you are missing the greatest blessing in life.

Many people think that receiving Christ eliminates all of the joy in life. Nothing could be further from the truth. The Lord Jesus Himself says: **"The thief comes not but for to kill to steal and to destroy, but I am come that they might have life and that they might have it more abundantly"** (**John 10:10**, KJV). The New International Version says **"that they may have life and have it to the full."** Are you living your life **"to the full"?** Do you have **"life more abundantly"?** Many of my dear friends can tell you this describes their life. God does not do tricks to impress people. To those who *realize God*, who genuinely put all of their trust in Him, God reveals Himself to them in many Divine ways.

"When Herod saw Jesus, he was greatly pleased, because for a long time He had been wanting to see Him. From what he had heard about Him, he hoped to see Him perform some miracle. He plied Him with many questions, but Jesus gave him no answer" (Luke 23:8–9). Herod was a powerful king. He could have given the order to set Jesus free, but Jesus would not even speak a word to him, much less do a miracle.

To those who love Jesus and believe in Him, they see Jesus walk on water; they see Jesus speak to a storm and quiet the winds and the waves; they see the tremendous catch of fishes upon His instructions; they see five thousand men, not counting women and children, fed with a little boy's lunch; they see him heal withered limbs and cleanse leprosy; they see him raise the dead. They see Him die on the cross; they also see Him alive after he arose from the dead. They see Him ascend up into heaven.

"Jesus Christ is the same yesterday, and today, and forever" (Hebrews 13:8). It still works the same way today. Those who doubt—who refuse to receive Jesus—see nothing. Those who receive Him in faith experience the power of God in their lives through the Cross of Calvary. They *realize* God in all of His fullness.

Two coach class tickets on an airline to Bulgaria cost more than $2,000. We had been assisting a family member with financial difficulties. Our reserve funds were almost depleted. Since we would be away from our home and family for an extended time, we drove to Galva, Iowa, to see our son, his wife, and our granddaughter. From there we drove to New Jersey to see our other son, his wife, and our grandson.

After returning from this trip, we drove to Peachtree City, Georgia, outside of Atlanta, to visit with my sister. My sister and her late husband both retired from an airline. From the time that I was a little boy, my sister has been a very special friend. When she learned that we would be returning to Bulgaria to preach the Gospel, she pulled-out some papers and said, "As a retired airline employee, I am entitled to special flying privileges for my family." She was able to book us two tickets from Charleston to New York to Athens, Greece. The cost was negligible. Not only that, but, our tickets over the Atlantic Ocean were in the elite business class instead of the coach. Would you call this just a coincidence? Or, would you say it was "good luck." If you *realize* God, you are sure that God keeps His word and provides for those who trust in Him.

Shortly after we arrived in Bulgaria, I checked our online banking account on the Internet. Our bank balance was $2,000 over what we anticipated. When I opened the information on deposits to our account, we discovered that our loved ones at Pittman Street Baptist Church had deposited the money into our account for us to use in our new assignment. I repeat: "If you realize God, you are sure that God keeps His word and provides for those who trust in Him.

We have since used that "extra" money to help feed the poor, clothe children in need, and to assist a former member of our church who is now a pastor in Ghana building a church. We helped a refugee from Nigeria with funds to acquire documentation papers so that he will no longer be required to travel several kilometers every day to the police station to register. We helped provide dental work for a poor lady in great, serious pain. We helped with a nose operation for a young believer. We provided milk for hungry infants. We helped to provide spectacles for an elderly lady who could not see. Many poor and needy people have been blessed by the love of those folks in America.

Bulgaria reminds me of America when I was a small child. During the Great Depression, jobs were scarce, wages were low, food was often difficult to obtain. Just as the people of the United States banded together and grew into a great nation, Bulgaria has a similar opportunity. Bulgaria is beautiful. It is blessed with many natural resources and people who are determined to succeed. Recently, workers discovered

— Realizing God *or* a form of godliness? —

a tremendous lode of gold ore in the little town of Pernik outside of Sofia.

The biggest difference I see between Bulgaria and early America is in God. America was founded by basically Christians who were free to worship as they pleased. For fifty years the Communists outlawed God. Bulgarians could not even celebrate Christmas. Now that the people of Bulgaria are free, it may take some time to overcome the past fifty years of Godlessness.

Although activist judges and radicals in America are trying to outlaw God just as the Communists did, history, as well as our heritage, shows that America grew from a handful of colonists into the greatest nation in the world because God was an integral part of everyday life, as well as, the government. Every citizen has the right to worship and believe in God or a god or to be an atheist without interference by the government. However, the Founding Fathers have inscribed the Almighty God onto the walls of the buildings, monuments, and documents. The very first thing the sun shines upon when it rises in the United States is the tip of the Washington Monument. Two words inscribed in Latin on the tip of the Washington Monument glisten in the early morning light. They read "Laus Deo," which translates into "Praise God." Every piece of American currency is inscribed with the motto "In God We Trust." Every state constitution in America acknowledges the Almighty God.

Some folks today are striving to undermine God in America. They claim the U.S. Constitution provides for "separation of church and state." If you read the Constitution, these words cannot be found. The Constitution provides that we cannot have a national church as many nations have. This gives every person in America the same rights to exist and operate according to their beliefs. The second part of this section of the Constitution prohibits the government from interfering with the free exercise of religion by our citizens. Many present day activist judges are violating this section of the Constitution by their prejudiced rulings.

I was in about the third grade in elementary school when I first saw the present-day problems beginning. We were talking about the issue of the government and the many different denominations and religions in our country. The teacher explained that we had to remove all mention of religion from the public square so that we would not offend anyone of a different faith. When the teacher said this, my first thoughts as a child were, "What about God?" I would much rather offend everyone than offend God. How can we say (and sing) "God Bless America" when we are trying to throw God out of our country?

While I was working with the U.S. Customs Service, I served as a member of Gideons International. The Gideons are a Christian business men's organization. Their goal is to place Bibles in hotels, motels, hospitals, jails, etc. The organization is active in almost two hundred countries throughout the world.

After the fall of the "Iron Curtain," I listened to a Gideon from Sumter, South Carolina, who had gone to Russia to help organize the Gideons there. As this man was driving into a former Communist city from the airport with a local businessman, he saw banner after banner stretched across the street leading into the city. The Gideon asked, "What do those signs say?" The Russian said: "The signs read: 'JESUS CHRIST LIVES!' "

Then the Russian said, "In Russia we are gaining our freedoms. In America you are losing yours." What a profound statement.

After Our First Year as Missionaries

A wonderful retired Baptist pastor named Darrel, along with his wife, Faith, volunteered to preach for us for more than a month so that we could return to the United States for annual physical examinations and another year's supply of vital medicines. They attend a large Baptist church in Texas. Their church provides tremendous quantities of medical equipment, clothing, shoes, and support for the orphans of Bulgaria.

As we were preparing to return to the United States, I realized that our friends in church at home would want to hear about our work in Bulgaria. In my mind I reviewed the past year. We had many very special experiences. For a week we traveled across Bulgaria with Paul and Judy Ridgway and a Christian team. Two couples from a large Baptist church in Marietta, Georgia, came to Sofia to assist in distributing aid that their church donated through the Ridgway Ministries, Inc.

Our team spent a full week traveling from orphanage to orphanage fitting children with new shoes. We also gave fresh fruits, clothes, and other treats. During the week we fitted more than 750 pairs of new shoes on the children. One of the directors told us that their budget includes only pennies per day for each child. The amount of money is not enough to provide adequate food for the children, much less, other necessities such as clothing, shoes, medical care, etc. Many times the Ridgway family makes special trips to orphanages when they learn that their food supply is exhausted..

As I began fitting shoes on the children, my heart broke. Virtually every child that I touched had very cold hands and feet. They were unable to escape the bitter cold weather. Many were struggling with respiratory ailments. As I sat, leaning over to fit shoes, a couple of those children sneezed. Before the week was finished I had contracted a serious respiratory infection.

When we arrived back in Sofia on Saturday evening, I realized that my voice was failing. I told Charlene, "I do not think I will be able to preach in the morning." I had no one to call at this late hour to help. The telephone rang. A good Christian friend who travels across Eastern Europe assisting in churches and bringing people to a saving knowledge of Christ had just returned from a trip. When he heard the sound of my voice, he said: "Ray, I don't see how you can preach tomorrow with a voice like that. I will come over and preach for you."

Was this just a coincidence? A lucky break? We believe it was the Lord answering the prayers of so many people who are praying for us.

One night our good friend Paul called. He and Judy had returned from a trip to the United States, where they were enrolling their third son in college. The young son had chosen a college in Oklahoma. However, some necessary forms that they were supposed to submit by the end of the week had inadvertently been brought back to Sofia. To mail the forms from Bulgaria would take approximately three weeks. Paul asked if I knew anyone who was planning to return to America. I told Paul that I was sorry but I did not know anyone.

Almost as soon as I finished talking with Paul, the telephone rang. A special American friend who attends our church mentioned that a mutual friend was leaving early in the morning to return to America. I immediately called Paul. His son's college application arrived on time.

Was this just a coincidence? A lucky break? We believe the Lord answers the prayers of many people who are praying for us.

Each July the International Baptist Convention (IBC) presents a weeklong Summer Assembly in Interlaken, Switzerland. More than sixty English-speaking churches from Europe, Asia, and Africa comprise the IBC. People from these churches come to Interlaken for a time of fellowship, singing, preaching, and sightseeing. We enjoyed meeting fellow believers from many places. One night we gathered in an auditorium with a very large screen and saw Italy edge out France to win the 2006 World Cup in soccer.

When the meetings were finished, we caught a train back through the Alps to Milan, Italy. Arriving at the airport, we were in line to board the aircraft. We presented our passports and tickets to the flight agent. He ordered us to stand aside. He continued boarding people on our flight. We watched as that entire line of people boarded the plane. A few minutes later, he handed us two new tickets and told us to board the aircraft. He had "bumped us up" from tourist class to business class. If you are not familiar with flying, this means he assigned us to larger, plush seats up front with better food and better service.

Charlene said, "Who did that? Do you think our good friend Alexander back in Sofia arranged that?" I replied, "No. I think our great big loving Heavenly Boss did that."

Was this just a coincidence? A lucky break? We believe the Lord answers in many different ways the prayers of those who are praying for us.

While we are serving overseas, Charlene's sister, Brenda, lives in our home in North Charleston and takes care of things. In June we received a sad e-mail. Brenda was diagnosed with a "mass" on her pancreas. Since we have some friends who died with pancreatic cancer, the news was not good. Several weeks later the doctor said the mass had spread into her esophagus and stomach.

Charlene said she would need to return to the United States to take care of her sister if she needed long-term care to recuperate after the operation. Since her dad is in his mid-eighties, he would not be able to help much.

After numerous positive tests, Brenda was admitted to the Medical University of South Carolina hospital for surgery to remove the mass from her esophagus and stomach. The surgical team was prepared to operate. Before commencing the operation they began making final tests. Every test the doctors performed revealed that the mass could not be found—not in her esophagus, not in her stomach, and not in her pancreas. Brenda was discharged from the hospital with a clean bill of health. To this day she has had no further problem Was this just a coincidence? A lucky break?

We believe the Lord answers the prayers of many people who are praying.

The most impressive experiences of serving as missionaries indicate how our Heavenly Father provides for us in many ways. Some experiences seem small and relatively insignificant. Others are huge and awesome. *Realizing* God in all of His fullness validates the scriptures.

Recently, we received word that Charlene's dad, now eighty-seven years of age, received word from his doctor that his kidneys are filled with cysts and are shutting down. His kidneys only work from 10 to 15 percent of the time. The doctor said he only has three to four months to live.

I said to Charlene, "I will get you an airplane ticket home so that you can be with your father." A young Korean student who was presently staying with us asked: "Why aren't you going with her?" I explained, "As pastor of the church someone must preach each Sunday." She nodded in agreement.

The very next morning I received an e-mail from George and Dorothy in Texas. George said they were coming to Sofia to work with the Ridgway Ministry and the orphans. He volunteered to preach for me for five weeks. I was able to take my wife home to be with her dad.

Was this just another of those happy coincidences? Or was God answering the prayers of the many folks who are praying for us?

As the year ended, we needed to transfer a percentage of our offerings from our church to various budgeted accounts. Bank transfers are very expensive here. The sending bank charges a sizable fee, as well as the receiving bank. The former pastor had established a bank account in the United States. A check can be mailed without paying excessive bank fees. We decided to deposit our offering checks into the American account and simply mail checks to pay our budgeted accounts.

The problem: no one in our church could access our USA account. The former pastor could access the account, but he was not only in the United States, he was recovering from major surgery.

The last information we received indicated that we had almost $700 in the account. In addition we mailed checks totaling $2,800 to the bank. After computing the amounts we needed to pay, we mailed another check for deposit in the amount of $1,000. Our total deposits would total approximately $4,500. Our bills totaled just under $4,000.

After several weeks, our $1,000 check still had not cleared the bank. We called the friends who were taking the check to the USA to be mailed. We discovered that our check had inadvertently been left in Sofia. We still needed several hundred dollars in the account to pay our bills.

We received an e-mail where someone said they were sending $1,000 to our American account to be used for missions overseas. Great! We could use this money to pay our bills and take the check that was still in Sofia to pay for missions. However, we needed to be sure that we had adequate funds before sending out checks.

After several attempts to try to discover whether all of these funds had been added to our U.S. account, I finally spoke with a wonderful lady in the bank. After answering several very technical questions about our account, the lady decided to help us. She said, "Yes, the $2,800 was deposited in the account, as was the $1,000 check for missions.

Then the lady asked, "Would you like to know the total balance that you have on hand?"

"Yes! Please! Thank you very much! We would really like to know the total balance in our account. As I mentioned, it should be approximately $4,500 according to our information.

She replied, "You have $15,011.57." Do you understand? We had more than $10,000 above all of our recorded deposits and information. The seven cents at the end of that number rang a bell in my heart. Seven is the number of perfection that God uses in His word, the Bible. **"God does all things well!"**

Where did this huge amount of money come from? Who placed more than $10,000 in our meager account? The bottom line is: "God answers the prayers of His people." Although we do not know the details, I remember the former pastor saying that sometimes some people who love the Lord will anonymously contribute funds through the bank for our church to help us. Perhaps God inspired some fairly wealthy person to help us at the very time that we needed it the most.

The Apostle Peter says: **"Though you have not seen Him, you love Him and though you do not see Him now, but believe in Him, you greatly rejoice with joy inexpressible and full of glory, obtaining as the outcome of your faith the salvation of your souls"** (**1 Peter 1:8**, NASB).

In contrast I think of the millions who have not *realized* God: people who live their lives and turn their backs upon God's free gift of love, His Son Jesus Christ; people think that they must give up a great deal to become a child of God. Actually, the reverse is true. God tells us: **"No good thing will He withhold from them that walk uprightly"** (**Psalm 84:11**, KJV). Jesus says: **"I am come that they might have life, and that they might have it more abundantly"** (**John 10:10**, KJV). The New International Version says: **"I have come that they may have life, and have it to the full."**

To anyone who cannot tell me you are living your life abundantly, to the full, you need to invite the Lord Jesus to keep His promise to you personally. This is the starting point for *realizing* God. Simply trust God in faith to keep His Word in your life, personally.

Chapter 20

Conclusion

If you have not *realized* God, please understand the Lord's invitation to you: **"Here I am! I stand at the door and knock. If anyone hears My voice and opens the door, I will come in and eat with him, and he with Me"** (**Revelation 3:20**, NIV).

The choice is yours. You can say, "No thanks!" God loves you. He will not force Himself upon you. The choice must be yours.

If you say **"with all of your heart,"** "Yes, Lord! I know You are the Son of God. I know You died on the Cross of Calvary for my sins. I believe in my heart You arose from the dead and You are alive today. I invite You to come into my life and save me from my sins. I now confess You as my Lord and Savior." If you can say this prayer with all your heart, your life will never be the same again.

If you have made a profession of faith in Christ Jesus in the past, what is your relationship with the Lord today? Are you reading His Word daily and trusting God to keep His promises in your life? Or, are you like so many who only have a form of godliness but deny the power of God to keep His promises to you personally?

Some time ago I preached a sermon titled "Starving Believers." Moses said in **Deuteronomy 8:3**: **"man does not** live on bread alone but on every word that comes from the mouth of the Lord." At the beginning of the Lord's earthly ministry, He was tempted by the devil. **Matthew 4:1–4: "Then Jesus was led by the Spirit into the desert to be tempted by the devil. (2) After fasting forty days and forty nights, He was hungry. (3) The tempter came to Him and said, 'If you are the Son of God, tell these stones to become bread.' (4)**

Jesus answered, 'It is written: <u>Man does not live on bread alone, but on every word that comes from the mouth of God</u>" ' " (emphasis added).

Please notice when the Lord Jesus was tempted by Satan, Jesus quoted from God's Word. What do you do when the devil comes knocking on your door? How do you deal with temptation? King David, **"a man after God's own heart,"** said **(Psalm 119:10): "I have hidden your word in my heart that I might not sin against you."** In **verse 105**, David says: **"Your word is a lamp to my feet and a light for my path."**

Moses and the Lord are emphasizing the necessity of feasting on God's Word every day of our lives. Many Christians are spiritually starving themselves. The Apostle Paul wrote to young Timothy **(2 Timothy 2:15): "Do your best to present yourself to God as one approved, a workman who does not need to be ashamed and who correctly handles the word of truth."** How many of us eat three meals every day, not counting between meal snacks? We need to feed our souls with the same amount of concern on the Word of God.

How many of us read God's Word every day? How many of us use a Bible Reader's Guide and are reading a portion

— Conclusion —

of God's Word every day? Do you understand: "Starving Christians"?

Why should we take time to read the Bible every day? First, the Lord Jesus confirms the words of Moses. **"Man does not live on bread alone, but on every word that comes from the mouth of God."** Why read the Bible every day? Because God tells us to! Just as we need food for our bodies to grow and stay healthy, in the same way we need to read God's Word to feed our souls.

I was very impressed by a tall, young lady with black hair from Germany. She visited our church several times when she came to Sofia. I openly commended her before the church. I am always impressed when I see a young person who is miles away from their home and friends and on Sunday they take time to come to church to worship the Lord.

After church that Sunday, as I was speaking with those who were leaving, this young lady shook my hand and said, "Pastor Ray, you do not understand. <u>I need to come to church</u> to worship the Lord. <u>I need to find strength and power from the Lord to live my life each day</u>." This is what Moses and the Lord Jesus tell us: **"Man does not live on bread alone."** We need to learn and pay attention to **"every word that comes from the mouth of God."**

My prayer for you is that you will begin to read God's Word. Underline God's precious promises in your Bible. Then, in simple, childlike faith, ask and trust God specifically to keep His promises in your life. In the same way you trust God for salvation, now trust Him to keep His promises to you personally. You will discover indescribable blessings and power from God in your life. Instead of having a "form of godliness," you will enjoy the dynamic force of the Almighty God that empowers you to live your life to the full.

Solution

"If My people, who are called by My name, will humble themselves and pray and seek My face and turn from their wicked ways, then will I hear from heaven and will forgive their sins and will heal their land" (2 Chronicles 7:14).

This scripture is written for Christians—not for unsaved people. Notice: God says: **"If <u>My</u> people, who are called by <u>My</u> name…"** Who is called by the name of God? What are the first six letters of the word "Christian"? C-H-R-I-S-T-i-a-n. We are indeed CHRISTians! We are called by the name of CHRIST, the Son of God—God, when He took upon Himself a body of flesh!

Churches pray for revival and look for the lost to come to Christ. This should always be the goal of every child of God, but in order to have a revival in the church or in a nation, the first key element for success is the believers. Christians must first put their house in order before God will bless His house, His Church, or their nation. The way Christians must put their house in order is cited in **2 Chronicles 7:14.**

Although the church is comprised of a group of baptized believers, each believer, each member, is vital to the well being of the church as a whole. When one part of the body suffers, the entire body suffers with it. So it is with the church we rejoice with those that rejoice and weep with those that weep. Never underestimate the importance of each and every believer—each member of the church.

Genesis 18:16–33: "the outcry against Sodom and Gomorrah is so great and their sin so grievous" that God has decided to utterly destroy both of these cities." (Verse 23): "Abraham approached (God) and said: 'Will you sweep away the righteous with the wicked? What if there are fifty righteous people in the city? Will you really sweep it away and not spare the place for the sake of the fifty righteous people in it?" (Verse 26) "The Lord said, 'If I find fifty righteous people in the city of Sodom, I will spare the whole place for their sake.' "

Then in verse 27–28 **Abraham says:** suppose the number is five less, will you destroy the city because of five people?

God says, **"If I find forty-five there, I will not destroy it."**

"Once again (Abraham) spoke to Him, 'What if only forty are found there?'

"(God) said, 'For the sake of forty, I will not do it.' "

Then Abraham said, **"What if only thirty can be found there?"**

(God answered): "I will not do it if I find thirty there."

Abraham said: **"What if only twenty can be found?"**

"God said, 'For the sake of twenty, I will not destroy it."

Finally, Abraham said **(verse 32)**, "May the Lord not be angry, but let me speak just once more, what if only ten can be found there?'

The Lord answered, **"For the sake of ten, I will not destroy it."**

"When the Lord had finished speaking with Abraham, He left, and Abraham returned home."

Then in **Genesis 19:27: "Early the next morning Abraham got up and returned to the place where he had stood before the Lord. He looked down toward Sodom and Gomorrah, toward all the land of the plain, and he saw dense smoke rising from the land, like smoke from a furnace."** God had destroyed the two cities. Why? BECAUSE GOD COULD NOT FIND TEN RIGHTEOUS PEOPLE LIVING THERE.

Suppose God announced this morning that He plans to utterly destroy your country because of its sin and unrighteousness. But, God will spare the entire country if He can find ten righteous people living there. Examine yourself and ask yourself, "Could I be counted upon to be one of the ten righteous people? Or, would I be one that would cause God to destroy my country because of my sin?"

When I was a young man, Harry S. Truman was president of the United States. On his desk he had a paperweight with these words: "The Buck Stops Here!" When you go to a person to get something accomplished, and the person, instead of helping you, refers you to someone else, we call this "passing the buck." Sometimes you may be referred to many different people before you can find someone to help you.

But President Truman said when you come to him for help, "The Buck Stops Here." He meant that he would resolve your problem without referring you to someone else.

As Christians, we need to say, as did President Truman, "The buck stops here"—with me. As a Christian, I alone am accountable to God. I must answer to Him and not look to another to try to hide behind them. I will be one of the ten righteous people that God can count upon."

— Conclusion —

As Christians, what are the four steps to success that can change our lives as individuals, and change our church, and change our nation? What can bring revival?

Step 1 to success: **"will humble themselves."** You don't find many humble people today. Everyone wants to be number one! Everyone is rushing to get to the head of the line—especially in traffic. In Charleston, South Carolina, a radio station once advertised that it was the number two radio station in Charleston. They reasoned, "We must be number two—everyone else says they are number one!" ("Wonderful WOKE radio").

Not so for Christians! Jesus says in **Matthew 23:12: "For whoever exalts himself will be humbled, and whoever humbles himself will be exalted." Matthew 20:16: "So the last will be first, and the first will be last."** The Apostle Paul says: **"Do nothing out of selfish ambition or vain conceit, but in humility consider others better than yourselves" (Philippians 2:3).**

This was a great problem with the Pharisees. They were more interested in exalting themselves than being humble and letting God exalt them. They always wanted to be first and acknowledged by all. Practically everything they did was out of selfish ambition or vain conceit. But, the Lord explains we need to humble ourselves and consider others better than ourselves.

Paul advances this thought by saying: **"Your attitude should be the same as that of Christ Jesus: Who being in very nature God, did not consider equality with God something to be grasped, but made Himself nothing, taking the very nature of a servant, being made in human likeness. And being found in appearance as a man, He humbled Himself** and became obedient to death – even death on a cross! Therefore God exalted Him to the highest place and gave Him the name that is above every name, that at the name of Jesus every knee should bow, in heaven and on earth and under the earth, and every tongue confess that Jesus Christ is Lord to the glory of God the Father" (Philippians 2:5–9).

Step 2 to success: **"and pray."** As Christians we need to examine our prayer life. How much do you pray each day? The Apostle Paul exhorts us: **"Pray continually" (1 Thessalonians 5:17).** "Do you not know that your body is a temple of the Holy Spirit, who is in you, whom you have received from God? You are not your own; you were bought at a price, Therefore honor God with your body")1 Corinthians 6:19-20).** Realizing that the Holy Spirit is continually a part of our lives, we should always be in an attitude or spirit of prayer. Just as you would not ignore, but instead acknowledge continually a dear loved one who may be close to you.

In the Sermon on the Mount, Jesus said: **"Ask and it will be given to you; seek and you will find; knock and the door will be opened to you. For everyone who asks receives; he who seeks finds; and to him who knocks, the door will be opened" (Mathew 7:7–8).**

However, we need to be careful as we pray. **"When you ask, you do not receive, because you ask with wrong motives, that you may spend what you get on your pleasures" (James 4:3). "If I had cherished sin in my heart, the Lord would not have listened" (Psalms 66:18).** If we have wrong motives or if we cherish sin in our hearts, the Lord will not listen and answer our prayers.

— Conclusion —

Jesus gives us further instruction about how we should pray. **"And when you pray, do not be like the hypocrites, for they love to pray standing in the synagogues and on the street corners to be seen by men. I tell you the truth; they have received their reward in full. But when you pray, go into your room, close the door and pray to your Father, who in unseen. Then your Father, who sees what is done in secret, will reward you. And when you pray, do not keep on babbling like pagans, for they think they will be heard because of their many words. Do not be like them, for your Father knows what you need before you ask him" (Matthew 6:5–7).**

Some years ago, after our Sunday evening worship service in North Charleston, South Carolina, almost everyone had left the church. A man whom I'll call Don came and asked, "Could you take a moment and pray with me?" "Certainly," I replied, "I'll be happy to pray with you!"

Don had a wife and several children. He was an honest, hardworking man, but he had some problems. Don could not read and write very well. He spoke with a speech impediment. His problem: his wife was scheduled to spend a month in the state hospital for tests and he could not continue to work and take care of his children at home. He needed to work in order to buy food for his children. We went into the choir room and shut the door. We humbled ourselves on our knees. Don poured out his heart in prayer to God and asked the Lord for help in his time of need. Together we agreed upon his request to God **("Again, I tell you that if two of you on earth agree about anything you ask for, it will be done for you by My Father in heaven," Matthew 18:21).**

After we finished praying, we got up to depart. All of the lights in the church were turned off except for the lights in the hallway that led to the back door of the church. Everyone had departed except for one deacon who was standing by the back door. As we approached the door, the deacon asked, "Could you take a few minutes to talk with me?" My reply, of course, was, "Yes."

We went back into the choir room, and the deacon told me that he and his wife had talked the situation over. They decided that Don had a serious problem and they would like to offer to take care of Don's children while Don's wife was in the hospital. The deacon asked me, "Do you think Don will be offended if we offer to take care of his children?" **"Before they call I will answer; while they are still speaking I will hear" (Isaiah 65:24). "Call to me and I will answer you and tell you great and unsearchable things you do not know" (Jeremiah 33:3).**

I think this is what Jesus meant: **"Until now you have not asked for anything in My name. ASK AND YOU WILL RECEIVE, AND YOUR JOY WILL BE COMPLETE"** (John 16:24, emphasis added). When we come to the Lord in heartfelt prayer and cry out to Him for help, God answers our prayers. Help comes—He makes our lives happy and complete. Every Christian should experience the joy of answered prayer.

Step 3 to success: **"and seek My face."** James gives us the key to getting closer to God. **"Come near to God and He will come near to you" (James 4:8).** Throughout the Bible, as well as in life, we see people running away and trying to hide from God. We discover a loving Heavenly Father seeking to save the lost. The moment we decide to come near

— Conclusion —

to God, we discover that the Lord is already knocking at our heart's door, waiting to be invited into our lives. **"Here I am! I stand at the door and knock. If anyone hears my voice and opens the door, I will come in and eat with him, and he with Me" (Revelation 3:20).**

This invitation is found in **Isaiah 55:6–7: "Seek the Lord while He may be found; call on Him while He is near. Let the wicked forsake his way and the evil man his thoughts. Let him turn to the Lord, and He will have mercy on him, and to our God, for He will freely pardon."**

When I worked with the U.S. Customs Service around 1960, we found a crewmember on board a ship that had just arrived from overseas. When we searched him, we discovered his pocket filled with marijuana. We also learned that he was guilty of violating Title 18 of the United States Code (as I remember, the Section was 1409). The law at that time stated that a person who uses drugs or has been convicted of using drugs or selling drugs must register with the Customs Service immediately upon arrival in the United States or immediately prior to departure from the country. Since that time, the U.S. Supreme Court has removed this law, but in 1960 it was valid.

The man hired the former mayor's son as his lawyer. He was perhaps the best attorney in the city. The lawyer convinced my boss that his client should be tried under the registration law, since the penalty for the violation is one year in jail. The pocket-full of marijuana would have resulted in a much lesser sentence and, therefore was not of great consequence.

Finally, the day for the court case arrived. We were there in the Federal Courthouse, located on the second floor of the Post Office Building in downtown Charleston on the corner of Meeting and Broad streets. We were ready to testify against this man.

When the judge rapped his gavel on the desk to begin the trial, the defendant asked for permission to speak to the judge with his attorney. The judge allowed him to approach the bench. The man gave the judge a white paper that he had brought to court. The judge read the paper, rapped the gavel on his desk, and said the case is dismissed the man is free to go. The man walked down the isle of the courtroom waving his white paper like a flag of victory and walked out into the freedom and sunshine of Broad Street in Charleston.

What was this "white paper"? The man had served in the merchant marine during the Second World War. In those days many ships were torpedoed by enemy submarines resulting in a great loss of life. Since the man had risked his life in the service of the United States of America, President Harry Truman issued him a presidential pardon for any and all crimes that he might have committed. When the judge saw this presidential pardon, he realized that the man's criminal record had been wiped completely clean. He could not be held accountable for his crime and the six months that he served in jail.

Why do I mention this? Because the Lord says: **"God will have mercy and freely pardon" (Isaiah 55:7).** Would you like to receive a free pardon from the Lord from all of your sins? God says it is yours, if you will seek Him right now **"while He may be found."**

Step 4 to success: **"and turn from their wicked ways."** Quoting from the great prophet Isaiah, Jesus says, **"These**

— Conclusion —

people honor Me with their lips, but their hearts are far from Me. They worship Me in vain; their teachings are but rules taught by men" (Matthew 15:8–9). So many people today have a religion of do's and don'ts—rules about what is proper and what is not. God expects more than this from us. God wants to have a close personal relationship with each one of us; God wants to write His Word in our hearts. We need to turn from everything and everyone who would keep us away from living in Christ Jesus and Jesus living in us.

Why should we take these four steps to success? Because when we do, God says: "**Then will I hear from heaven and will forgive their sin and will heal their land.**" Does your nation need healing today? I see daily on the television of countries around the world that are faced with calamity, with riots, with bloodshed, with foreclosed loans, with insurrection, with disruptive behavior from their citizens. How can we correct these problems?

In order to correct these problems, we need not be concerned with criminals or foreigners or atheistic elements within the country. WE CAN CORRECT THESE PROBLEMS WHEN GOD'S PEOPLE, THE CHRISTIANS, THOSE WHO KNOW AND LOVE THE LORD: **(1) HUMBLE THEMSELVES; (2) PRAY; (3) SEEK HIS FACE; (4) TURN FROM THEIR WICKED WAYS.**

When Christians are ready to get serious with God and obey His Word, then God **"will hear from heaven and will forgive their sins, and will heal their land."**

Many years ago, we attended a church in North Charleston. The pastor said we had attempted to have a revival in the church for several years, but to no avail. He said, "We brought in quality, professional singers, musicians, and evangelists, but the results were very disappointing." The pastor said, "Revival comes from God and from within His people." He said, "This year I will preach and Ray will lead the music." Let me tell you—if revival comes from his preaching and my singing, it would indeed require a miracle from God.

The pastor's handwriting was almost as neat as a third-grade child's. Have you ever noticed a doctor's handwriting on a prescription? That is what our pastor's handwriting looked like. He took a piece of typing paper and wrote an invitation to our revival. Then, he made copies of his handbill and we delivered them to the houses in our community. I was posting one of these in a service station near our church. A friend at the service station showed me a quality printed invitation to a revival meeting in his church. His church had photographs of the evangelist and music director on their invitation. Our flyer was just a scribbled invitation.

A couple of weeks before our spring revival, about twenty-five of our key leaders became upset about some literature that had been published by our Southern Baptist denomination. They left the church. Among these was the chairman of the deacons, the music director, the Sunday school superintendent, some deacons, etc.

In the past a man and his wife had some serious disagreements with the pastor and the church. They humbled themselves and changed their entire attitude. They began to pray and to seek to do God's will. The entire church joined in this humility, the prayers, seeking the Lord and His will, and turning from every way that is displeasing to God.

— Conclusion —

Before the revival began, people started coming to receive Christ and to be baptized. Every night during the revival more people came to profess Christ Jesus as Savior and Lord. During the revival and the days surrounding it, we had fifty-five people who came to Christ and into our church - most of them on profession of faith. This was the first time in my life that I saw a church grow vigorously during the summer. Usually, a church experiences a summer slump when school is finished and vacations begin.

This experience is a small indication of what happens when we take God's promises to heart and (1) humble ourselves; (2) pray; (3) seek God's face; and (4) turn from our wicked ways. It happens exactly as God says it will! These are God's four steps to success!

Overview

When the Lord called me out of retirement and sent us to Bulgaria, I thought God was enabling me to help a missionary get a vehicle. Now, as I look back, I realize the Lord had much more than I could imagine in store for us. The International Baptist Church Sofia called me as its pastor, and I am still there actively serving the Lord. Last year we had folks from thirty-five countries to come and worship with us. We have baptized new believers from Bulgaria, Iran, many African and European nations, the United States of America, and even from China, Japan, and Korea.

Believers have transferred from our church to actively witness for the Lord. They have established a church in Greece for Afghan and Iranian immigrants. Another began a church in Ghana, Africa. Many others have been scattered around the world, witnessing for Christ.

When I look back over my seventy-seven years, I remember as a small child my older brothers, along with some other young neighbors. They were planning to walk to Charleston's famous Battery to go fishing. Charleston is a peninsula bordered on two sides by the Ashley and Cooper rivers. Residents enjoy saying, "The Ashley River and the Cooper River flow around Charleston and join together at the Battery to form the Atlantic Ocean." As you stand on "High" Battery, you can see Fort Sumter out in the harbor where the War Between the States began on April 12, 1861. Beyond Fort Sumter is the Atlantic Ocean.

Since I was not as old as my brothers and their friends, I was not to be included in the fishing trip. Of course, I let out an immediate cry of "unfair!" My dear mother, who arbitrated such disagreements, decided that I should also be included in the trip. "But Mom," my brother said, "he does not even have a fishing line!"

"Then help him fix one," was her reply.

We tied a piece of old fishing string to a small stick and wound up enough cord for a fishing line. With a flat piece of lead for a sinker, my brother Gene showed me how to make loops in the cord to attach three fish hooks. Soon, we were off for an almost two-mile trek to the battery. We stopped at Carroll's Fish Market to buy a few shrimp for bait. My brothers decided we should fish near the end of South Battery. A small strip of beach there is not obstructed by sharp rocks.

Spreading out along the very small beach, we began to fish. Several other folks were fishing there that day. Soon, I hooked and landed a nice drum fish. It weighed probably a little more than a pound. As we continued fishing, I caught seven drum fish. No one else among all of those people even got a bite. As a child, I thought about the Lord and His disciples. I remembered in Sunday school that Jesus said to them: **"Follow Me, and I will make you fishers of men" (Matthew 4:19**, KJV).

A couple of years later, my mother was sick and in the hospital. In those days the hospital was across the street from Colonial Lake in downtown Charleston. When my dad came home from work, he took me, my fishing pole and some bait, and we went to see Mom. He left me across the street to fish in the lake. While Dad was in the hospital, I caught several nice, frying-sized whiting fish. A man fished nearby with a nice rod and reel. I kept catching fish, but he could not get a nibble.

Finally, the man came to me and said he would give me his rod, reel, and fishing tackle box if I would let him fish with my pole. I told the man that he could keep his nice equipment, but he was welcome to use my pole. The man fished and fished but never got a nibble. In disgust, he gave me all of his fishing gear, including the nice rod and reel. Even though I insisted that he keep his things, he said, "I am through with fishing forever!"

Once again, those words of Jesus echoed in my heart: **"Follow Me, and I will make you fishers of men."** As a little boy I could not understand. "What can I do? I am only a child!"

Most Baptist churches conclude their worship services with what they call "a hymn of invitation." As the congregation sings this final hymn, members of the congregation are urged to come forward to confess their faith in Lord Jesus Christ and invite the Lord to forgive their sins and be their Savior. They are also invited to come forward to dedicate their life for full time Christian service, or to come for prayer to resolve any special need.

This is a most important part of the service. Jesus said: **"If you confess Me before men I will confess you before My Father in heaven. If you deny me before men, I will deny you before My Father."** Think of it! The Lord gives His Word that he will **"confess you before His Father in heaven"** if you publicly acknowledge Him before others.

As a child in church, we sang the hymn, "Wherever He Leads I'll Go" (B. B. McKinney). One Sunday the pastor gave a special invitation: "Anyone who will answer God's call to go wherever God leads them, please come forward." In my heart I said to God: "Lord, I am the least of the six children in our family. But, I am willing to go wherever you want me to go. I'll do whatever you want me to do. I'll say whatever you want me to say. I'll be whatever you want me to be. However, Lord, the only way I can and will do this is if You will go with me and help me." In my early teens I went forward. I agreed to follow God's leading only if God would go with me. Where would God lead me?

As a college student I attended a Christian retreat at Ridgecrest, North Carolina. Once again the minister gave such an invitation. I went forward again with the same stipulation: "Lord, I'll go, if you will go with me." Where, when, and how could God use me? During the years that followed, I

— Conclusion —

tried to remain true to the Lord. I worked with children and youth; I served as a lay preacher; I taught Sunday school and Bible studies; I testified of God's great love in the army and on the streets of New York. Whatever I could do for the Lord, I tried to do my best.

Now, as an old man, I have the advantage of looking back over the years. The Scriptures I have mentioned, the direct promises God has kept in my life, the blessings including the harrowing experiences, the miraculous way God has kept His Word in so many different situations—all of these confirm: **"When He said this, all His opponents were humiliated, but the people were delighted with all the wonderful things He was doing" (Luke 13:17).**

The Lord is still touching people's lives today. I hear many "opponents" who are very vocal in denying the Lord Jesus. However, those who *realize* God are **"delighted with all the wonderful things He is doing."**

Peter said **(1 Peter 3:15): "But in your hearts set apart Christ as Lord. Always be prepared to give an answer to everyone who asks you to give the reason for the hope that you have. But do this with gentleness and respect."**

If you rely wholly upon God and His Word; if you yield your will to God, you will not only realize God's power in your life, but God will use you to accomplish His will through your witness—regardless of other factors, such as age, health, economic status, etc. You realize the power of God in your life. You will not merely have a form of godliness, denying the power thereof.

Inscription in the Cathedral of Lubeck, Germany:

"Thus speaks the Spirit of Christ our Lord to us:

You call Me Master	and obey Me not.
You call Me light	and see Me not.
You call Me the way	and walk with Me not.
You call Me life	and desire Me not.
You call Me wise	and follow Me not.
You call Me fair	and love Me not.
You call Me rich	and ask Me not.
Your call Me eternal	and see Me not.
Your call Me gracious	and trust Me not.
You call Me noble	and serve Me not.
You call me mighty	and honor Me not.
You call me just	and fear Me not.
If I condemn you	blame Me not."

Second Peter 1:4: "Through these He has given us His very great and precious promises, so that through them you may participate in the divine nature and escape the corruption in the world caused by evil desires." God tells us plainly that we may participate in the divine nature and escape the corruption in the world through **"His great and precious promises."**

Let us say with King David: **"Search me, O God, and know my heart; test me and know my anxious thoughts. See if there is any offensive way in me, and lead me in the way everlasting" (Psalm 139:23).** My prayer for you is that you will

— Conclusion —

begin living your life in the power of the Almighty God. Turn away from any form of godliness that denies God's power in our lives today.

Second Corinthians 9:15: "Thanks be to God for His indescribable gift!"

Made in the USA
Charleston, SC
26 March 2011